HISTORIC TAMPA CHURCHES

Best Wishes
John V. Cinchett

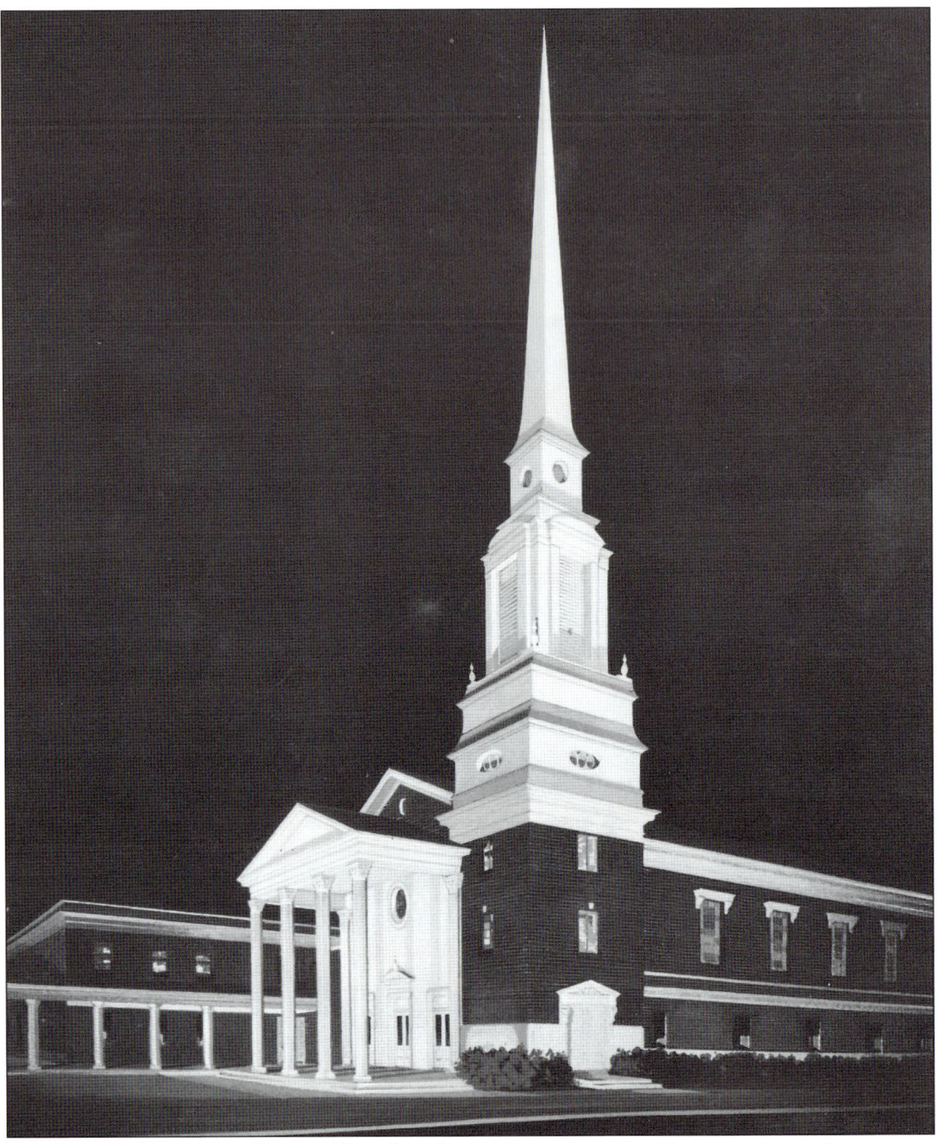

For travelers coming into Tampa, Florida, along the interstate, the towering white steeple of Seminole Heights Baptist Church welcomes them like a lighthouse guiding ships in the night. The history of this church begins in 1921, when an organizational meeting was held by the pastors representing all the Baptist churches in Tampa to establish a new church in the developing community of Seminole Heights. The church is a familiar landmark on East Hillsborough Avenue and is pictured here in 1958. (Courtesy of Seminole Heights Baptist Church.)

ON THE COVER: The congregation of Sacred Heart Catholic Church is pictured on December 3, 1944, attending a novena mass in honor of St. Francis Xavier. This saint was a cofounder of the Society of Jesus (the Jesuits) and is one of the most revered missionaries of the Catholic Church. The Jesuits served the church from 1888 until 2005, when the Franciscan Friars assumed care of the faithful. This beautiful historic church was dedicated in 1905 and is a downtown landmark visited by thousands of tourists each year. (Courtesy of University of South Florida Special Collections Library.)

IMAGES
of America

HISTORIC TAMPA CHURCHES

John V. Cinchett

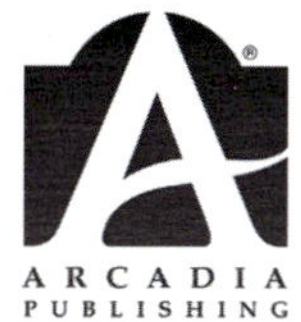

ARCADIA
PUBLISHING

Published by Arcadia Publishing
Charleston, South Carolina

Printed in the United States of America

Library of Congress Control Number: 2017952174

For all general information, please contact Arcadia Publishing:
Telephone 843-853-2070
Fax 843-853-0044
E-mail sales@arcadiapublishing.com
For customer service and orders:
Toll-Free 1-888-313-2665

Visit us on the Internet at www.arcadiapublishing.com

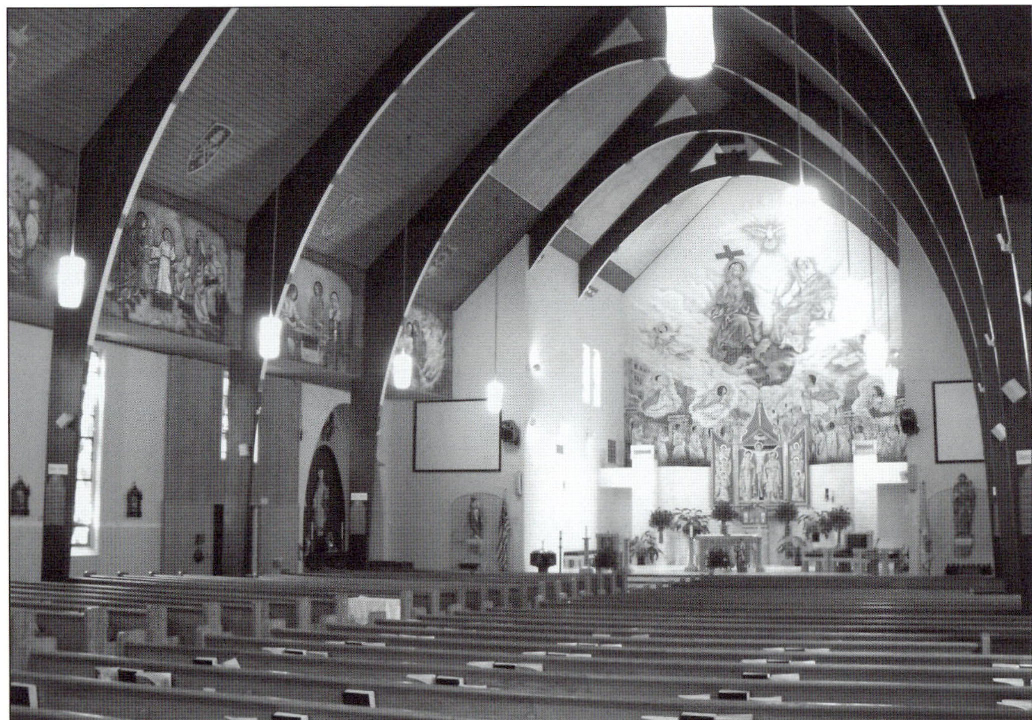

St. Joseph Catholic Church is the oldest Catholic church west of the Hillsborough River, established in 1896. During the Spanish-American War, in June 1898, the church was converted into a hospital for wounded soldiers. The Sisters of the Holy Names, who staffed the school, cared for the soldiers, offering them rosaries and religious medals as they led them in prayer. It is recorded that the nuns cooked meals for more than 800 soldiers on the first day they began arriving at the church. In appreciation, the following day, the soldiers collected $210 and donated the funds to the sisters for the school. (Author's collection.)

CONTENTS

ACKNOWLEDGMENTS

The author first and foremost must thank the gracious pastors and their dedicated church staff members, who welcomed me into their churches to interview them about the history of their congregations and collect their historical pictures.

My sincerest appreciation to the Tampa–Hillsborough County Public Library staff and librarians Todd Ciardiello and Bill Harris for their assistance with several images from the Burgert Brothers Collection (HCPLC). The University of South Florida Special Collections Library is gratefully acknowledged for its efforts to preserve the historical Robertson-Fresh Collection. Several images from that collection include the acknowledgement (USFSCL).

My sincerest appreciation to Jennifer Dietz and Alison Smith, archivists for the City of Tampa who assisted me with several photographs (Tampa Archives). In appreciation of assistance with locating historical photographs, special thanks to Rev. Raul Fernandez, Rev. Brett Snowden, Pastor Brian Brink, Marguerite Brennan, Pam Ferron, Virginia Green, Nancy Turner, Heather Baxter, Sarah Walker, Barbara Allen, Paige Carlson, Kiersty Cox, Stephen Jerkins, Carl Zielonka, Tammy Snyder, Meagan Kempton, Andrew Rametta, Lona Elly, and Carlos Ranon at Ranon and Jimenez Construction. I am also very grateful for the assistance of several historians from religious orders that served in Tampa: Patrick Hayes, archivist of the Redemptorist Fathers; Lisa Mobley, archivist for the Diocese of St. Petersburg; and Sr. Catherine Bitzer, archivist for the Sisters of St. Joseph of St. Augustine (SSJSA) for her assistance with several photographs. All other photographs are from the collection of author John V. Cinchett and may not be used without exclusive permission.

I am very grateful to the owners of the *Penny Saver News*, historian Linda Hope and editor Gail Hope; and the owners of *La Gaceta* newspaper, Patrick and Angie Manteiga, for their continued support of my book projects and for their tireless efforts to further historic preservation initiatives in the city of Tampa.

The author wishes to offer sincerest gratitude to these individuals for their kind assistance with photographic restoration work: Sam Sellers at Golden Triangle Photography and Bill Krautler of Bill Krautler Photographic Service.

INTRODUCTION

The people of Tampa love their churches and temples. To the members of these faith communities, their church is their second home. When they come together for worship, it is a family gathering. In their church home, they not only pray and sing together, they share a special bond with each other through their spiritual connection.

The storied halls of Tampa's oldest religious institutions are deeply rooted in the longtime journey of dedicated faithful who gave their all to build these glorious structures. Many of these congregations built their churches themselves, devoting countless months of hard labor with a vision to create a special place where the new community could begin the work for which they had been called.

Just as the historic preservation community in Tampa can celebrate the architectural significance of Tampa's many historic churches, the citizens of Tampa must also celebrate the efforts of the congregations that have selflessly worked together to help establish and offer support to many of the most successful benevolent organizations throughout the city. Among these are Mission Tampa at Seminole Heights Baptist Church, the Portico Ministry of Hyde Park United Methodist Church, the McClain Foundation Home at St. John Presbyterian Church, Metropolitan Ministries, the St. Vincent De Paul Society, the Judeo Christian Health Clinic, Catholic Charities, Lighthouse Ministries, Love INC, the Florida United Methodist Children's Home, Lighthouse Gospel Mission, and One Church One Child of Florida. Many of Tampa's churches have also established housing developments for low-income residents and seniors. Among these are the Presbyterian Home Foundation of Florida, Tampa Baptist Manor at First Baptist Church, Methodist Place, and the Palm Avenue Baptist Tower. These organizations are only a few of many that represent the collective efforts of Tampa's faith communities dedicated to their mission of outreach.

Long before the establishment of government agencies to assist families in need, it was the faith communities that opened their doors to the poor and homeless. Tampa's churches, schools, and hospitals have a long relationship with many religious orders that have nurtured and assisted the community. The Sisters of St. Joseph established the first Catholic school in Ybor City, St. Joseph Academy, in 1891 and also ministered to residents, caring for the sick and feeding the homeless. The Redemptorist Fathers arrived in Tampa in 1934 and ministered to the Italian immigrants in Ybor City at Most Holy Name Church. The Salesian Fathers arrived in Tampa in 1926, established an orphanage, and began ministering to the cigar factory workers in Ybor City and West Tampa by speaking their native language to try to help them renew their faith. The Salesian Sisters developed a program of outreach and service to the inner-city youth, establishing Villa Madonna School in 1936. The Sisters of the Holy Names established Tampa's first parochial schools and secured homes for orphaned children living on the streets of Tampa. The Allegany Franciscan Sisters established St. Joseph Hospital in 1934.

Amidst the busy metropolis, between skyscrapers and apartment buildings, the steeples of Tampa's churches reach skyward reminding all who pass by of their mission on earth to lead the faithful to heaven. It is inside these churches and temples where the faithful come together united in their passion for spreading the love of God through good works and benevolent deeds for the greater good of the community. It is here where new life is celebrated through baptism. It is here where a young bride begins her new journey with her betrothed and widows bid farewell to their longtime beloved husbands. It is here where congregants renew their faith through confirmations, and ministers dedicate their lives to the church in ordinations.

His Holiness Pope Benedict XVI has shared his reflections on the importance of sacred churches and temples:

God's desire is to build a spiritual temple in the world, a community that worships Him in spirit and truth. But this observance also reminds us of the importance of the material buildings in which the community gathers to celebrate the praises of God. Every community therefore has the duty to take special care of its own sacred buildings, which are a precious religious and historical patrimony. The church building exists so that God's Word may be listened to, explained and understood by the faithful. It exists so that God's Word may be active among the members of its community as a force that creates justice and love.

Upon visiting St. Patrick's Cathedral in New York City, Pope Benedict also shared his thoughts on the symbolism of stained-glass windows that are the hallmark of historic churches and temples:

Stained-glass windows flood the interior with mystic light. From the outside, those windows are dark, heavy, even dreary. But once one enters the church, they suddenly come alive; reflecting the light passing through them, they reveal all their splendor. It is only from the inside, from the experience of faith and ecclesial life, that we see the Church as she truly is: flooded with grace, resplendent in beauty, adorned by the manifold gifts of the Spirit. It follows that we, who live the life of grace within the Church's communion, are called to draw all people into this mystery of light.

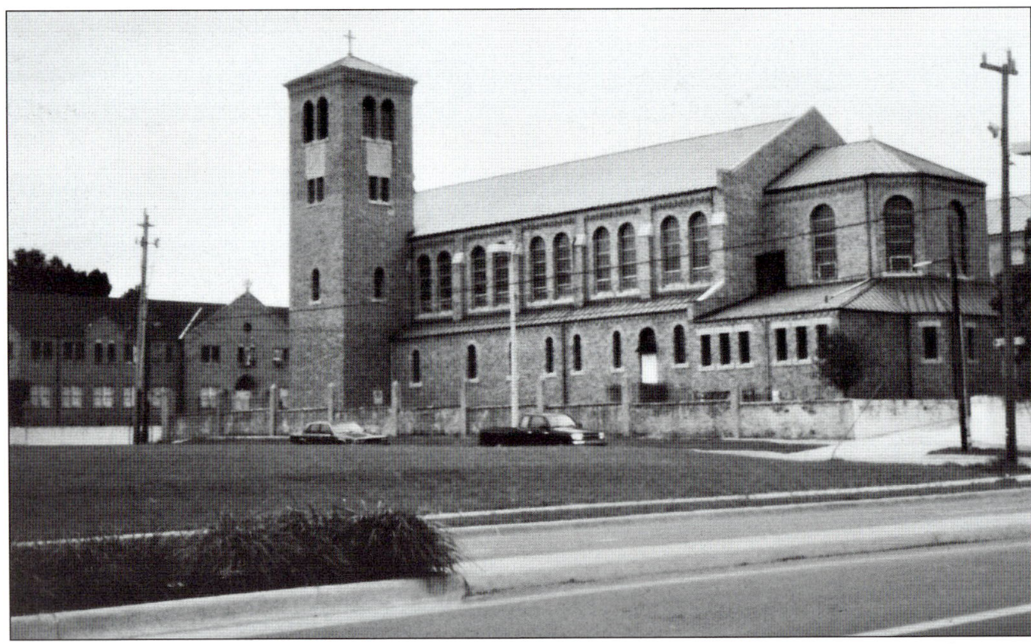

Our Lady of Perpetual Help Catholic Church is a familiar landmark on Palm Avenue welcoming visitors into the Ybor City Historic District. The church was established in 1891 and is one of the oldest churches in Tampa, originally founded to serve the many Cuban, Italian, and Spanish immigrant families living in Ybor City. On the morning of May 19, 2000, one of the largest fires in the history of the city engulfed an apartment complex across the street from the church. The fire encompassed two entire city blocks, destroying many buildings, but was kept away from the church by the diligent efforts of the Tampa Fire Department, whose members worked tirelessly to save the historic structure from damage.

One

DOWNTOWN, HYDE PARK, AND SOUTH TAMPA

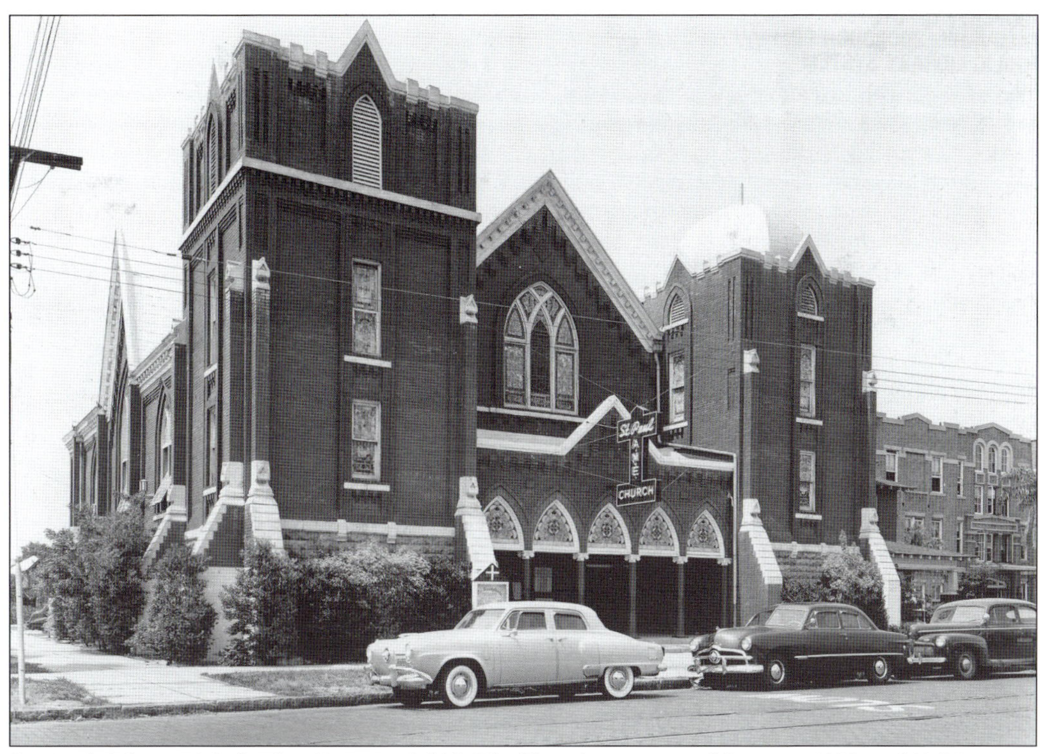

St. Paul African Methodist Episcopal (AME) Church is pictured here in 1939 at 502 Harrison Street. The church was constructed in 1914 during the tenure of Rev. S.A. Williams and was designed in the Neo-Gothic architectural style featuring 26 stained-glass windows and a pipe organ. One of the most distinguishing features of the design is the colonnaded portico entryway spanning the front of the church, flanked by impressive brick towers. (HCPLC.)

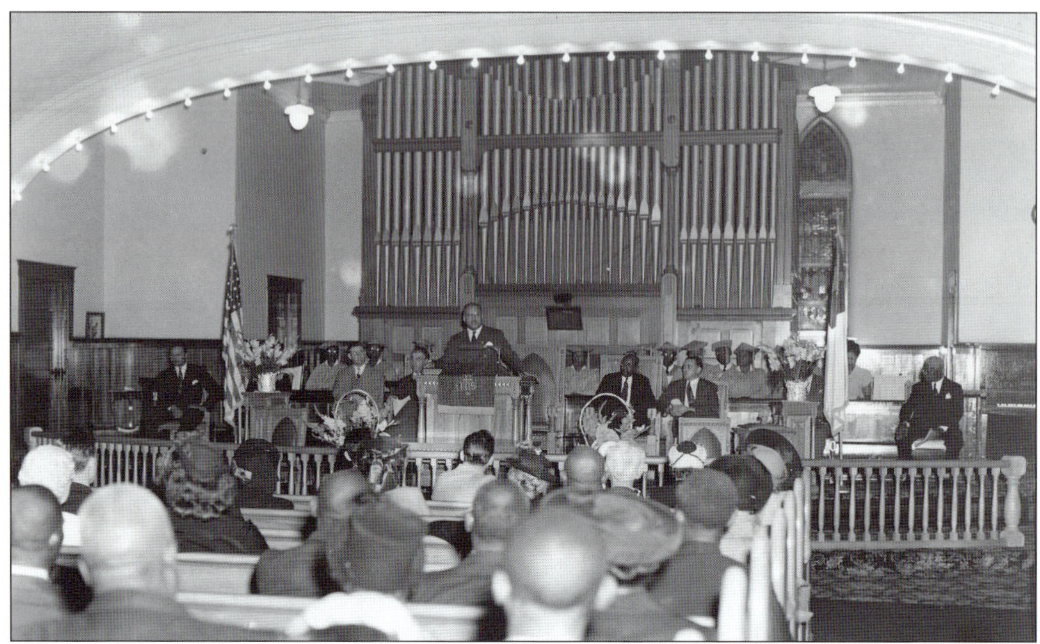

St. Paul AME Church holds a prominent place in the history of Tampa. Established in 1870 by Rev. Thomas Warren Long and Rev. John Thomas as Brush Harbor Mission, it is believed that former slaves helped hack away brush and shrubs at the corner of Harrison and Tampa Streets to create a makeshift sanctuary. This congregation built their first church structure in 1872; in 1879, they moved to a larger building at 1013 Marion Street named Mt. Moriah AME Church before changing the name to St. Paul AME Church. With its prominent downtown location, the church became a popular meeting place for Tampa's African American community. Pictured above in 1948 is the congregation attending a service. The photograph below of the usher's board was taken in 1946. (Both, HCPLC.)

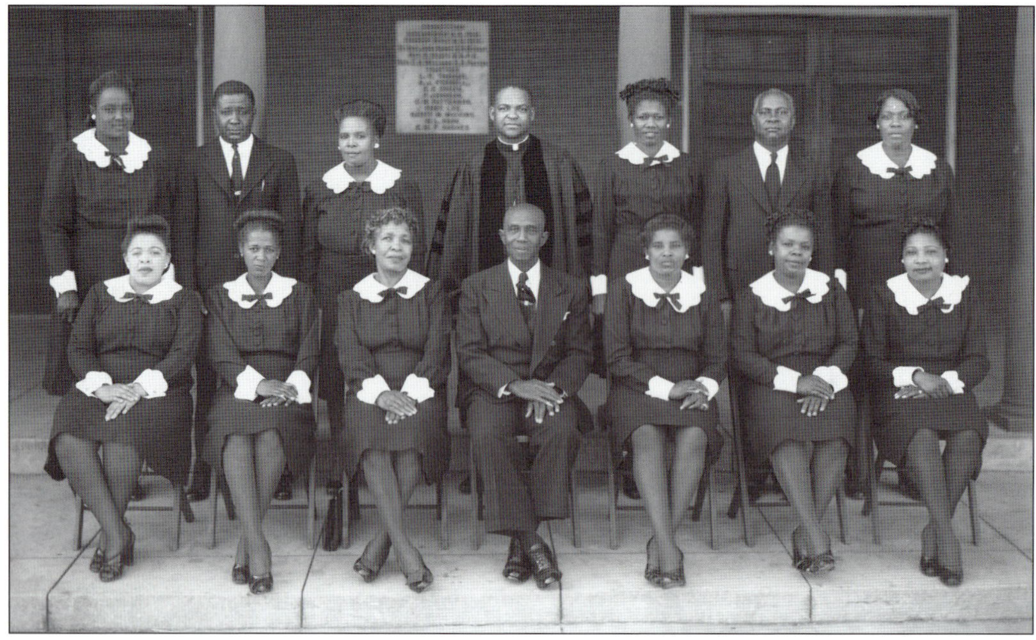

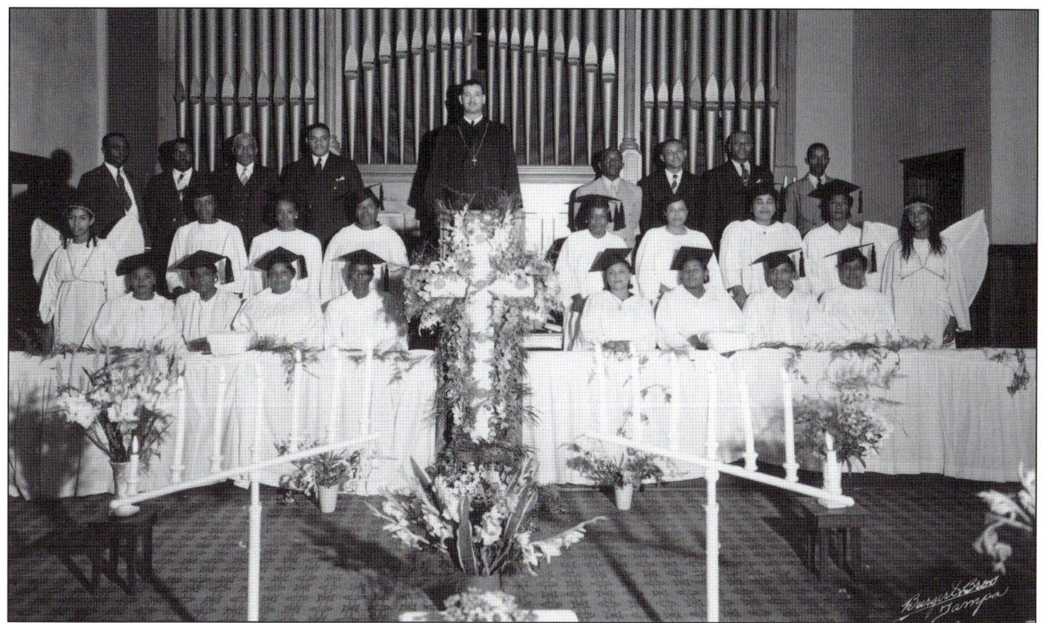

During the 1950s and 1960s, St. Paul AME Church was the center of civil rights activism in Tampa with appearances by many nationally recognized civil rights leaders, including Rev. Jesse Jackson, singer Ray Charles and Supreme Court justice Thurgood Marshall. Dr. Martin Luther King Jr. traveled to Tampa in November 1961 to meet with church elders and local leaders of the civil rights movement to discuss their vision for the advancement of civil rights in Florida. US president Bill Clinton made a speech at the church on November 3, 1996. The photograph above from 1946 shows the Sunday school graduation. Pictured below in 1948 is the church nurses' association. The historic church has been preserved and serves as an activity center for residents of a nearby downtown apartment community. (Both, HCPLC.)

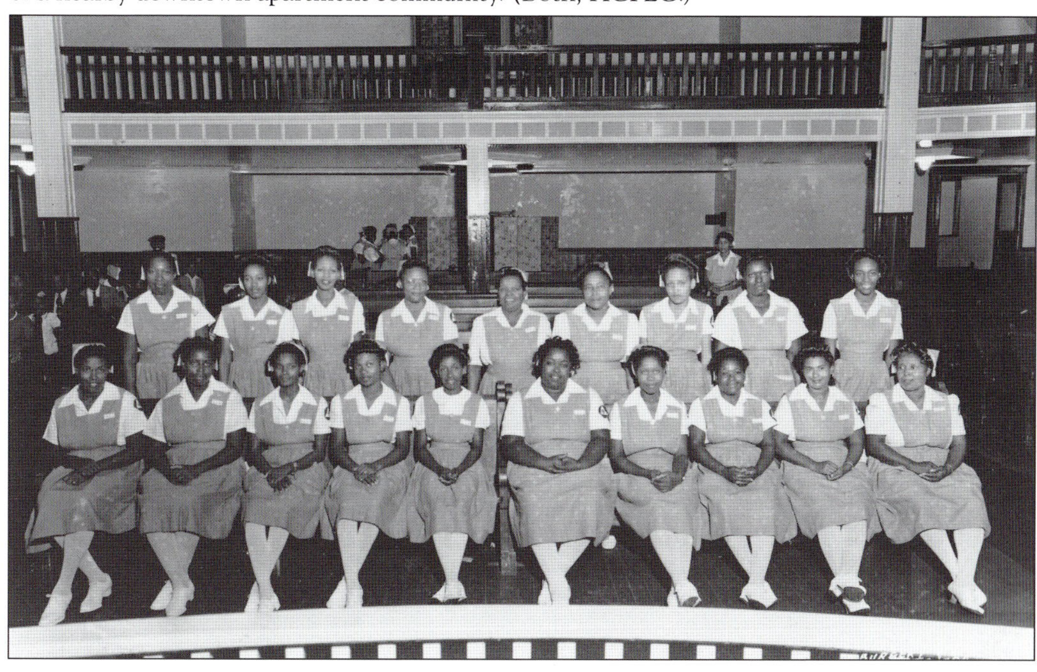

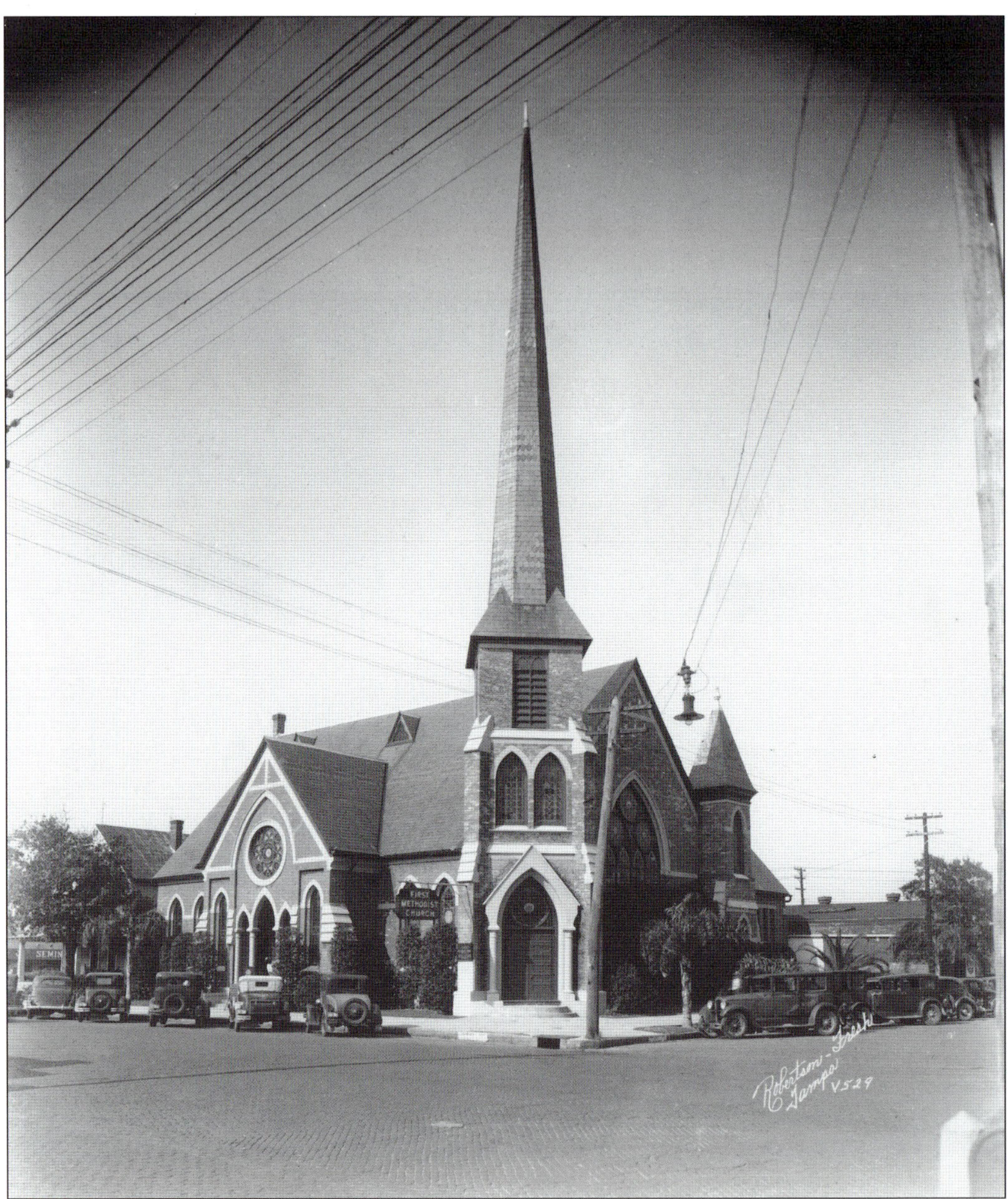

First Methodist Church was organized on July 26, 1846, under the pastorate of Rev. J.C. Ley and was Tampa's first organized church, meeting in a chapel built of wood from nearby Fort Brooke. In 1848, the church was destroyed by a storm and a new church was completed in 1853 at the corner of Lafayette (now Kennedy Boulevard) and Morgan Street. In 1857, Union general Oliver Howard was converted in the church and became known as the "Christian General" for his work as an advocate for freed slaves after the Civil War. He later became commissioner of the Freedmen's Bureau, an agency that assisted the black community, providing them health care and helping them find jobs. The church pictured here in 1939 at 1001 Florida Avenue was dedicated in 1891. The stately redbrick church featured a soaring 50-foot steeple, which was the tallest of any church in the city. During its many years of service, the church established five new congregations. The church closed in 2011 due to declining membership. (USFSCL.)

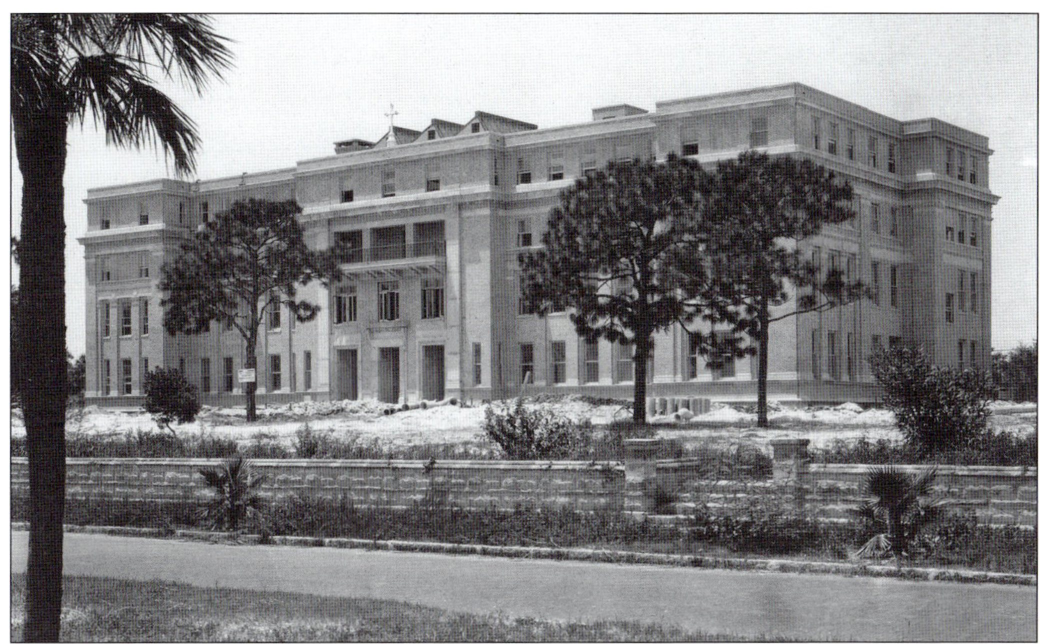

In 1881, the Sisters of the Holy Names arrived in Tampa with a mission, a vision, and a plan to develop and nurture the growing Catholic community in Tampa. Under their prayerful direction, the city's first Catholic school and several churches were established. On July 17, 1881, two Sisters of the Holy Names opened a two-room schoolhouse in a former blacksmith shop on Zack Street in Tampa. In 1891, the sisters opened the Academy of the Holy Names on the corner of Twiggs and Morgan Streets. In 1921, with a vision for future expansion, the sisters purchased property at 3319 Bayshore Boulevard for $17,500. In September 1929, the new school opened. Pictured above is the Academy of the Holy Names under construction in 1928. The Sisters of the Holy Names serving the school are pictured below in 1930.

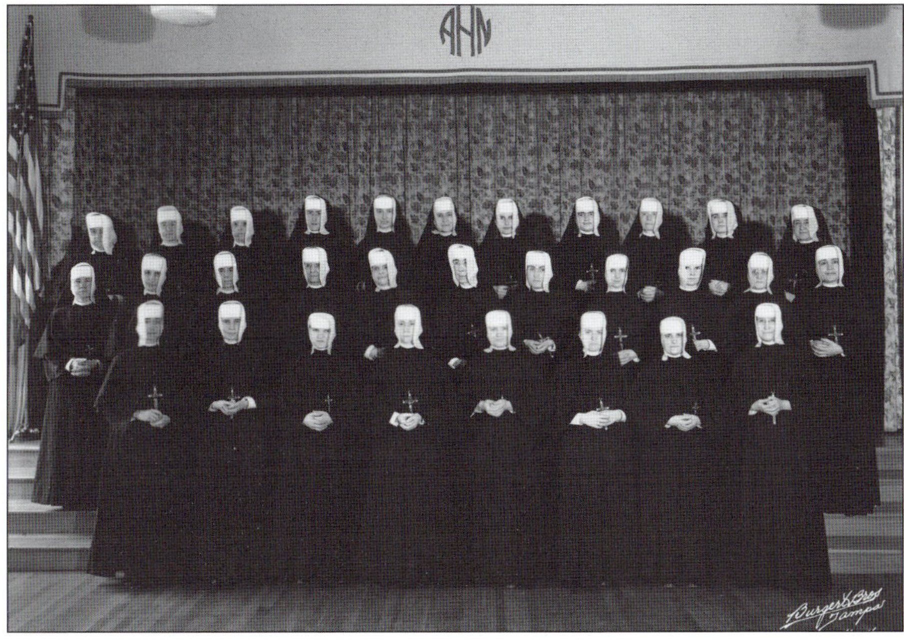

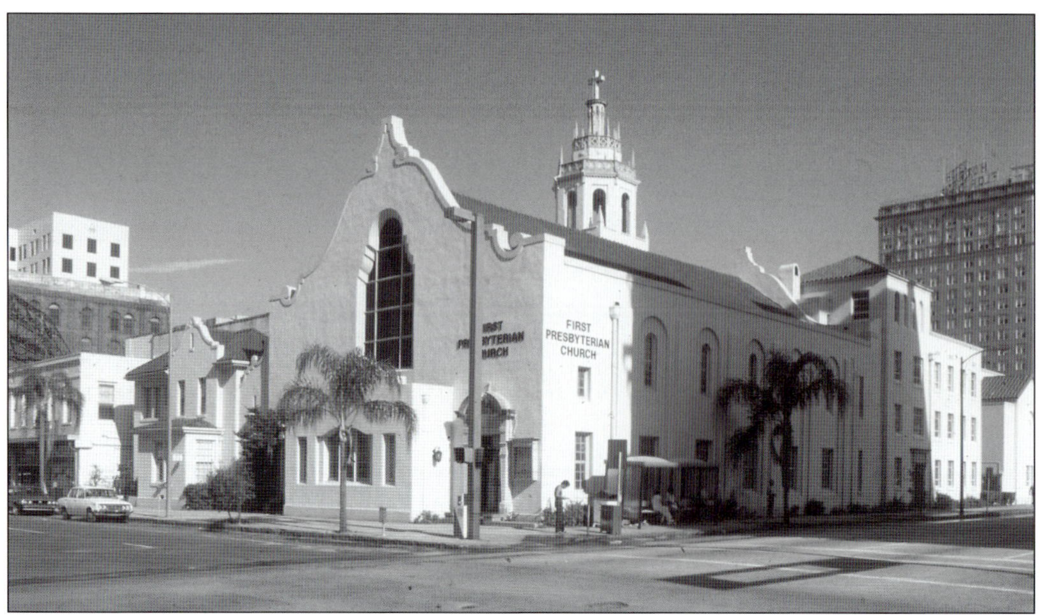

The history of First Presbyterian Church begins in 1878, when two devoted women, Ida Hale and Mrs. E.J. Cardy, established Presbyterian classes in the Hale home on Marion Street. The group later met in the Hillsborough County Courthouse. In 1882, Rev. W.G.F. Wallace was assigned to develop the community, and formally established the church in November 1884. The congregation then met in the Branch Opera House at the corner of Franklin and Lafayette Streets. In November 1885, a small chapel was built on Cass Street. In 1898, the congregation constructed a church on the south side of Zack Street between Marion Street and Florida Avenue at a cost of $8,000. The new church, pictured below in 1904, was a large structure with twin steeples and large stained-glass windows.

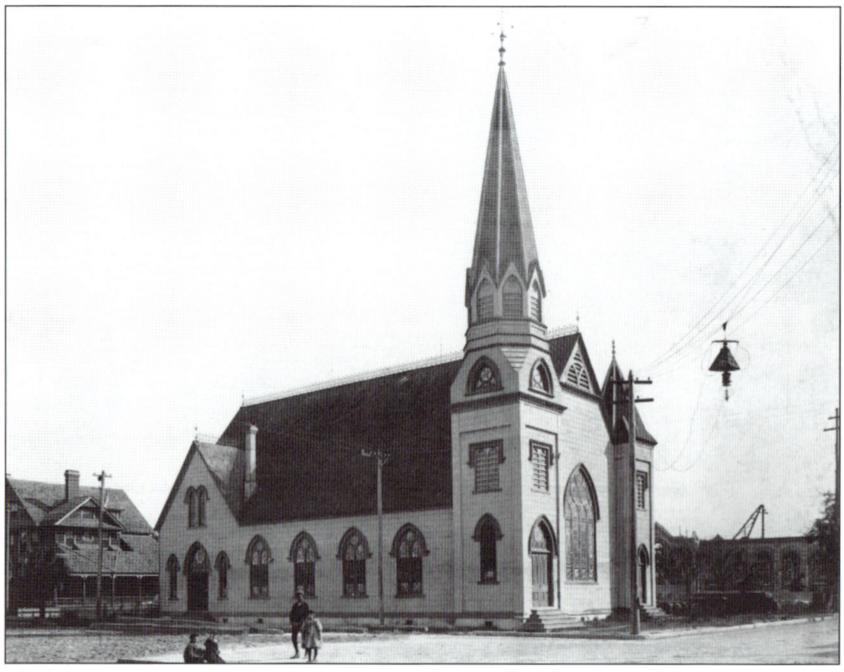

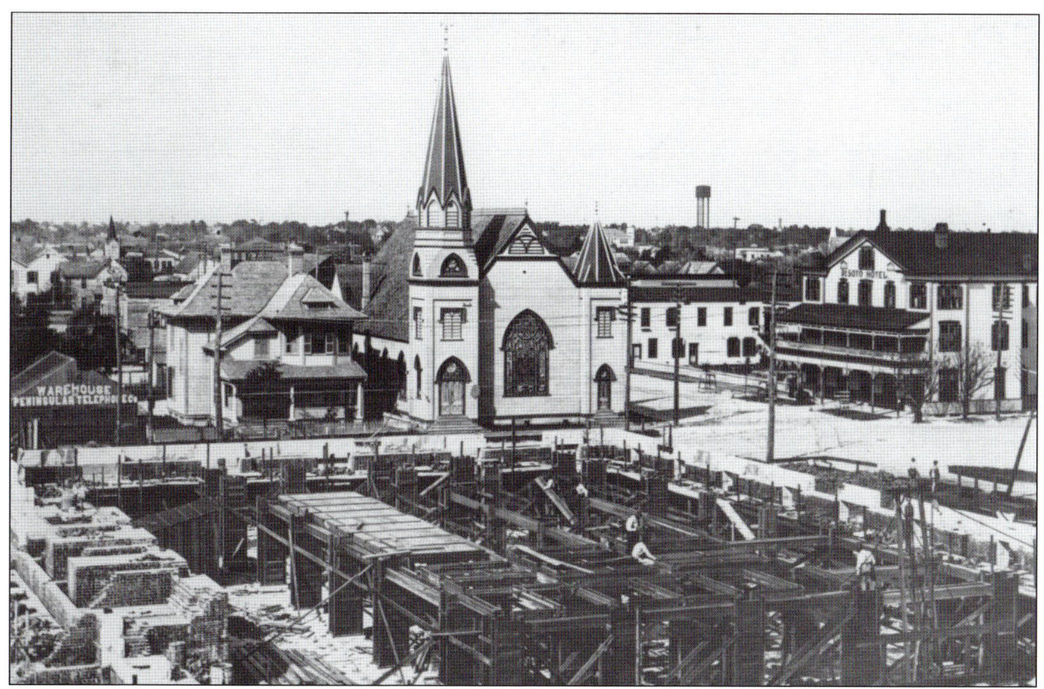

In 1900, the federal government decided to construct a new building on the same city block the church was on and told the congregation the church would have to be moved. The church was carefully moved across the street to the northwest corner of Zack and Marion Streets. The above photograph from 1905 shows construction of the new federal building; the church can be seen at its new location across the street. By 1919, the congregation had grown to more than 600 members and needed a larger church. The church secured a loan for $50,000 and moved forward with plans for the new church. The 1921 image below shows the original church being moved again to the southwest corner of Marion and Polk Streets.

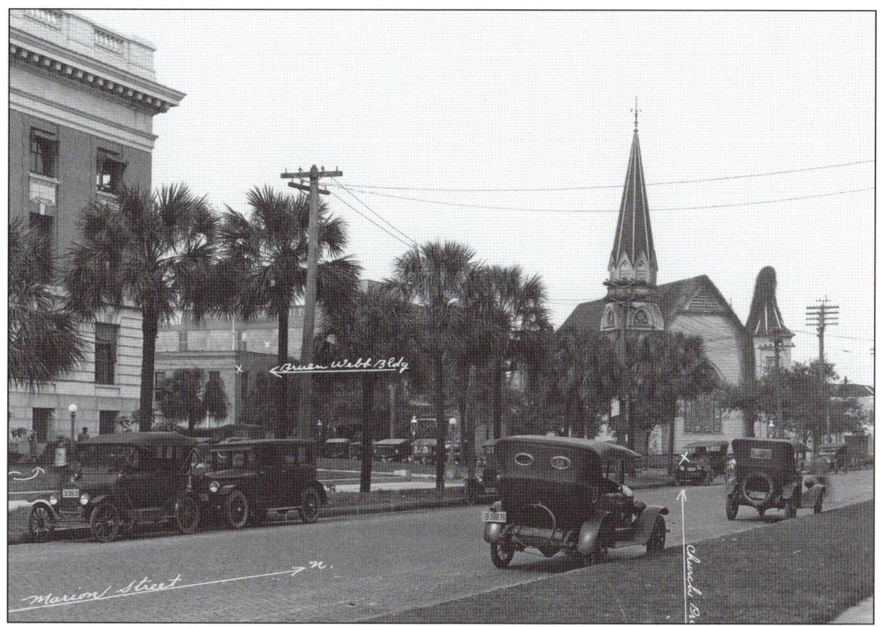

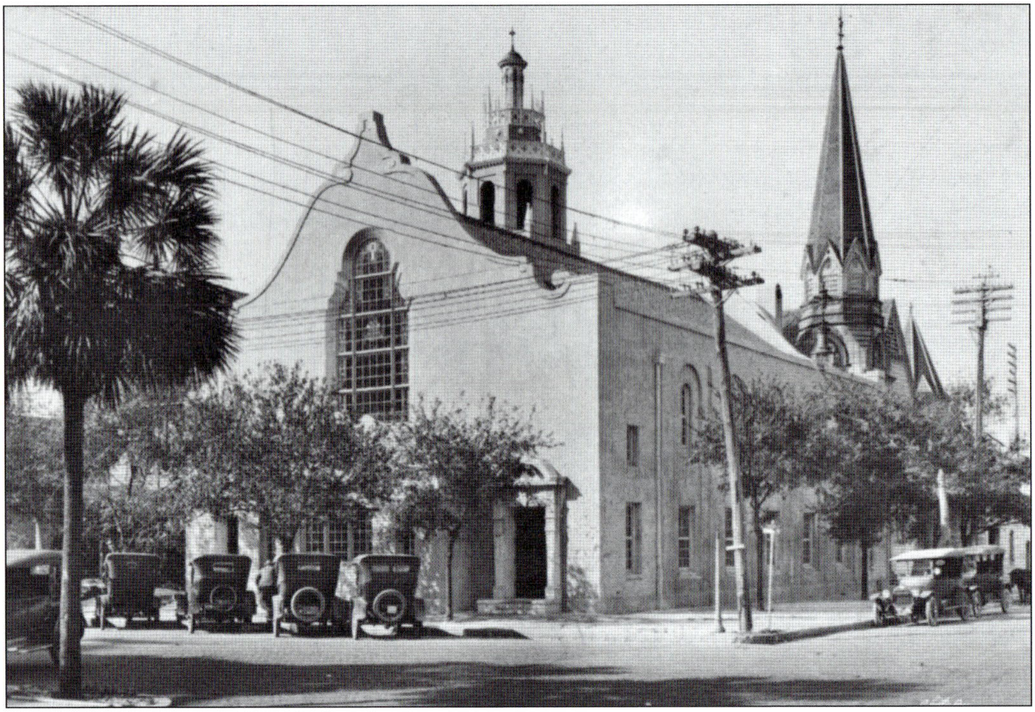

The new First Presbyterian Church was designed in the Spanish Renaissance style and was completed in 1922. In the above photograph, taken in 1922, the original church can be seen in its new location behind the new church that had just been completed. It was later razed for construction of a new education building. The first service in the new church was held on October 22, 1922. It is considered to be one of the finest examples of this type of architecture in the state of Florida.

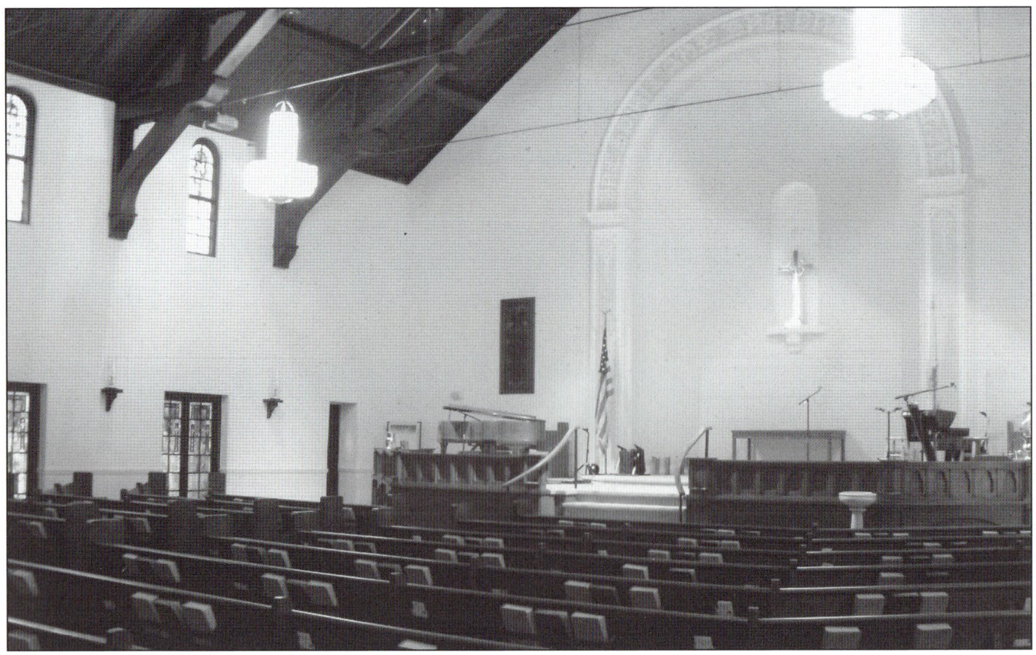

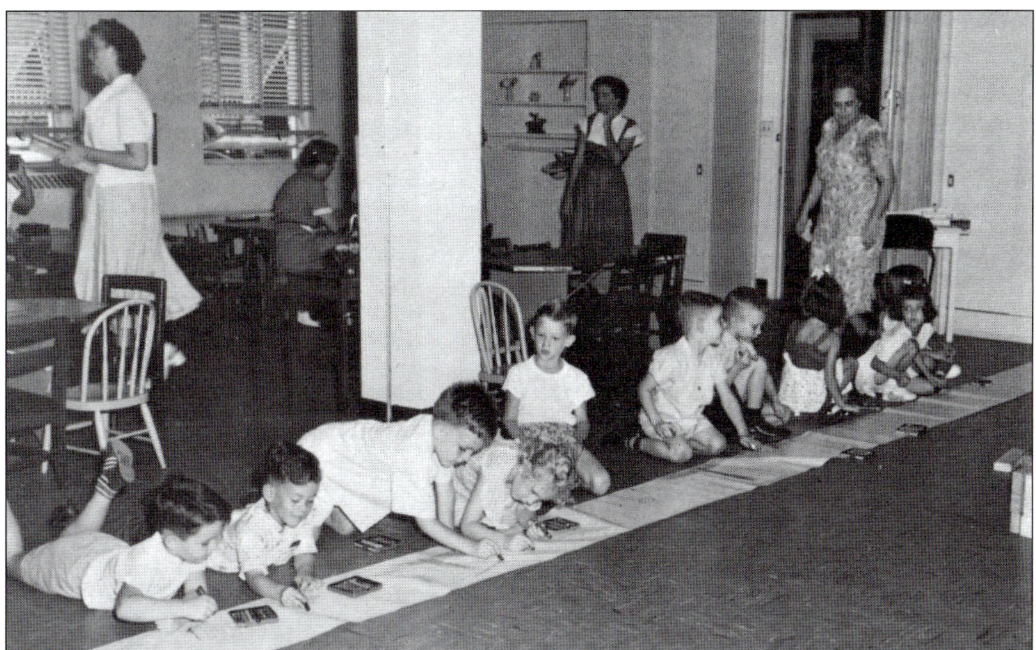

First Presbyterian Church continued to expand its campus with two new education buildings constructed in 1949. On November 13, 1949, the Tims Building was dedicated in honor of longtime pastor Dr. John Chapel Tims, and the Memorial Building was dedicated in honor of those parishioners who died serving in the armed forces during World War II. Pictured above is the kindergarten Sunday school shortly after completion of the new buildings. In 1958, the church began making plans for a new pipe organ to be installed; on March 27, 1960, the new organ was dedicated with longtime organist Margaret McAlister at the console. More than 1,600 organ pipes are located high above the choir loft, surrounding the stained-glass windows, as seen below.

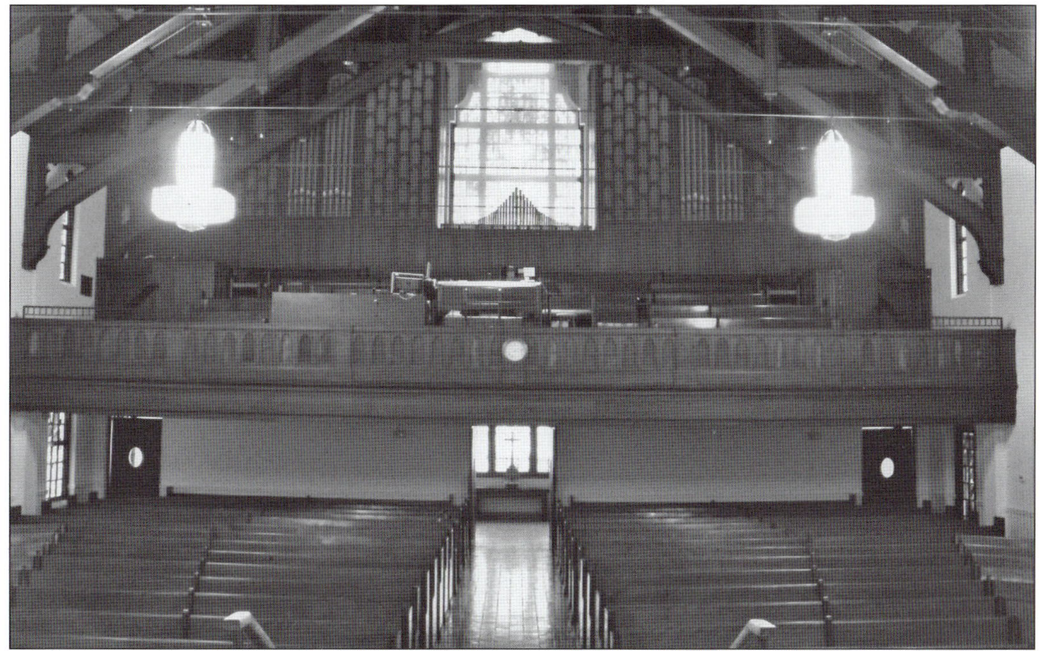

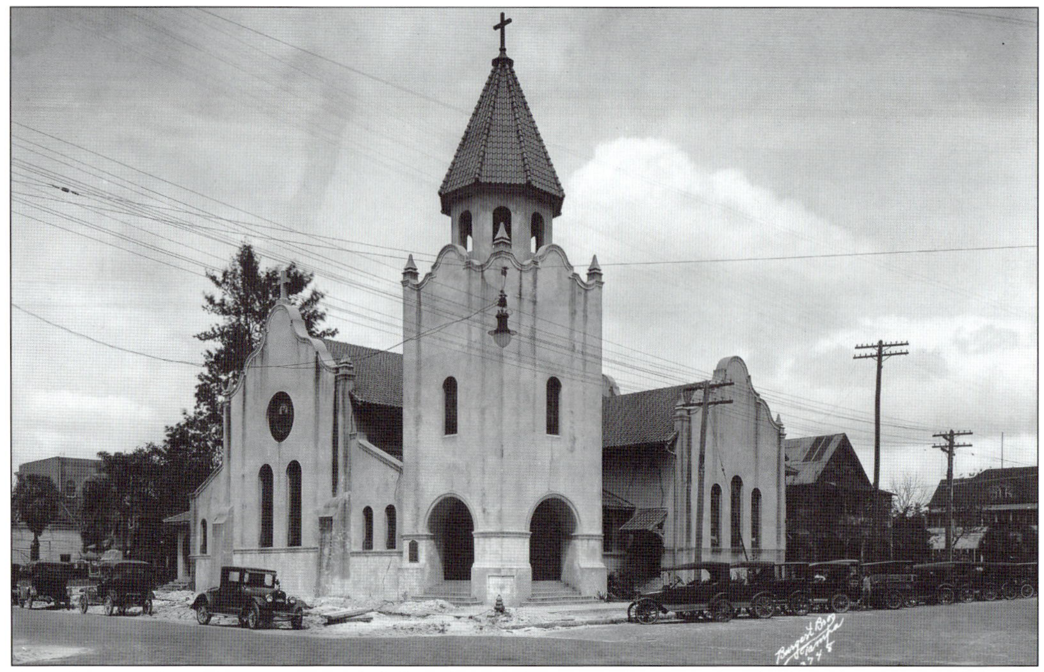

Another jewel in Tampa's crown of churches is St. Andrew's Episcopal Church, pictured here in 1925. This was Tampa's first Episcopal church, established on July 24, 1871. The church originally met for services in the Soldier's Hospital at Fort Brooke with Rev. R. Ainsworth Simpson. Services were later held at several locations including a hotel owned by Merobah Hooker Crane, a devoted parishioner. The diocesan records from 1877 show membership of five families and one dollar received from the church. The church owned one lot at that time, valued at $140. On that property bordered by Morgan, Twiggs, and Marion Streets, the original church was constructed in 1883. The church pictured here was dedicated in 1907.

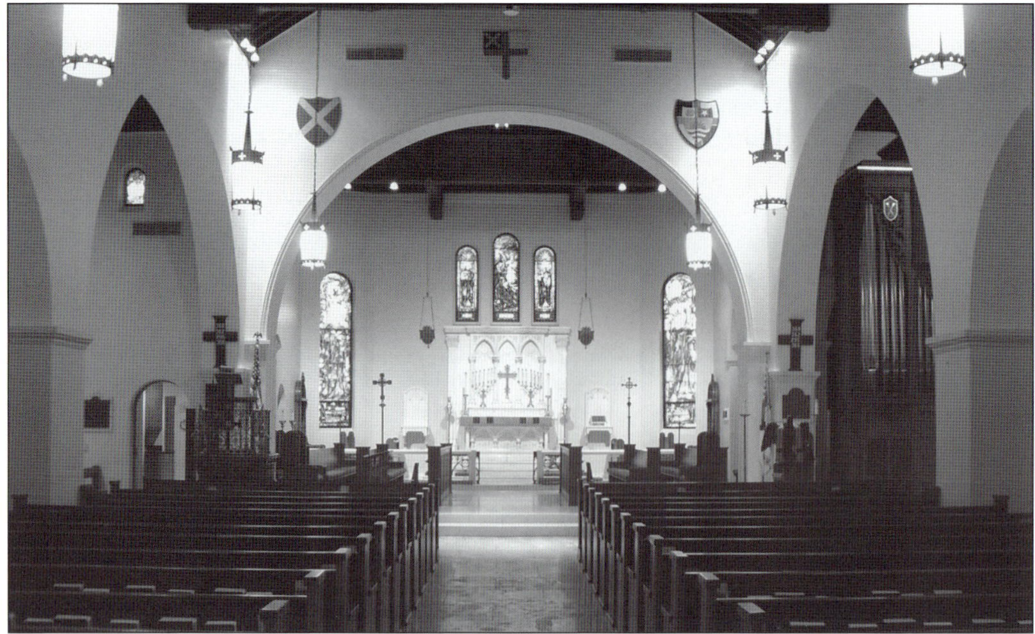

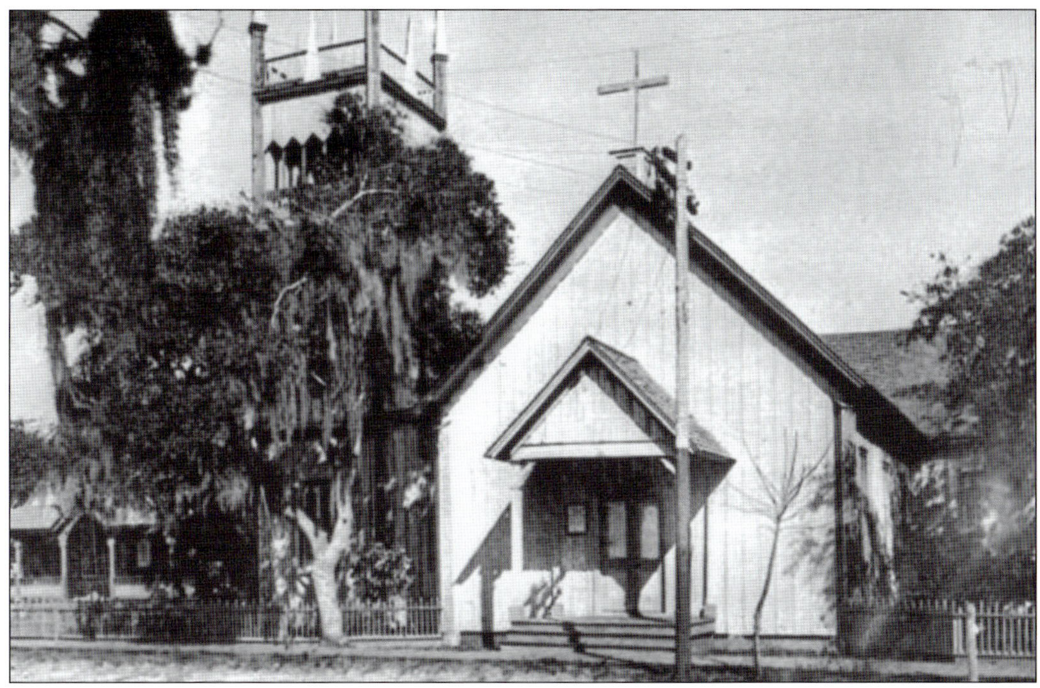

Pictured above is the original St. Andrew's Episcopal Church constructed at a cost of $1,000 under the direction of Rev. J.H. Weddell. In April 1883, the church hired the Jones Contracting Company to build the new church, which was completed in August 1883. The building was constructed in the Gothic Revival style, which was very popular for Episcopal and Catholic churches during the late 1800s. The below photograph shows the interior of the original church, which featured many stained-glass windows that were later moved to the new church.

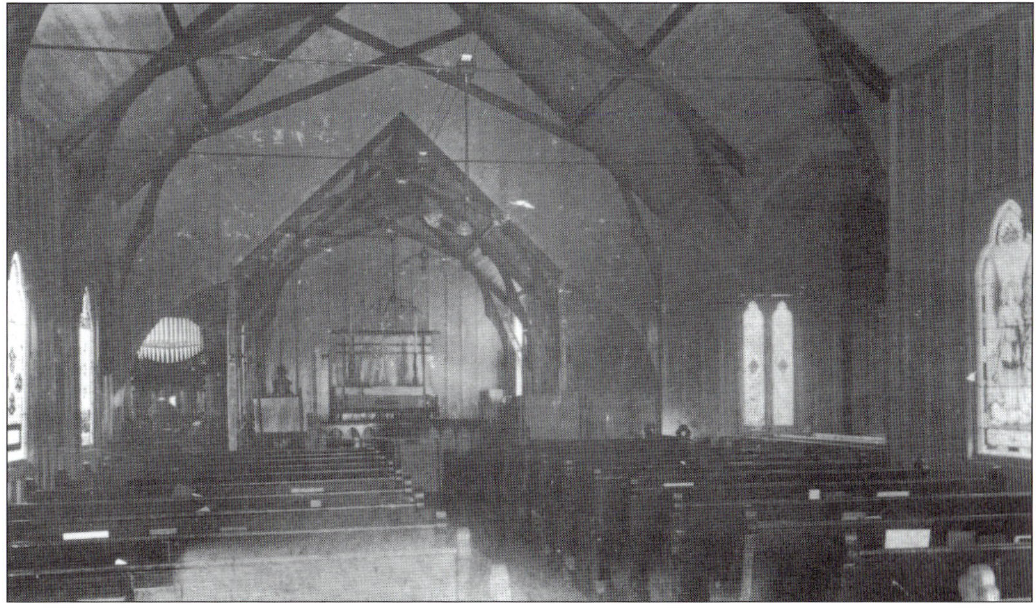

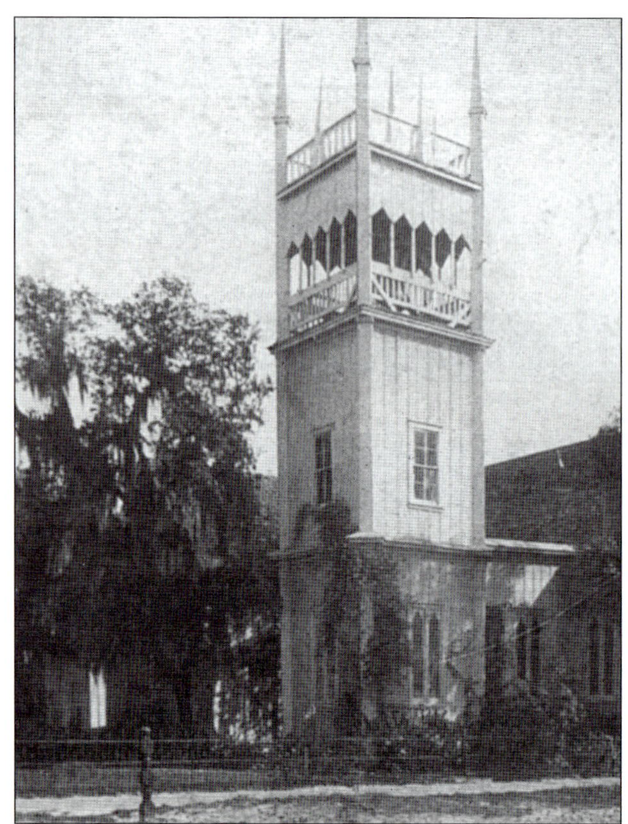

In 1890, Rev. Joseph Cross was appointed pastor and facilitated an expansion of the church and construction of a new Gothic Revival three-story bell tower, standing 52 feet tall, designed to hold four large church bells. Reverend Cross enjoyed ringing the bells very loudly, and some nearby residents began complaining that the bells were waking them up on Sunday mornings. Pictured below in 1925 is the Society of the Daughters of the King with Rev. Willis Clark (first row, center). This society was established to assist the pastor with any special needs of the church.

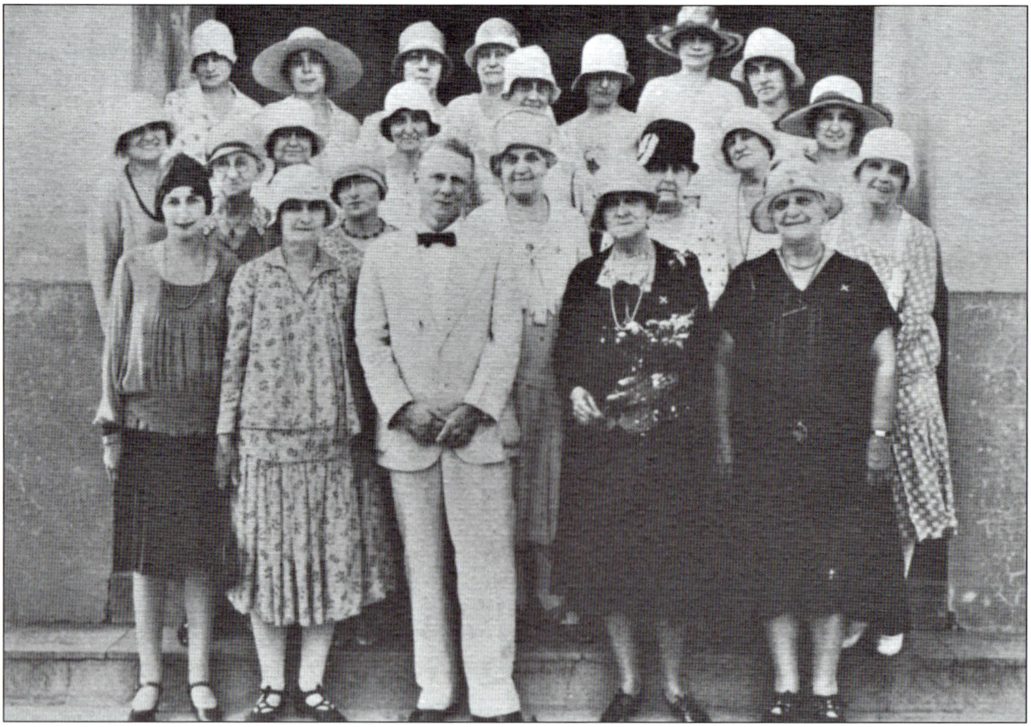

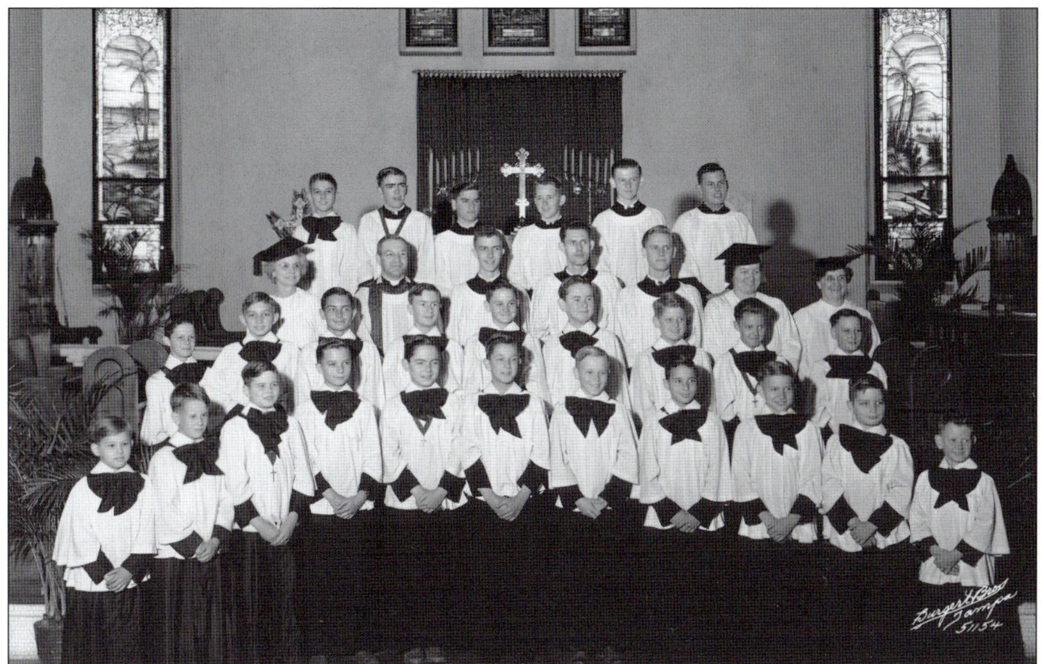

The photograph above from 1946 shows the St. Andrews Children's Choir. That same year, the church established a mission that later became St. Mary's Episcopal Church. The new church is a fine example of the Mediterranean Revival style and was designed by Tampa architects Michael J. Miller and Francis J. Kennard, who also designed several local landmarks including the Belleview-Biltmore Hotel. The new church was furnished with several articles from the original church built in 1883, including the communion rail and pulpit. The church was dedicated on May 26, 1907. In 2009, the church was listed in the National Register of Historic Places. (Both, HCPLC.)

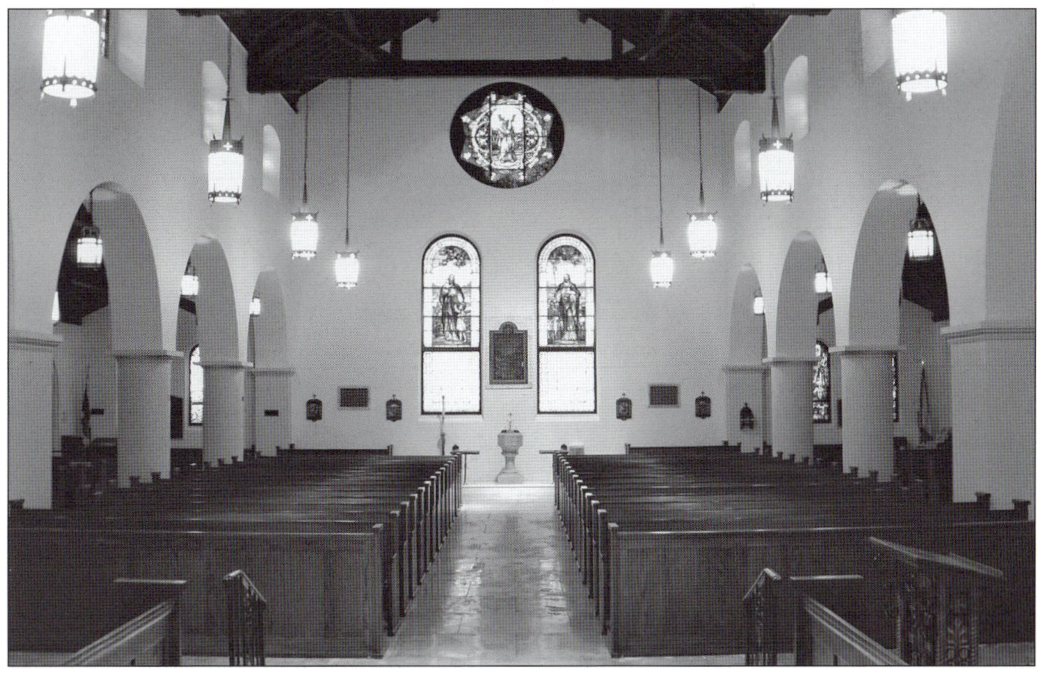

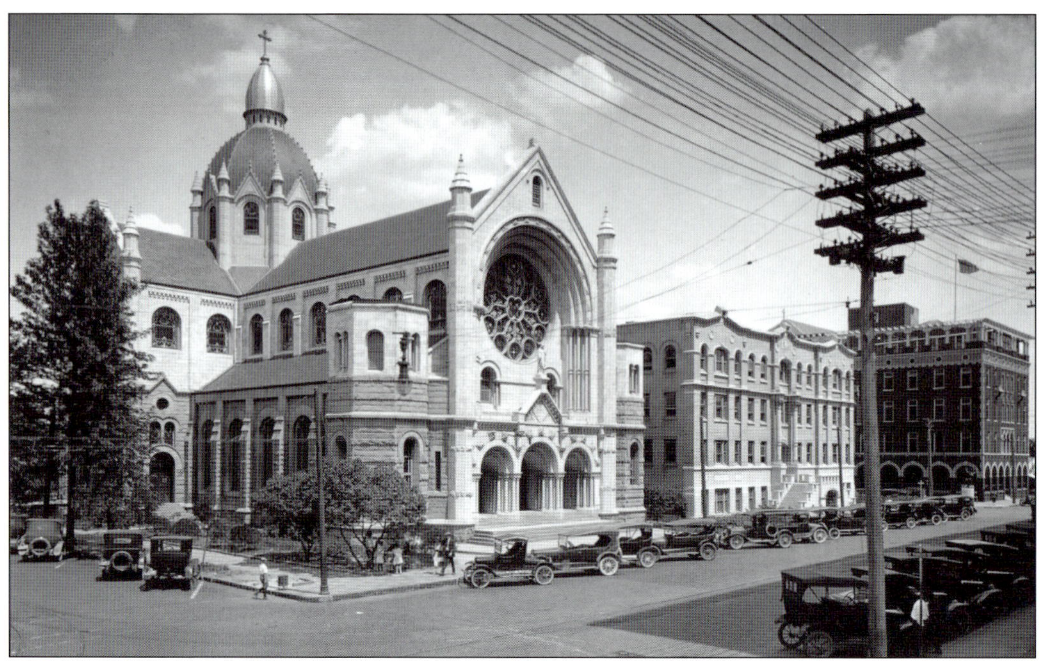

Pictured here in 1925 is Sacred Heart Catholic Church at 509 Florida Avenue. In the early 1850s, Hillsborough County commissioners deeded property at Ashley Drive and Twiggs Street for a Catholic church; it was later exchanged for land at Florida Avenue and Twiggs Street, where the original church was completed in 1859. St. Louis Catholic Church was named in honor of King Louis IX of France, a leader in the Crusades, and in memory of Fr. Luis Cancer, a Dominican missionary from Spain who was martyred on the shores of Tampa Bay in 1549. The church was officially constituted in February 1860 with the appointment of Fr. Charles S. Mailley as pastor. (Both, HCPLC.)

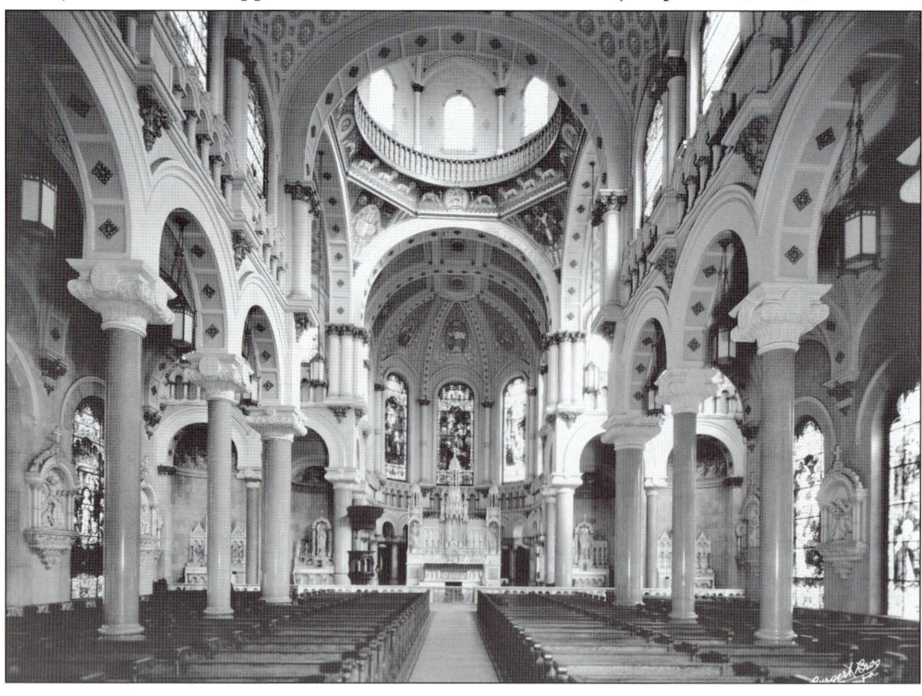

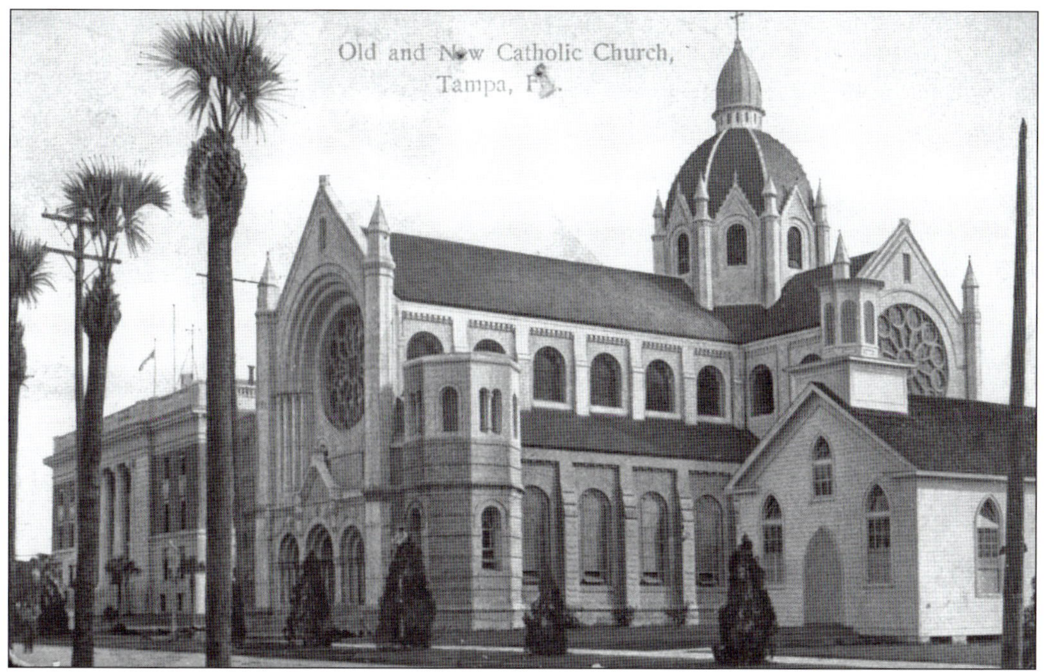

The rare 1910 photograph above shows both the original church, St. Louis Catholic Church, at right, and the new Sacred Heart Catholic Church. In 1897, Pastor Fr. William Tyrrell announced plans for a new church to accommodate the growth of the parish. Ground was broken for the new church on February 16, 1898, and construction began. The beautiful new structure was completed in 1905 at a cost of $300,000 and was named Sacred Heart Catholic Church. The smaller church was moved farther south on the property to allow for construction of the new church. The old church was then used by Sacred Heart College, which later became Jesuit High School. Below, the congregation is arriving for the dedication ceremony on January 15, 1905.

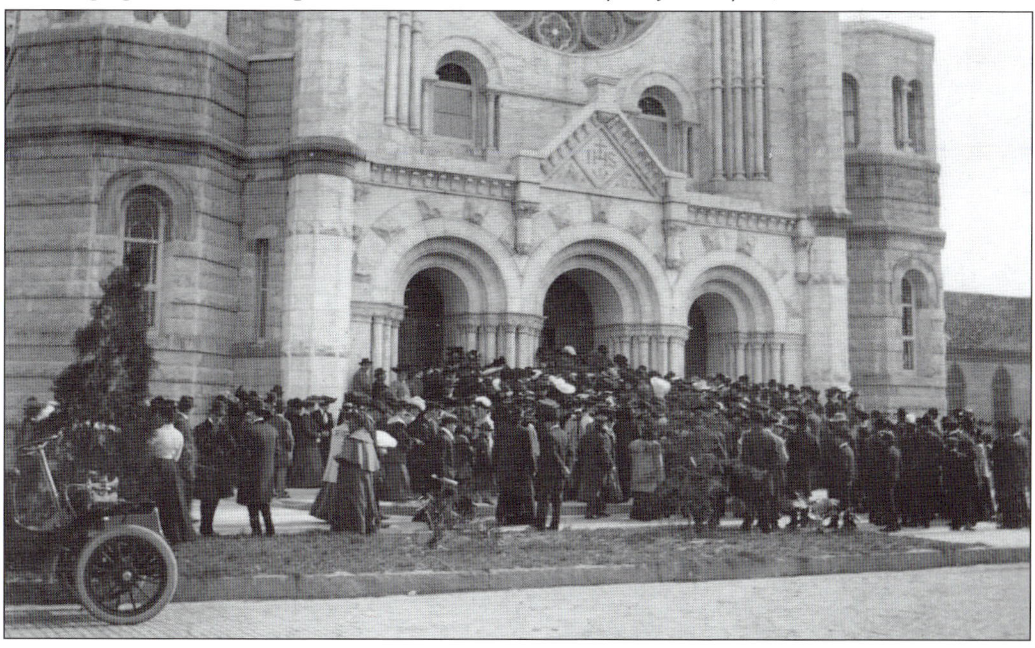

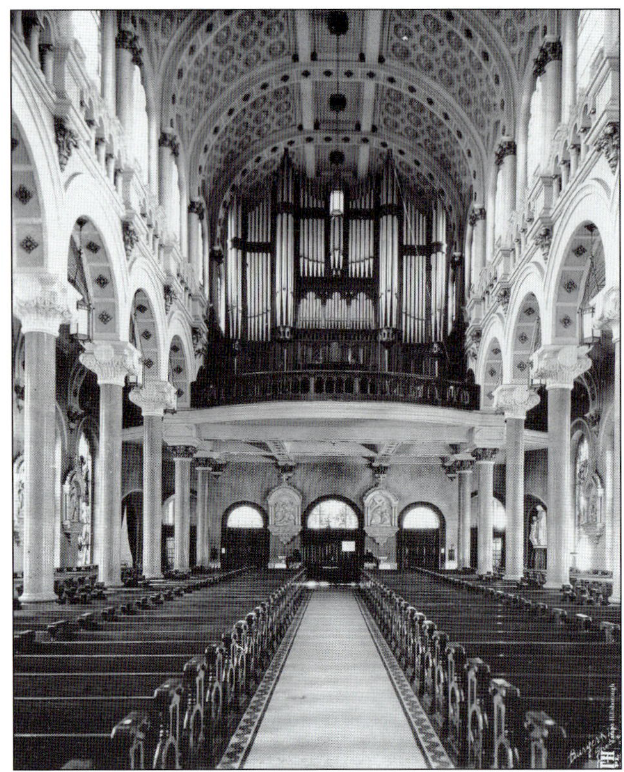

In the 1926 photograph at left, the massive pipe organ stands out prominently high above the nave of the church. The organ featured more than 4,000 pipes above the main entrance. In 2004, the church underwent a major renovation project to restore the historic stained-glass windows. During that process, the engineers discovered that the support structure for the church's dome had been made entirely of wood and was in a critical state of disrepair. The engineers had to lift the entire dome off the church to install a new steel structural support system. Below, the choir is assembled in the choir loft at the rear of the church in 1953.

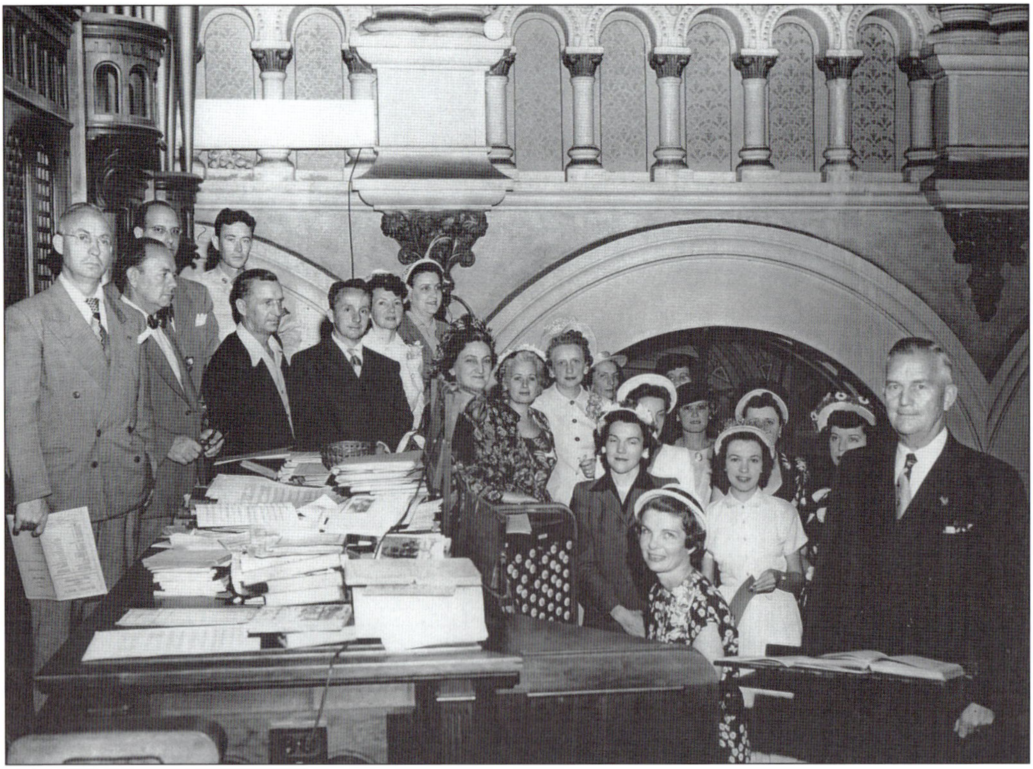

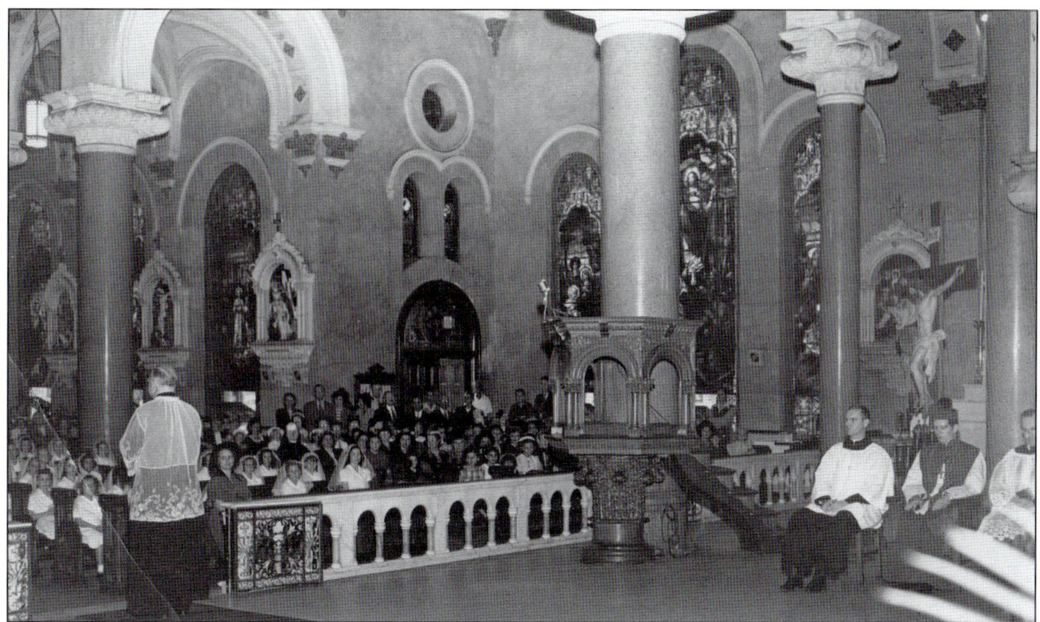

In the above photograph, taken in 1949, the stations of the cross along the north wall of the nave reveal the recent project to paint the hand-carved marble stations in vivid colors. This project was not well received by many within the congregation, and in a very short time, the paint began peeling off, which required the church to restore them to their original state. The church features 70 extraordinary stained-glass windows made by Franz Mayer Company of Munich, Germany. Pictured below in 1972 is the Resurrection Window, which is actually a triptych, with three panels. The center panel presents the risen Christ, triumphant over death. The two smaller panels depict the Virgin Mary with Mary Magdalene and Martha approaching the tomb, and two soldiers fleeing as it opens.

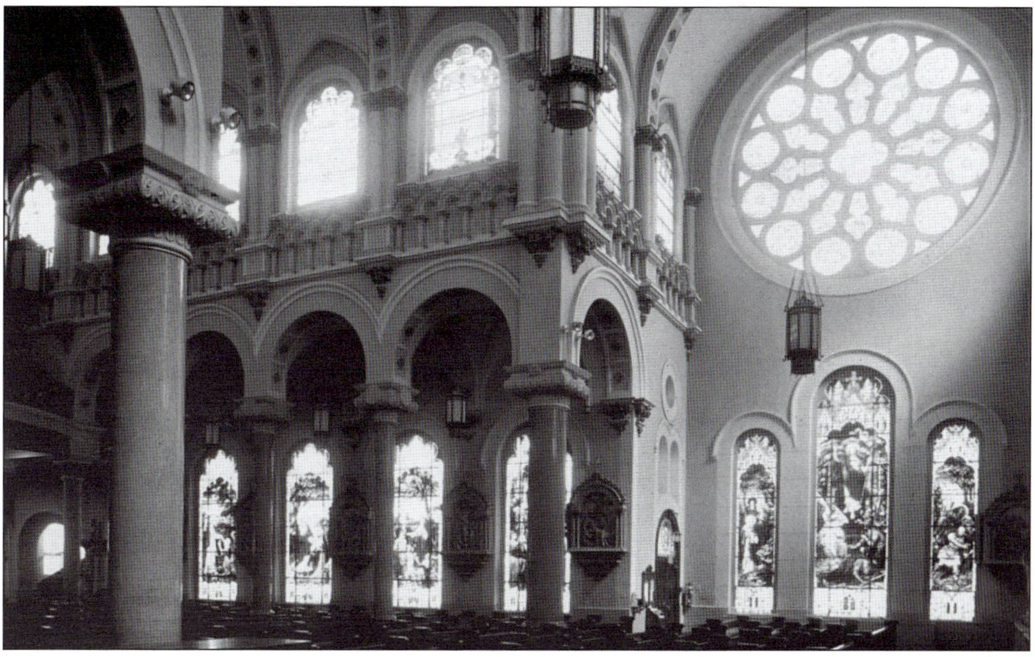

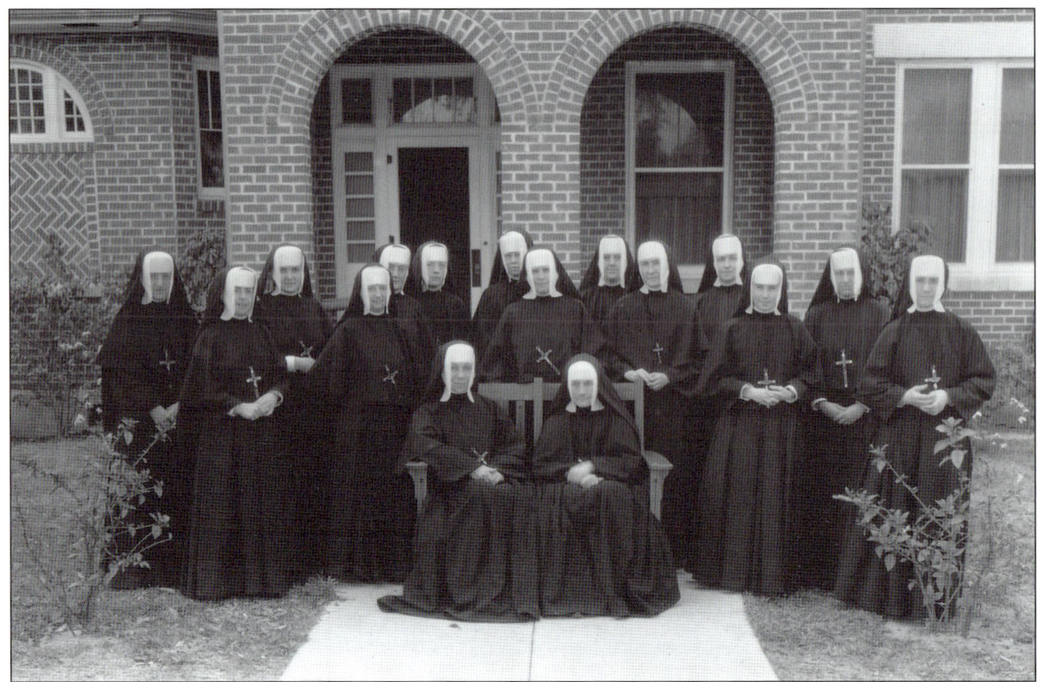

In 1930, Fr. Theodore Ray, pastor of Sacred Heart Catholic Church, started making plans for a new parish school to be constructed on property several miles north of the church at 3515 Florida Avenue. One year later, On September 13, 1931, Bishop Patrick Barry of the Diocese of St. Augustine presided at the dedication ceremony of the new school and convent. Sacred Heart Academy opened on September 14, 1931, with 326 students. The Sisters of the Holy Names staffing the school are pictured above in 1931 in front of their new convent. Below is the first graduating class on May 23, 1937. The school closed in 2012 due to a decline in enrollment.

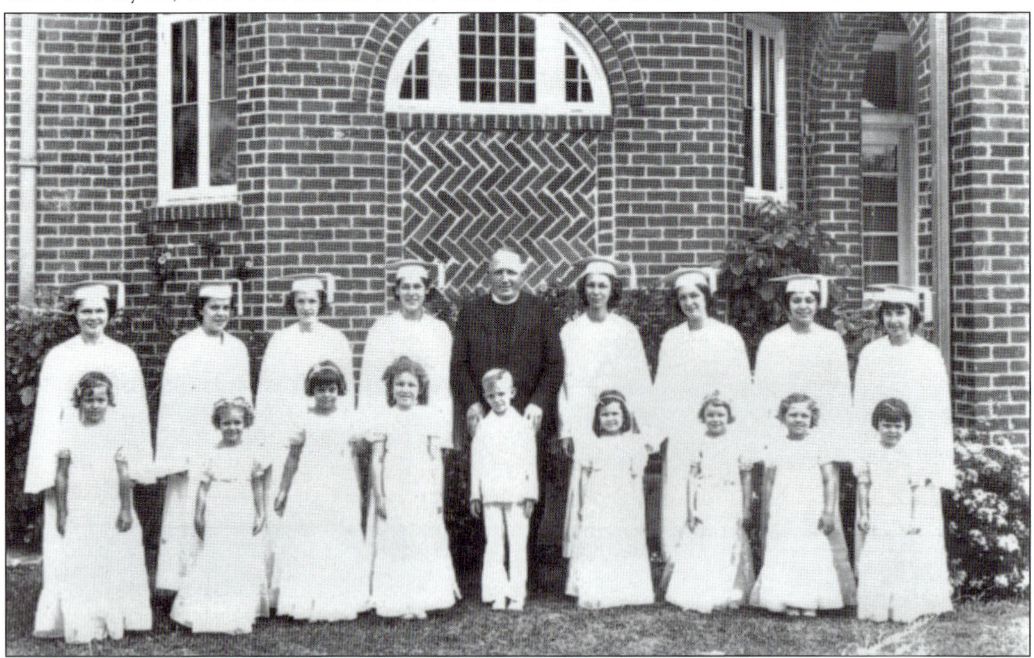

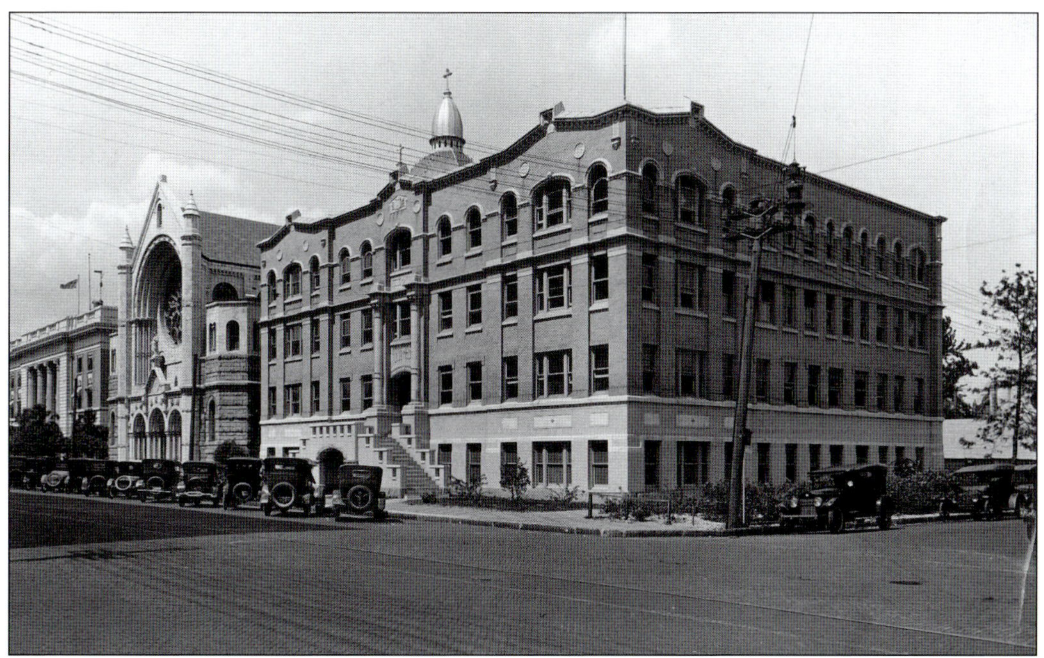

Jesuit High School was originally established as Sacred Heart College in 1899 at St Louis Catholic Church with five students. In May 1916, construction began on a new school building, and in May 1917, the new school was blessed by Rev. Michael McNally, pastor. In May 1929, the name of the school became Tampa College and enrollment reached 115 students. In 1940, Tampa College changed its name to Jesuit High School in honor of the 400th anniversary of the founding of the Society of Jesus. In March 1950, the Jesuit High School basketball team won the state championship under the direction of Coach Paul Straub, the first Catholic school in Florida to claim that honor. Pictured above is the school in 1922; below are students at Sacred Heart Academy in 1953.

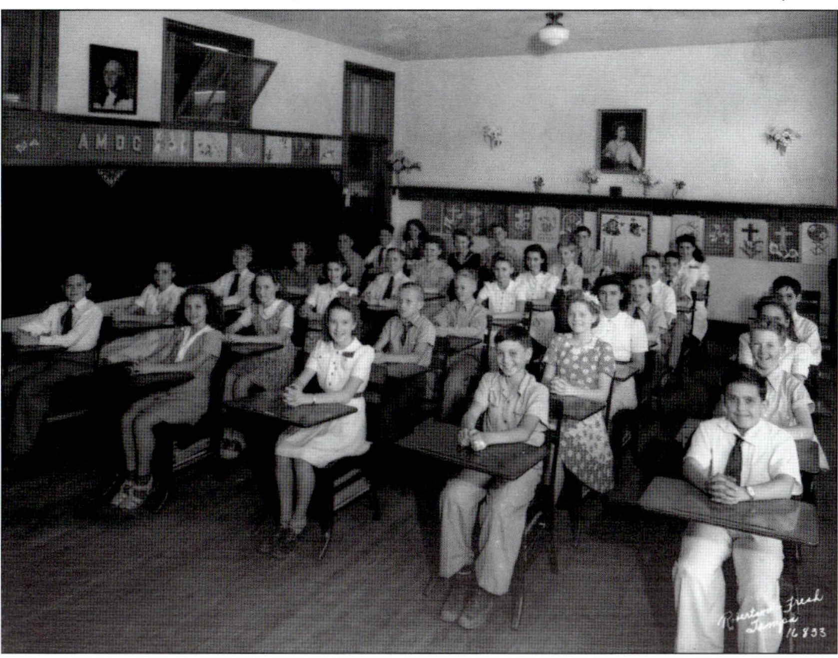

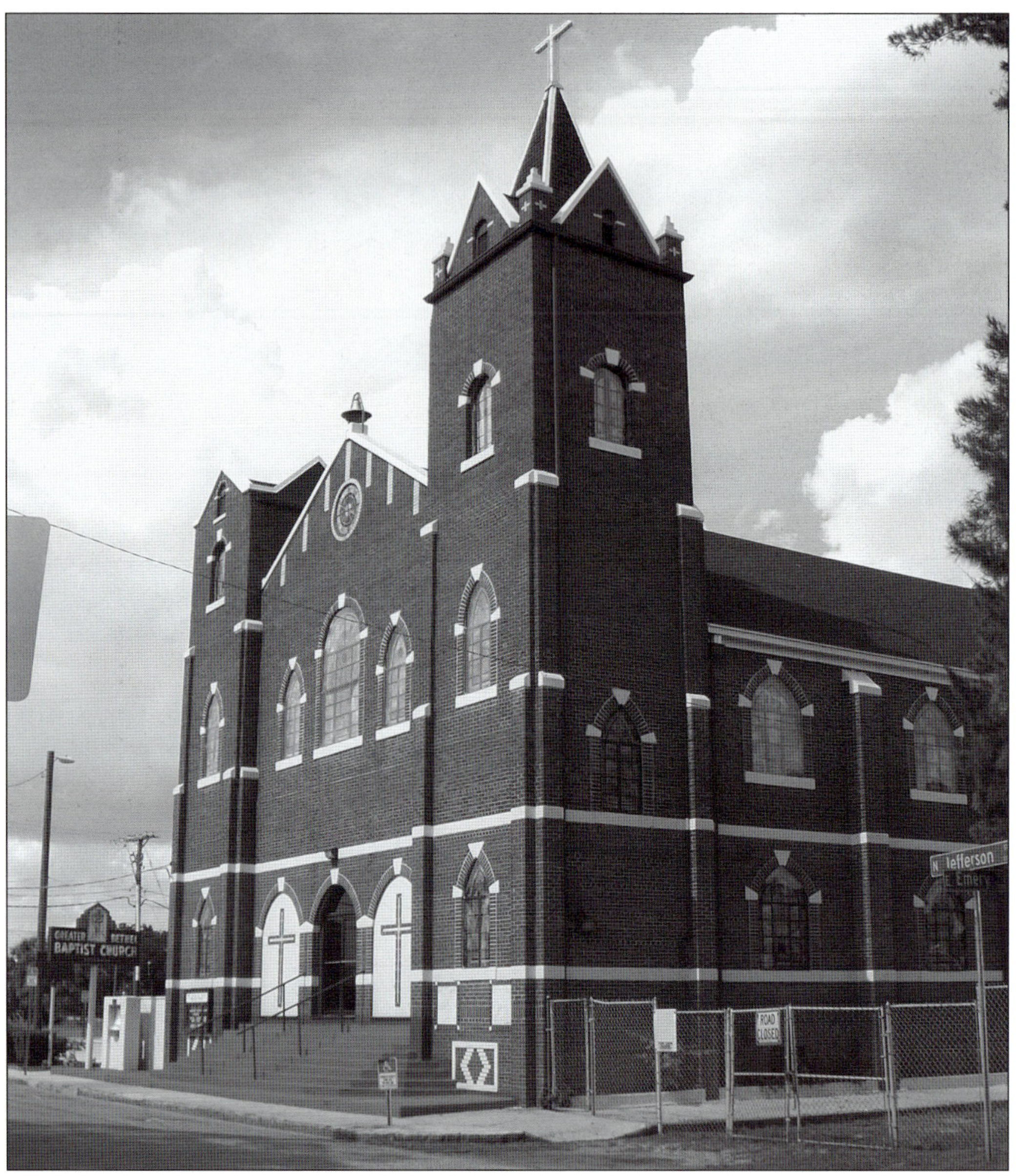

Greater Bethel Missionary Baptist Church was established in 1893 and is one of downtown Tampa's most historically significant churches. Its location on the western edge of the city, known as the "Scrub Neighborhood," made it a focal point for Tampa's African Americans. The congregation originally was named Ebenezer Baptist Church and met in a tent for worship until 1904 when their first church was built. That year, the church was reorganized and dedicated as Bethel Baptist Church. At the time, there were less than 50 members, but they were among the most influential in the community, many of them early settlers. Pastor Jacob Wesley Rhodes headed the church from 1936 through 1959. Under his leadership, the name was changed to Greater Bethel Missionary Baptist Church. In 1949, the community celebrated the completion of a beautiful new Gothic-inspired redbrick church dedicated as Greater Bethel Missionary Baptist Church. The church's facilities were expanded in 2001 to include the Rev. Oscar Johnson Jr. Fellowship and Educational Center, named after the church's pastor appointed in 1978.

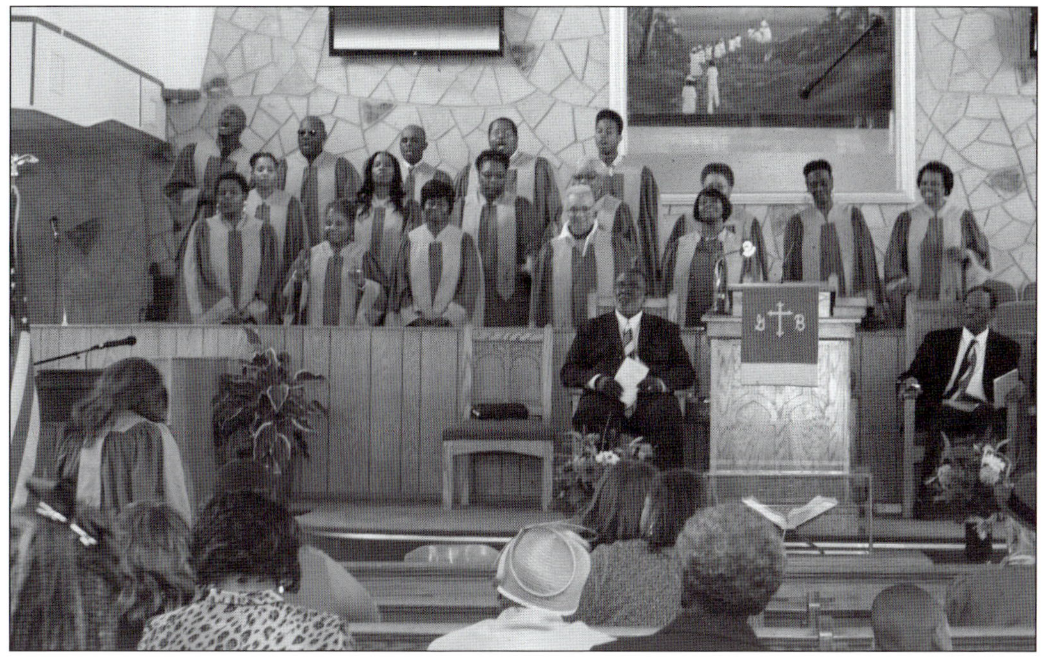

In 2004, the City of Tampa recognized the long-standing importance of the church when it designated it one of the local landmarks in the Historic Central Avenue District. In 2011, the church was designated a local historic landmark by the Hillsborough County Historical Advisory Council. The community of Greater Bethel Missionary Baptist Church continues the mission of those early founding members who met in a tent on a street corner to begin their service of outreach to the community. Pictured here are the choir and congregation in their historic sanctuary.

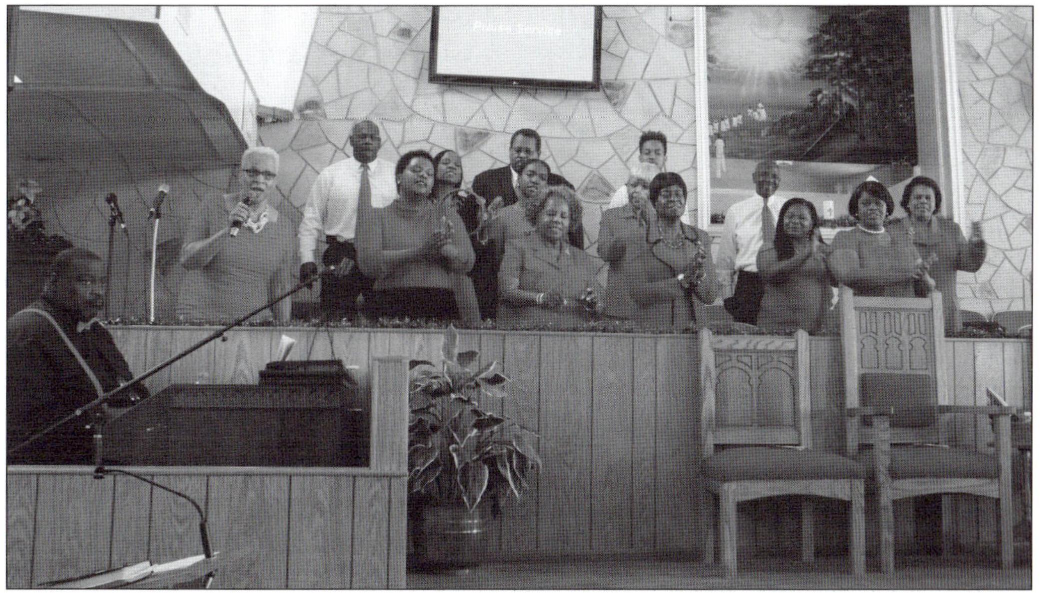

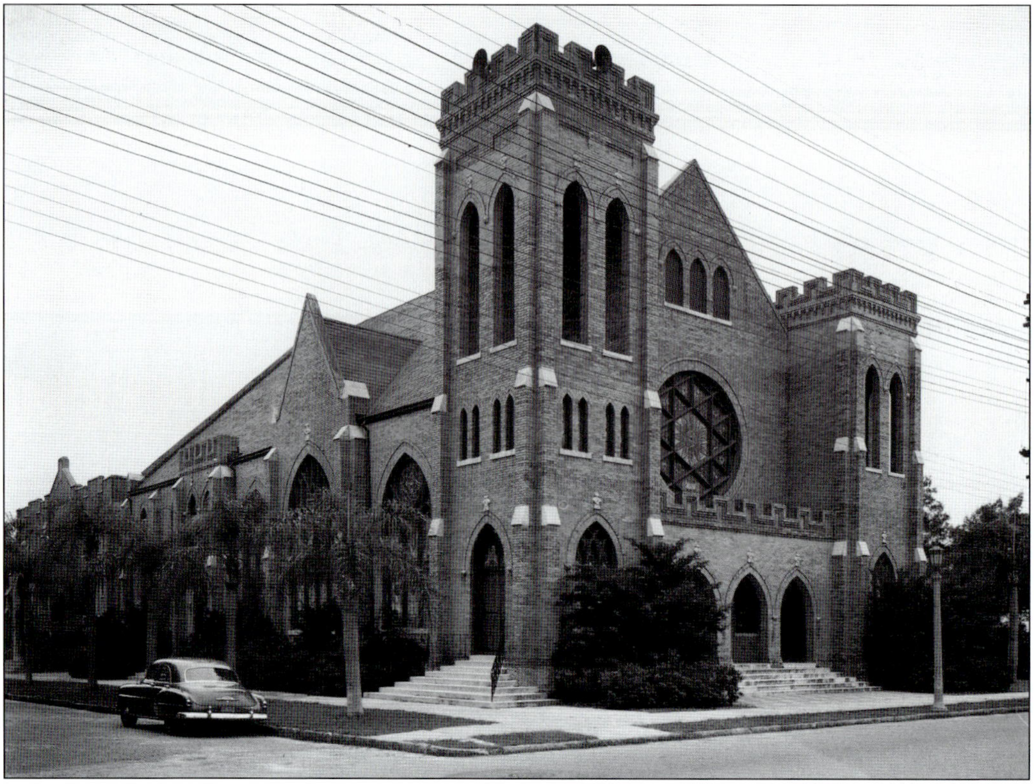

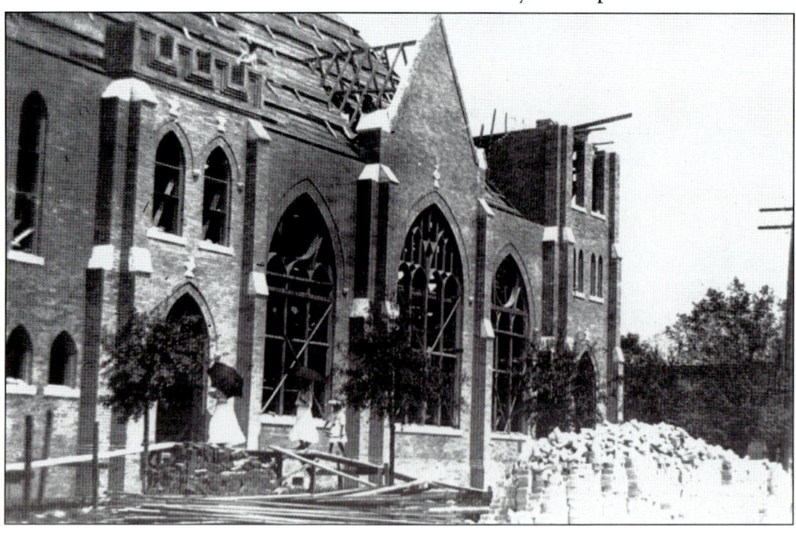

Pictured here in 1954 is Hyde Park United Methodist Church at 500 West Platt Street. In the late 1800s, Methodist families in Hyde Park rode by horse and buggy to First United Methodist Church on the east side of the Hillsborough River. One Sunday afternoon in 1899, three families met to start a Sunday school for neighborhood children and began a new congregation. On March 12, 1899, thirty people gathered for the first meeting in a two-room schoolhouse on the corner of Magnolia Avenue and Platt Street, where the Tampa Fire Station now stands. In 1907, the congregation completed their new church at a cost of $24,000. The photograph below shows construction of the new church in 1907. It was dedicated by Bishop E.E. Hoss.

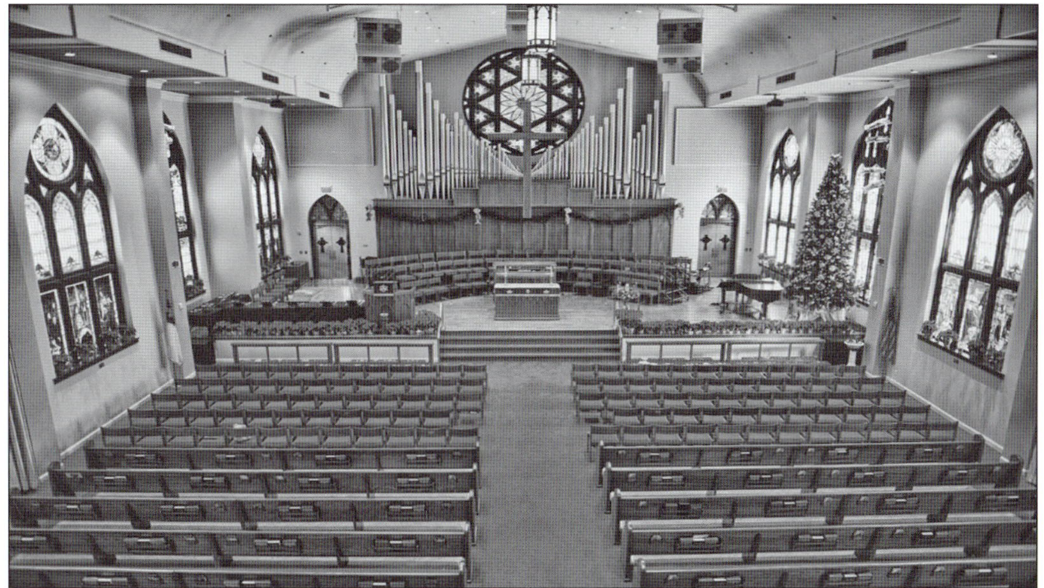

The congregation was officially organized as Hyde Park United Methodist Church in 1900, with 29 charter members and Rev. Henry Hice serving as pastor. Several of the grandchildren and great-grandchildren of those founding members remain active members of the congregation today. The church sanctuary pictured here was originally constructed in 1907 with a "half-round" worship space and two-story classrooms. The Gothic structure features 73 memorial stained-glass windows. In 1922, an education building was constructed with a fellowship hall on the first floor and classrooms on the upper floors.

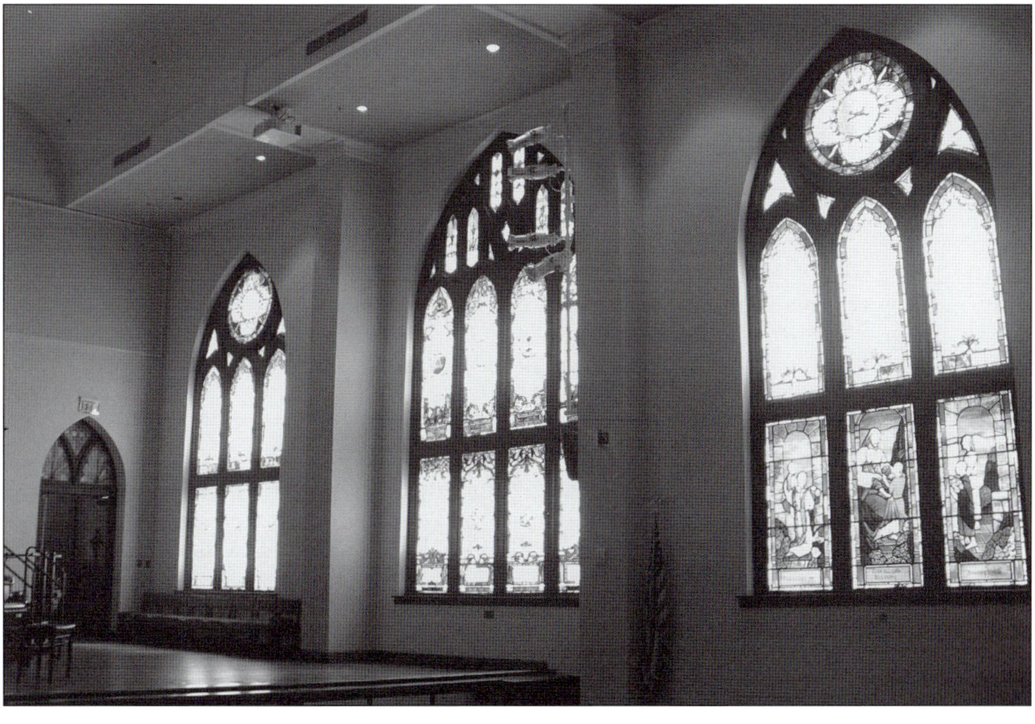

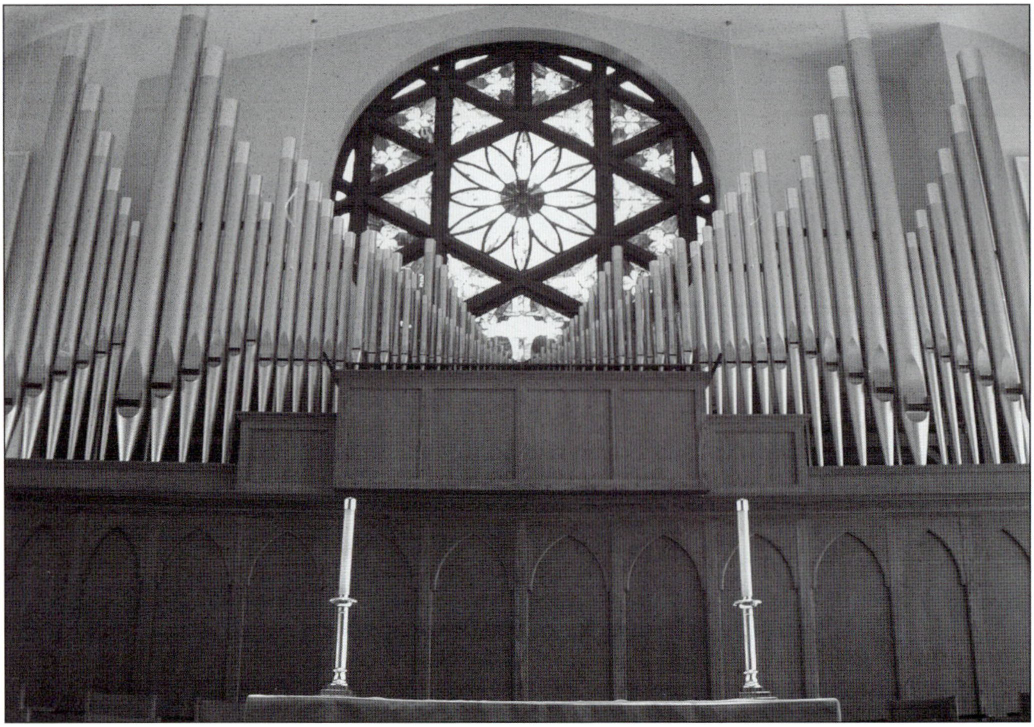

In 1953, Hyde Park United Methodist Church underwent a major renovation project to move the chancel and choir loft to the south end of the church in the area that had been classrooms, and new church pews were added to the enlarged sanctuary space. The fellowship hall and chapel were built in 1954. The chapel was dedicated to the memory of Dr. Laurie Ray, who led the congregation in the building program of 1953. The fellowship hall was named in honor of former pastor J. Lloyd Knox when he was elected to the episcopacy in 1984. The below photograph shows the chancel choir in the historic sanctuary.

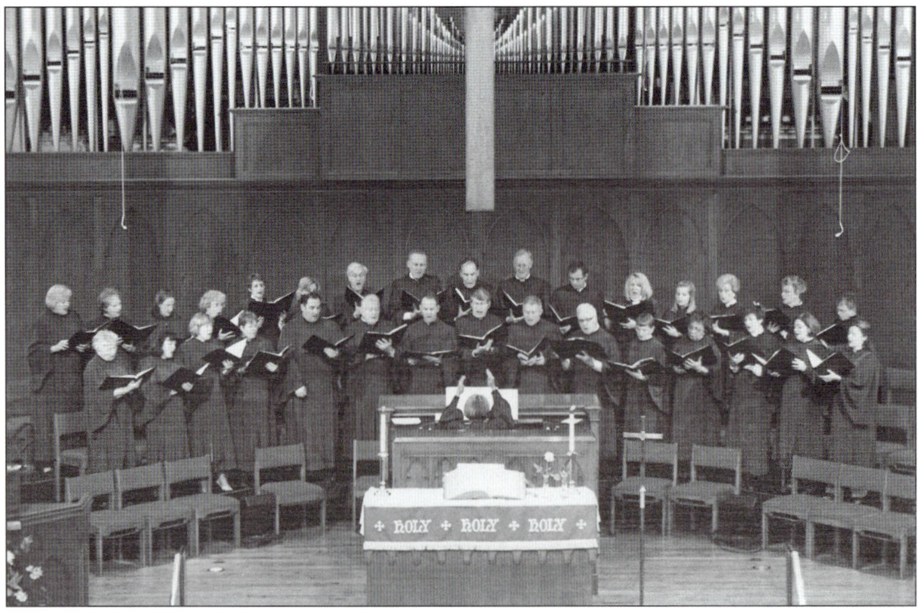

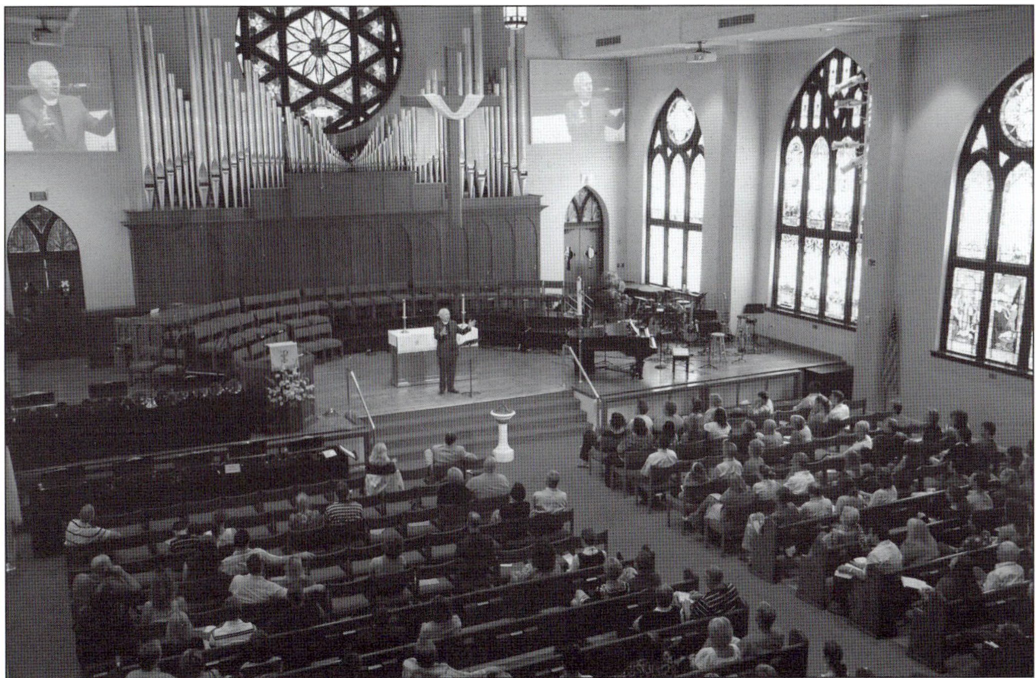

Hyde Park United Methodist Church continues the mission of those three founding families by offering ministries of outreach to the community including many programs of assistance to the underprivileged. One of the most extensive ministries is the Portico, located in the former First United Methodist Church building pictured below in 1982. The Portico is a community worship center and performing arts hall that also serves as the headquarters of Love INC, an interdenominational ministry providing assistance to the poor and homeless. The Portico Café serves as a means of fundraising to benefit church-sponsored outreach programs for those in need.

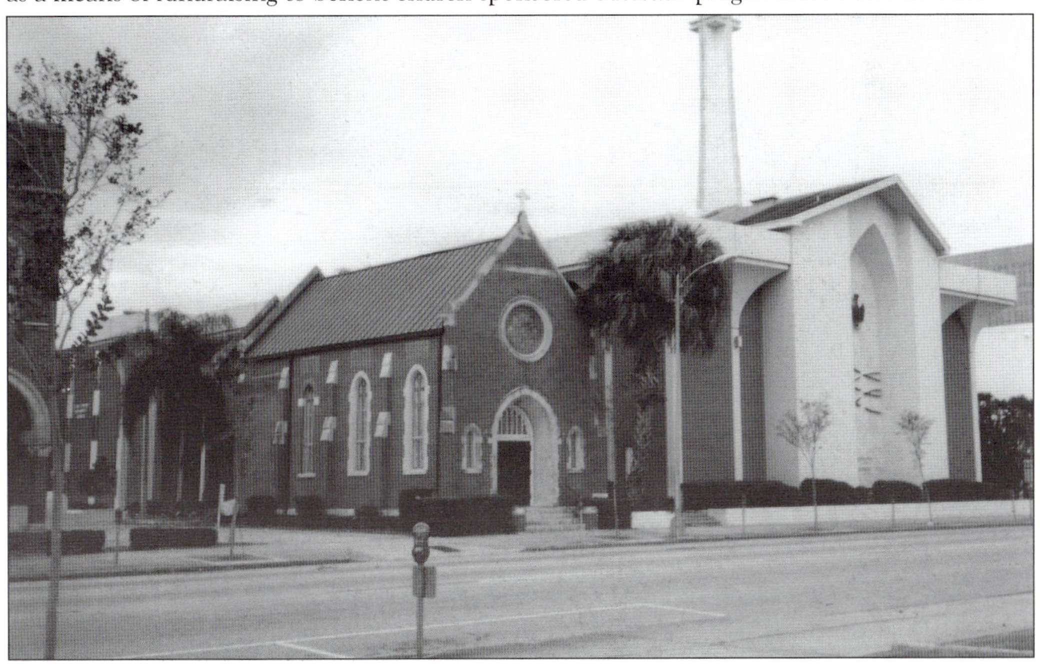

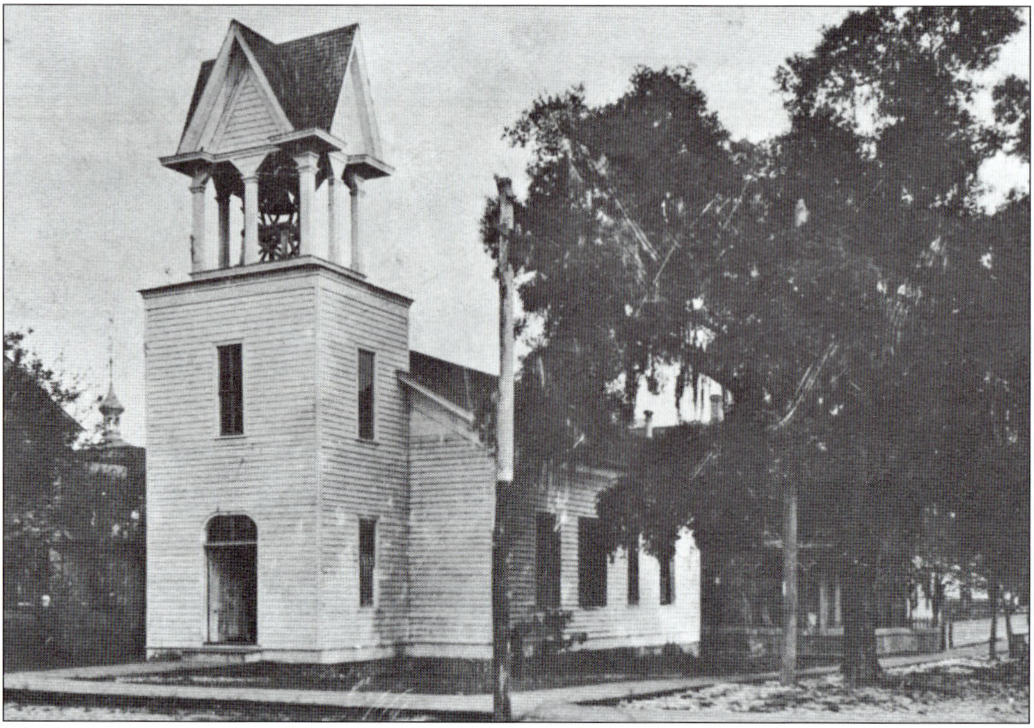

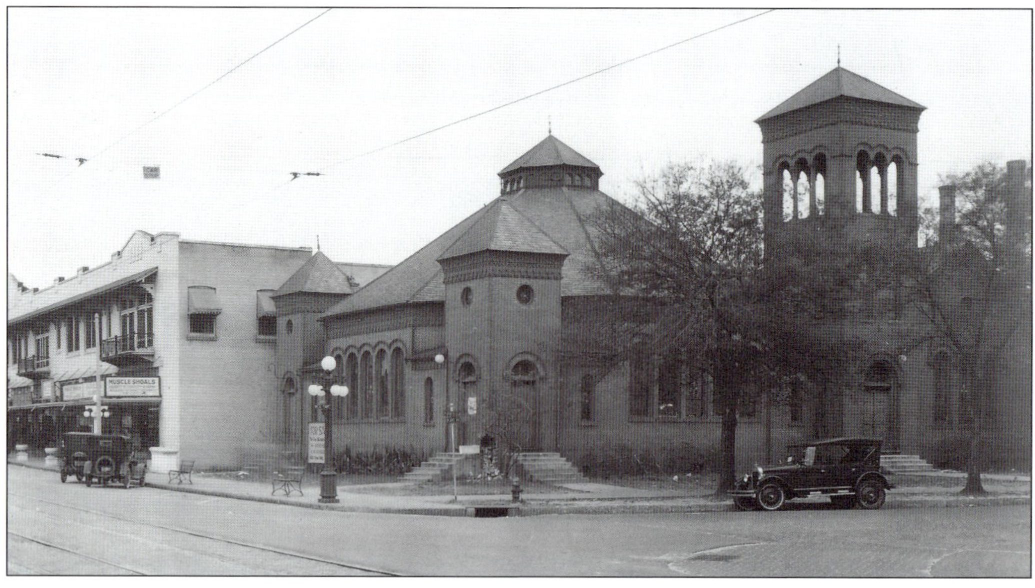

The history of First Baptist Church dates to 1855, when Rev. Jeremiah Hayman arrived in Tampa with plans to establish a new church. On July 23, 1859, the church was organized by Reverend Hayman, the first pastor. The Hillsborough County Commission voted to give the church a lot in downtown Tampa. The first church was constructed on the corner of Tampa and Twiggs Streets in 1892 (pictured above). In 1896, a larger church was constructed on the southeast corner of Plant Avenue and Lafayette Street, pictured below. In 1924, the congregation constructed a new church across the street from this church. The image below of the old church was taken in 1925, after the congregation had moved into their new church, and there is a "For Sale" sign in front of it.

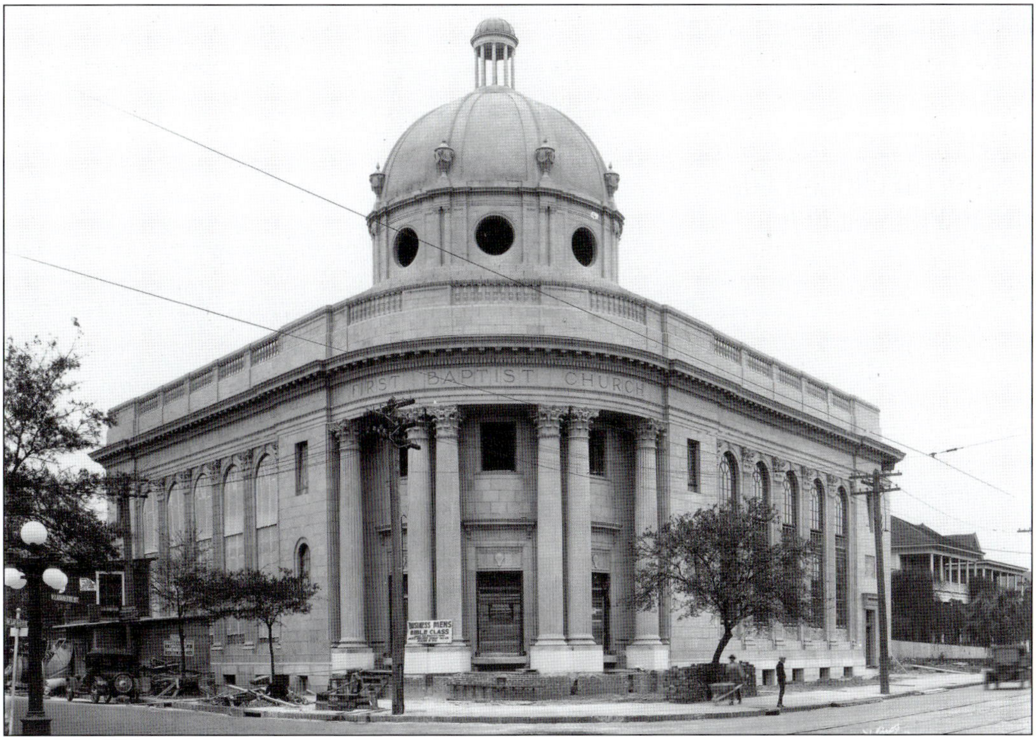

The new church was designed in the Colonial Revival style with a domed sanctuary and decorative balustrades adorning the roofline. The above photograph shows the new church nearing completion in 1924. The cornerstone was laid on March 30, 1923. In 1926, a set of bell chimes was installed in the tower. The vintage chimes have been restored by the church and are one of the last remaining sets of Deagan chimes still in operation in the United States. Below, the congregation of First Baptist Church is pictured on the church steps in 1937. (Both, HCPLC.)

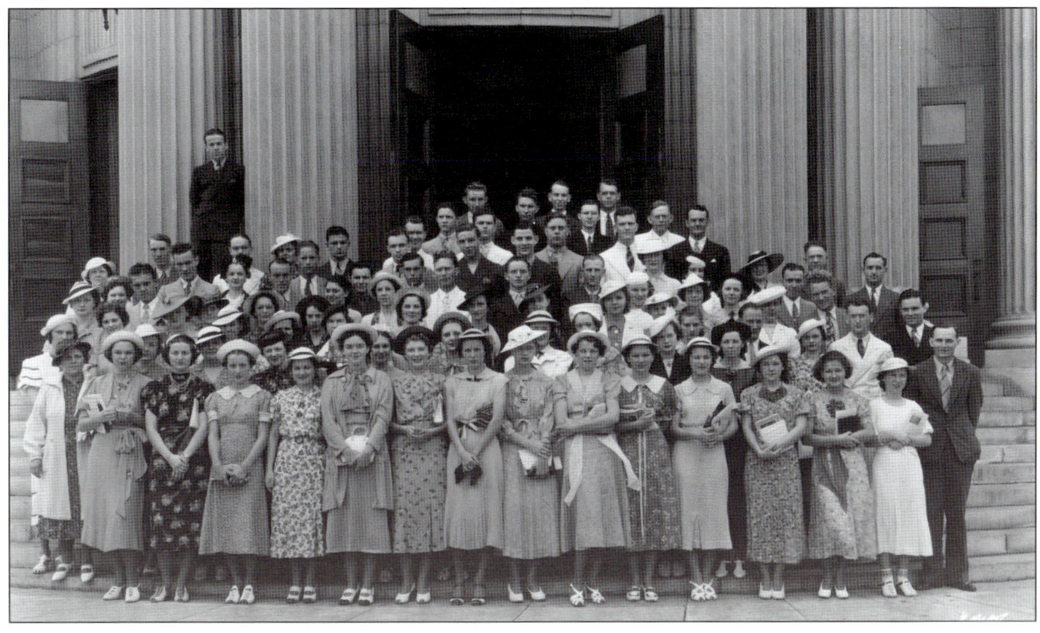

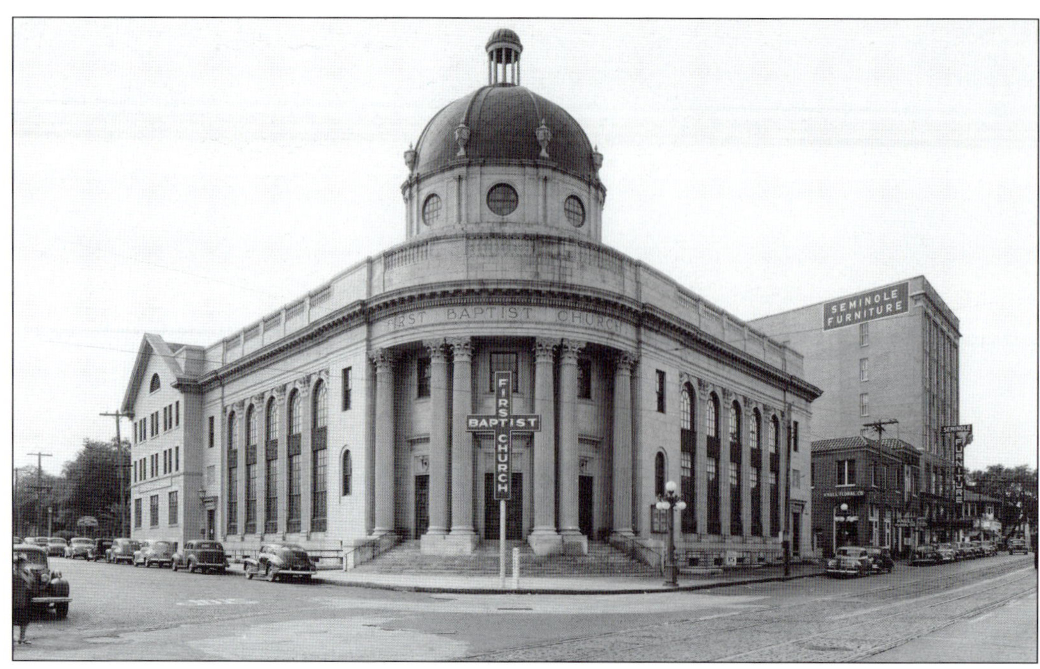

The new First Baptist Church is pictured here in 1947. The church holds a prominent place in the development of the Baptist community of Tampa. The first mission founded was in 1865, when Beulah Baptist Institutional Church was established for the African American community. The congregation has a long history of community outreach, establishing 18 missions during its years of service. Many of these missions have developed into longtime churches serving the neighborhoods of Tampa, including Palm Avenue Baptist Church, Concord Baptist Church, Sulphur Springs Baptist Church, Bayshore Baptist Church, and Northgate Baptist Church. The 1,600-seat sanctuary is pictured below in 1957.

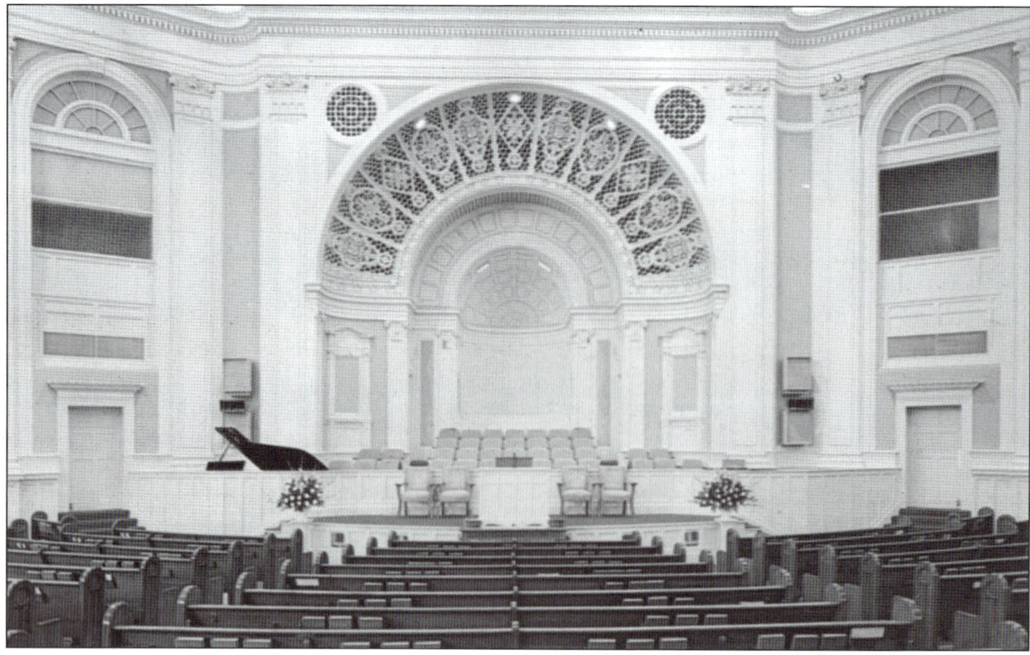

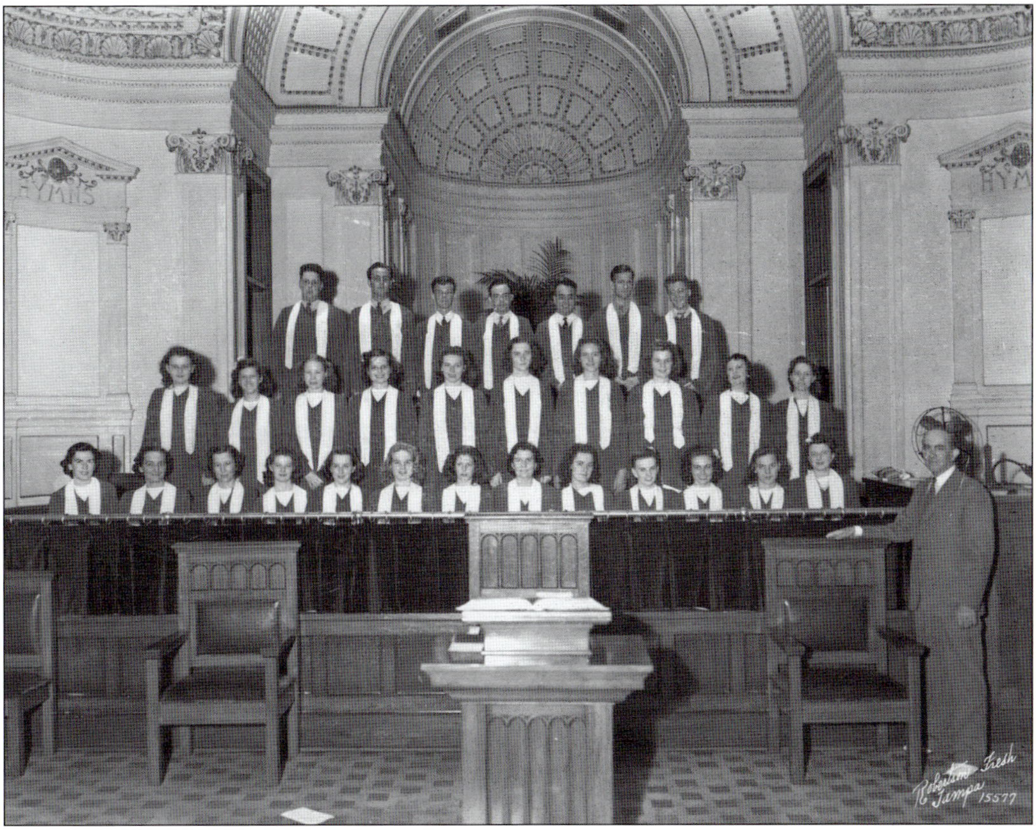

The church is also dedicated to missionary activities with many outreach projects including community missions for college students and children, and international mission trips. In 1973, the church constructed a 12-story apartment building across the street from the church for the benefit of low-income senior citizens. The above photograph shows the choir of First Baptist Church in 1941. Below, the children's Sunday school class celebrates at a party in 1947. (Both, HCPLC.)

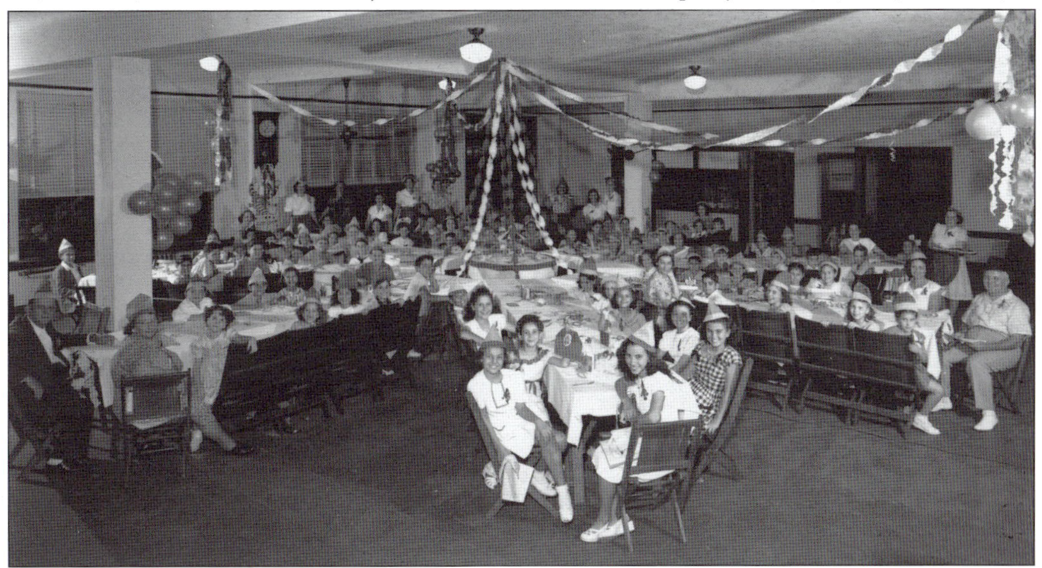

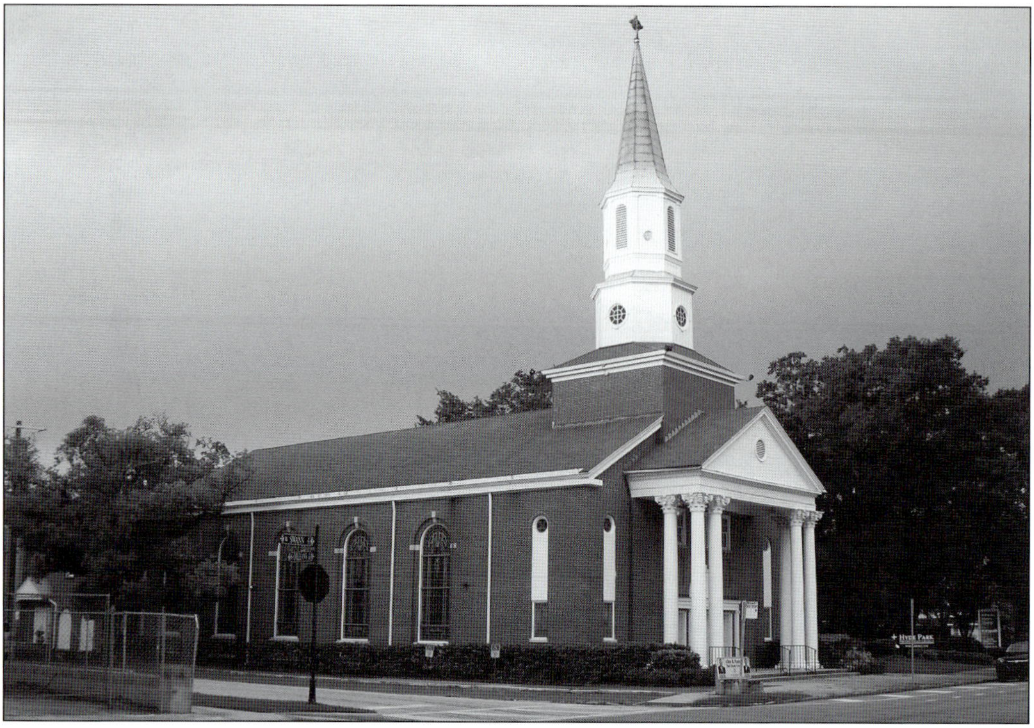

The history of Hyde Park Presbyterian Church dates to 1910, when a group of congregants met in the Olivet Chapel at the corner of Inman and Oregon Avenues. In 1914, the church was officially organized with 31 charter members under the guidance of Dr. J.R.C. Brown. The congregation then dedicated the first church, pictured below shortly after construction, in 1917. In 1947, the church secured property at 1309 Swann Avenue and made plans for a new church to accommodate the growth of the congregation. In 1952, the new church (above) was dedicated by the community. Hyde Park Presbyterian Church supports many programs including Metropolitan Ministries, Habitat for Humanity, the Judeo-Christian Health Clinic, Beth-El Ministry, the Good Samaritan Counseling Center, and many other special programs of assistance to the poor and underprivileged.

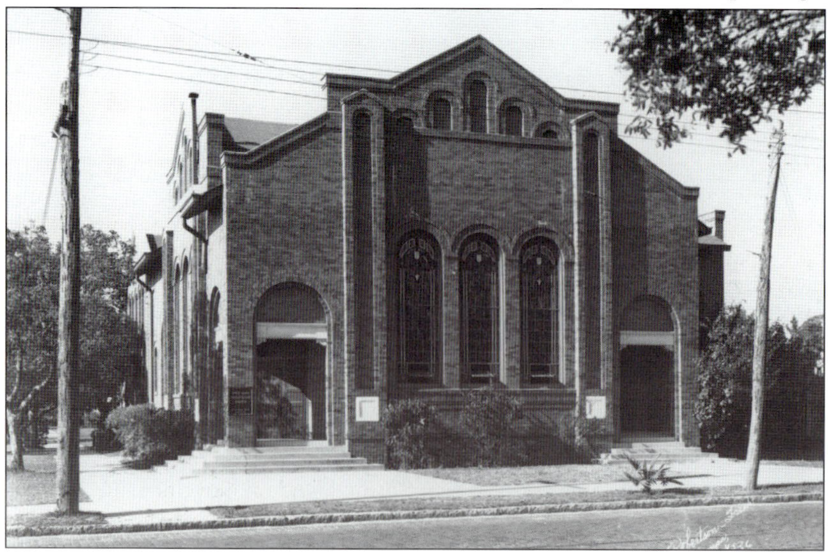

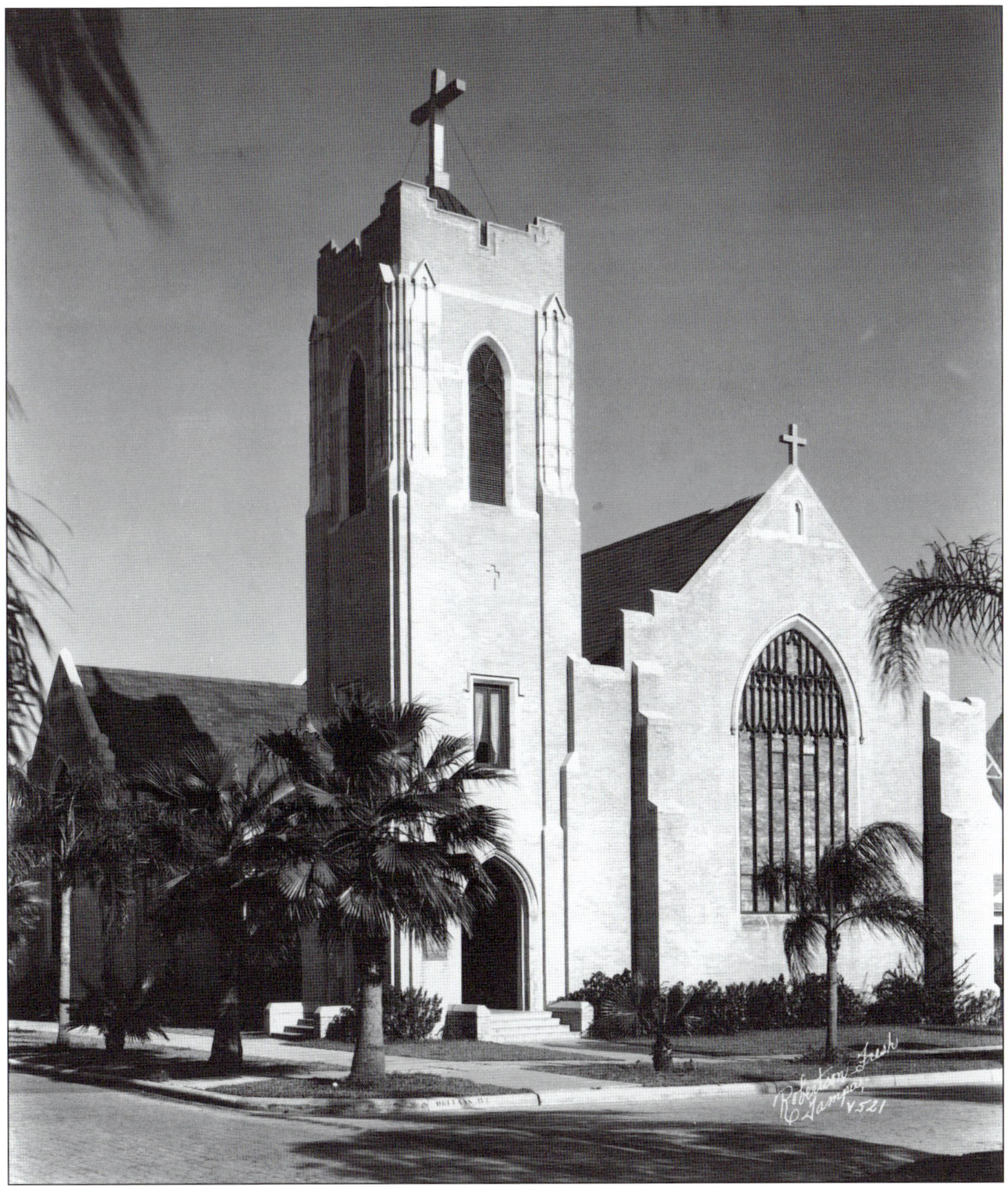

St. John's Episcopal Church was established on May 26, 1912, when it was officially consecrated by the Rt. Rev. William Crane Gray, bishop of the diocese. In 1911, Bishop Gray purchased property at the corner of Orleans and Morrison Avenues for a future church, which was a mission of St. Andrew's Episcopal Church. The original church was completed in March 1912. The first rector was Rev. John Friedenreich Porter. Bishop Gray wrote in his diary on November 21, 1911: "At St. Andrew's Rectory, after dinner, went in automobile with Rev. and Mrs. DeHart to where the first move for the new church, St. John's By the Sea, is being made. I thank God that we have such a good and promising location for the future welfare of the church." With the continued growth of the congregation, a larger church was planned, and on November 16, 1924, ground was broken for the new church. The church was completed at a cost of $60,000 and was dedicated on Palm Sunday, April 1, 1928.

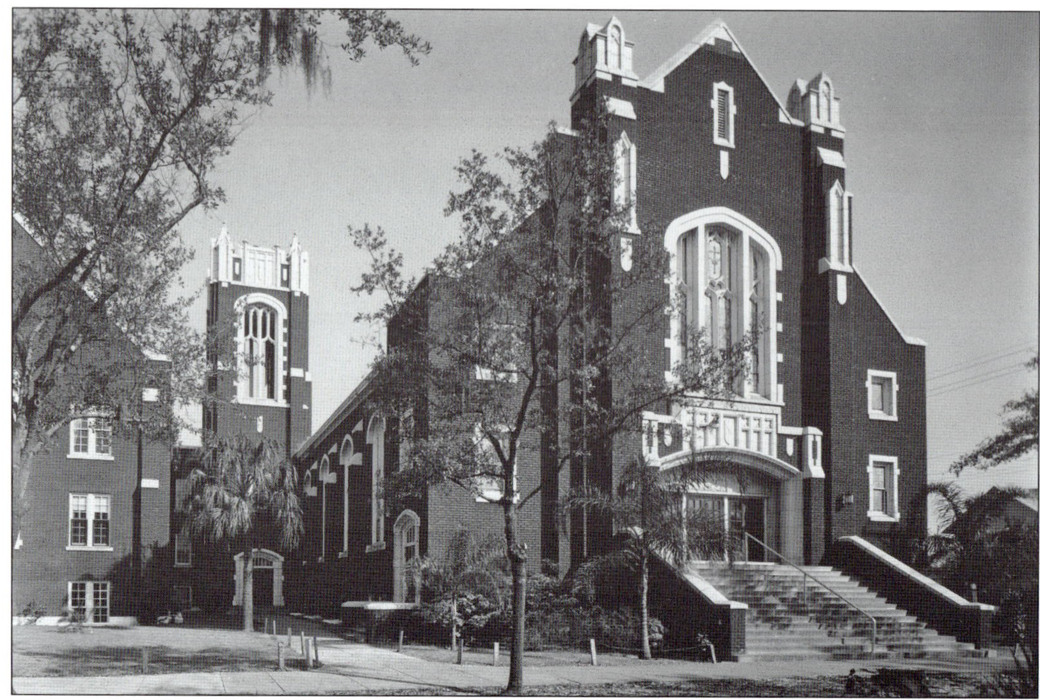

First Christian Church at 350 South Hyde Park Avenue is pictured here in 1927 shortly after its construction. The church was completed at a cost of $250,000. It was established on April 2, 1900, by Dr. S.D. Colyer, the first pastor. This magnificent church is a Hyde Park landmark of English Gothic architecture, overlooking the Davis Islands Bridge. The congregation established several missions, including Central Christian Church in 1928, Peninsular Christian Church in 1953, Hillsborough Christian Church in 1955, University Christian Church in 1957, and Brandon Christian Church in 1966. In 2008, the congregation left their beloved church due to a decline in membership. Pictured below is the church choir in 1953.

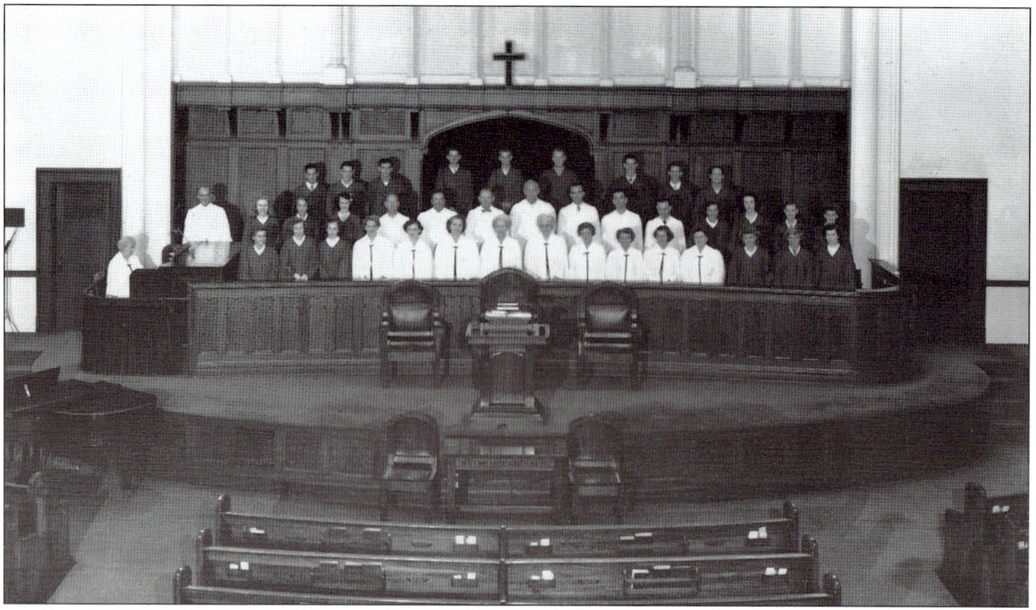

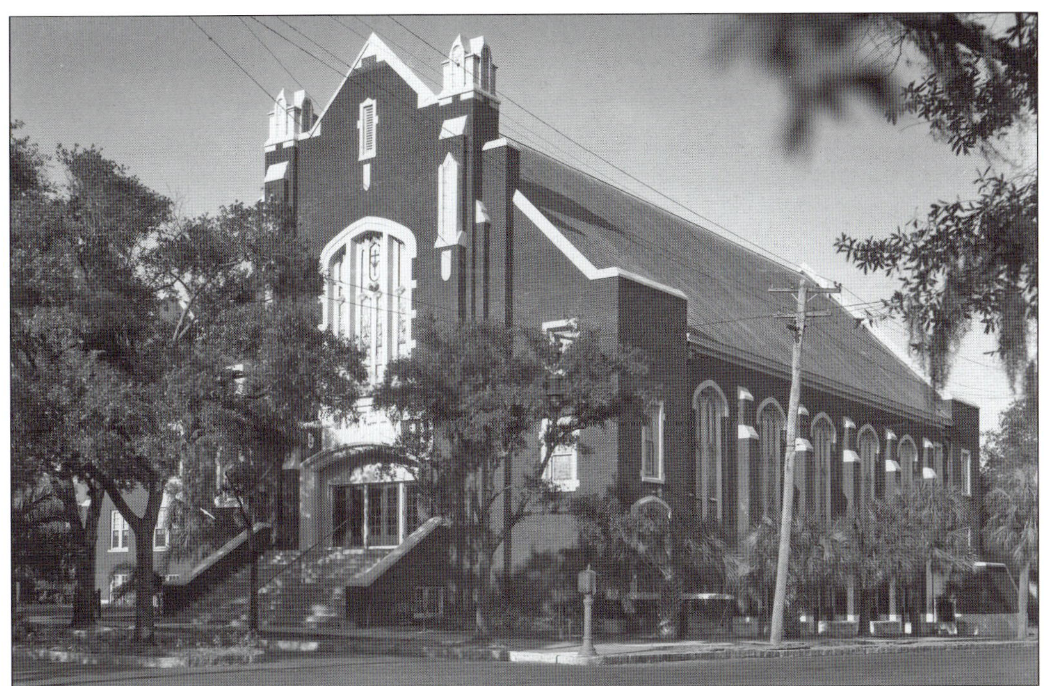

Today, this church is home to Holy Trinity Presbyterian Church. Established in 1995, the community began with 17 individuals from different church backgrounds who joined together to explore the possibility of starting a Bible-believing church. The community decided to join the Presbyterian Church in America, which best fit their beliefs. In 1998, Rev. Steve Casselli was called as the organizing pastor. Rental space was secured at Palma Ceia Baptist Church and the congregation held its first service on November 8, 1998, as Holy Trinity Presbyterian Church. In May 2009, the community purchased the historic First Christian Church building, pictured above in 1939, and began their community service to the Hyde Park neighborhood. The congregation is pictured below shortly after moving into their new church.

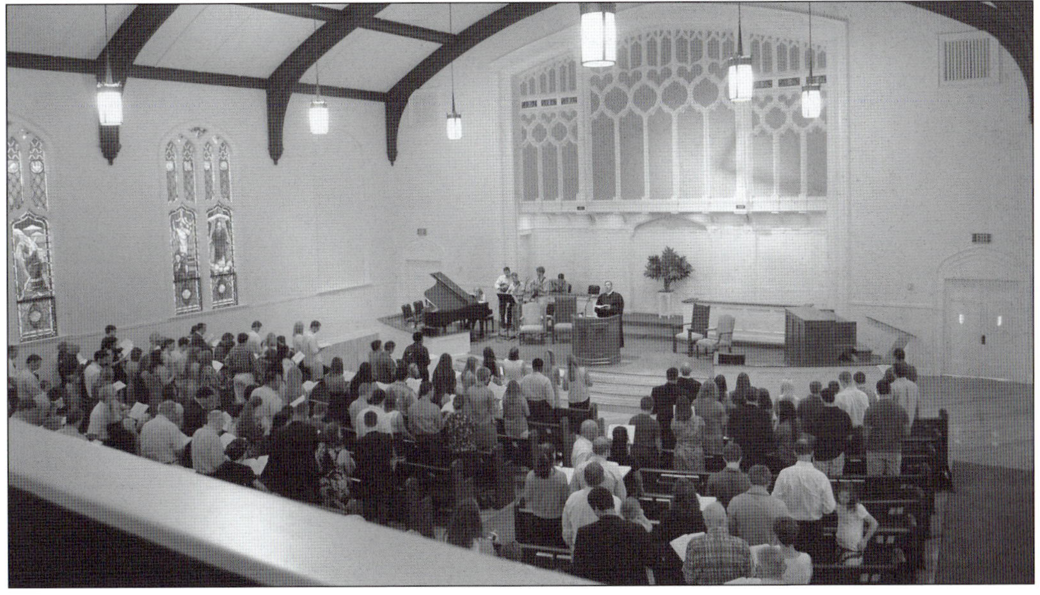

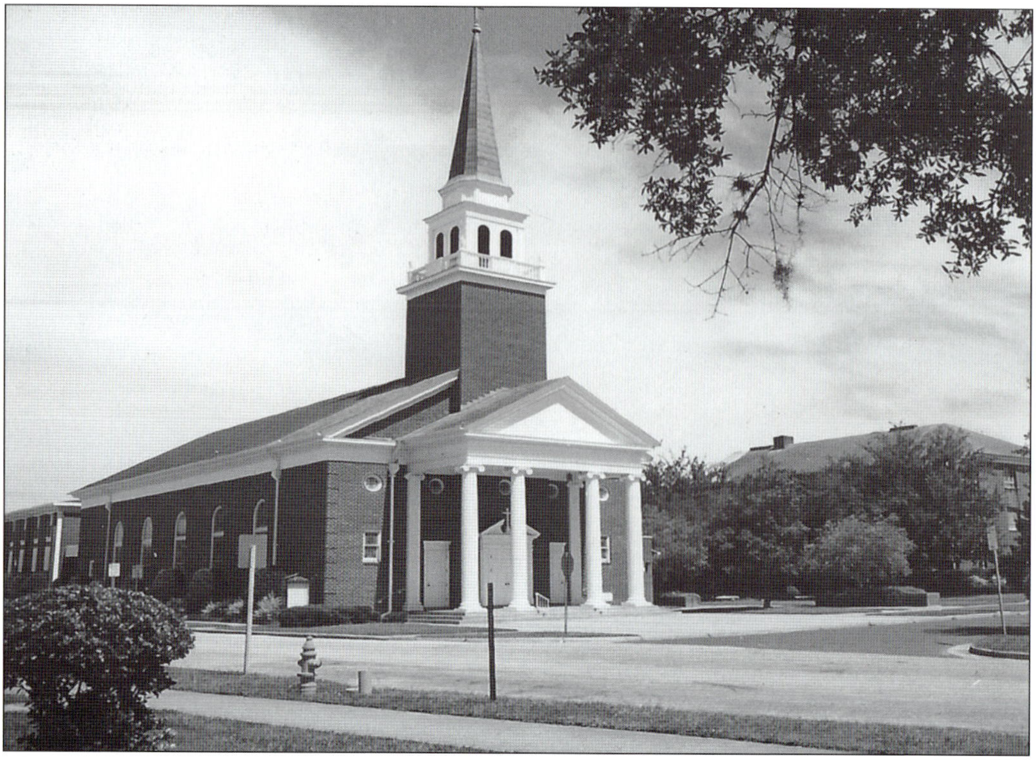

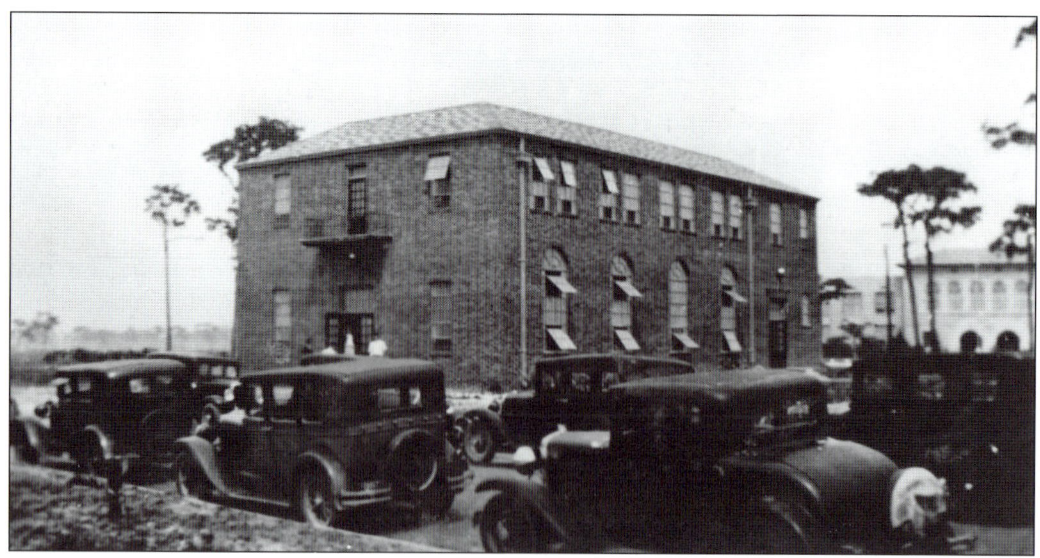

Palma Ceia Presbyterian Church was established on July 10, 1927, in the home of Mr. and Mrs. Frank Heaton by the superintendent of home missions, Rev. E.A. Lindsey. The church originally held services in a log cabin on the corner of Palmira Street and MacDill Avenue. In August 1927, three lots in Bayview Estates on San Jose Street were purchased for $6,000. In 1932, the congregation constructed a three-story church on their new property, pictured below shortly after completion. The first service in the new building was on January 24, 1932, with 300 faithful. The present church, pictured above in 1957, was completed in 1949 at 3501 San Jose Street.

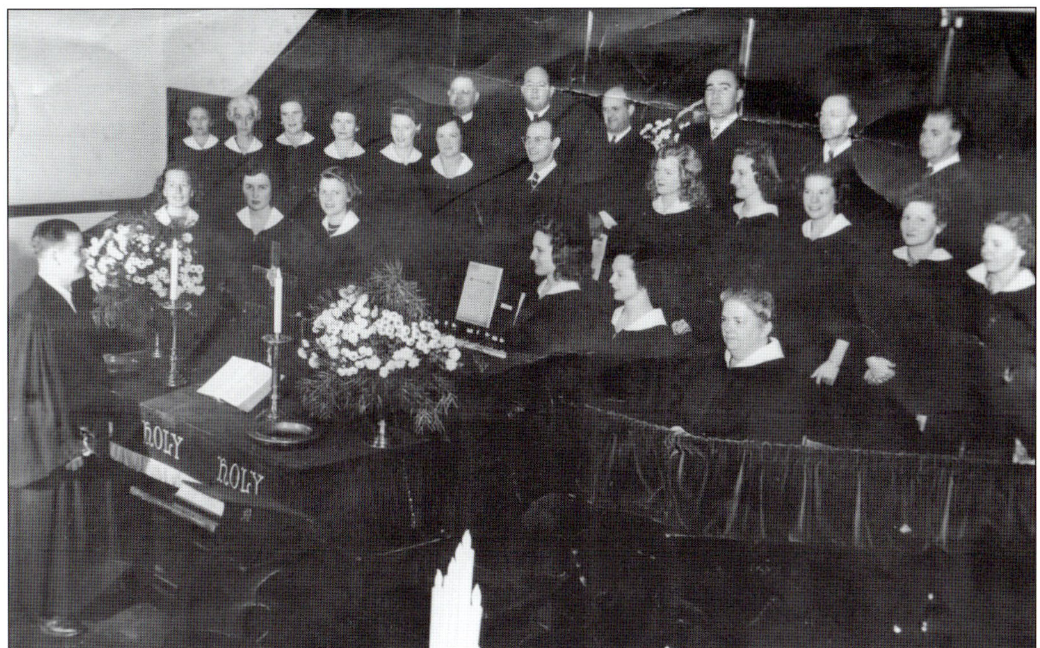

Pictured here is the choir in the original three-story church building on November 6, 1948. Palma Ceia Presbyterian Church celebrated the ground-breaking ceremony for the new church on March 28, 1948. It was built at a cost of $118,369. The Colonial Revival–style church was dedicated on Easter Sunday, April 17, 1949, and featured a columned portico and stained-glass windows. In 1956, the church membership reached 1,600. The below photograph shows the children's Sunday school class and their teachers in 1966.

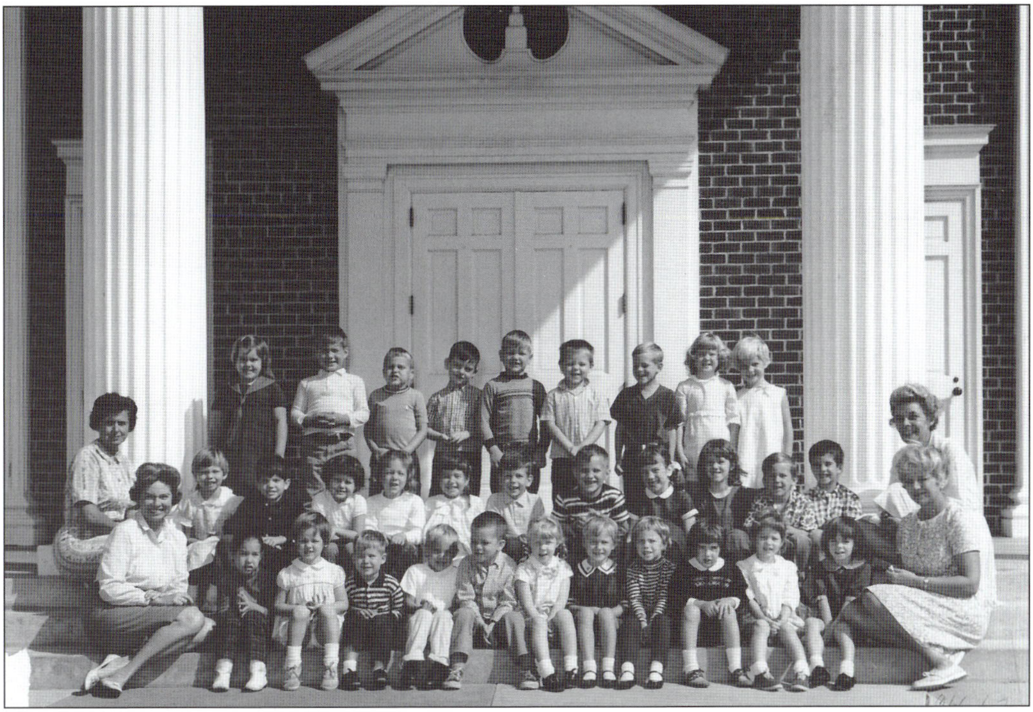

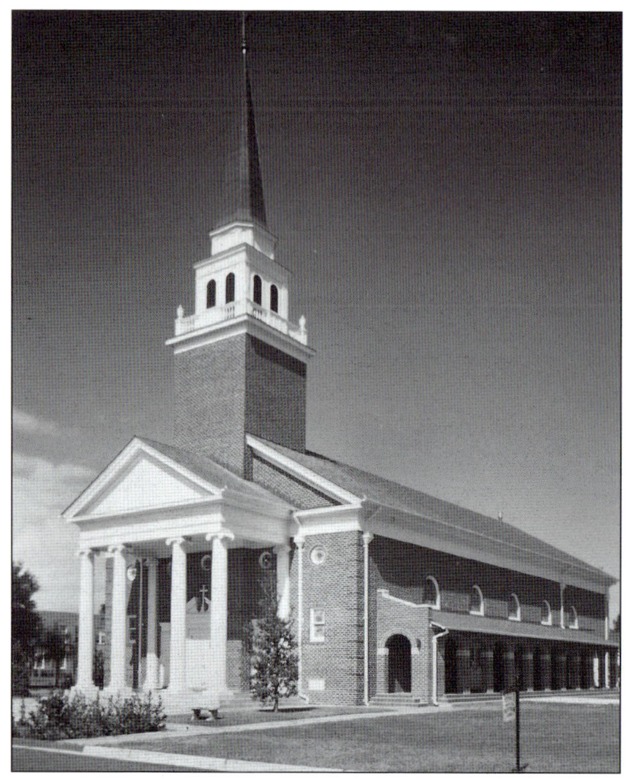

The steeple bell installed in the new Palma Ceia Presbyterian Church was originally acquired in 1946 by a local Methodist church only to discover it was too large for their belfry; at that time, the leaders of the church were making plans to build a new church. This opportunity led church leaders to purchase the bell from the Methodists. It stood on the church lawn for three years, and in 1949 was installed in the belfry that was specially designed for it. The church is pictured at left in 1957. The choir is pictured below inside the new church in 1949.

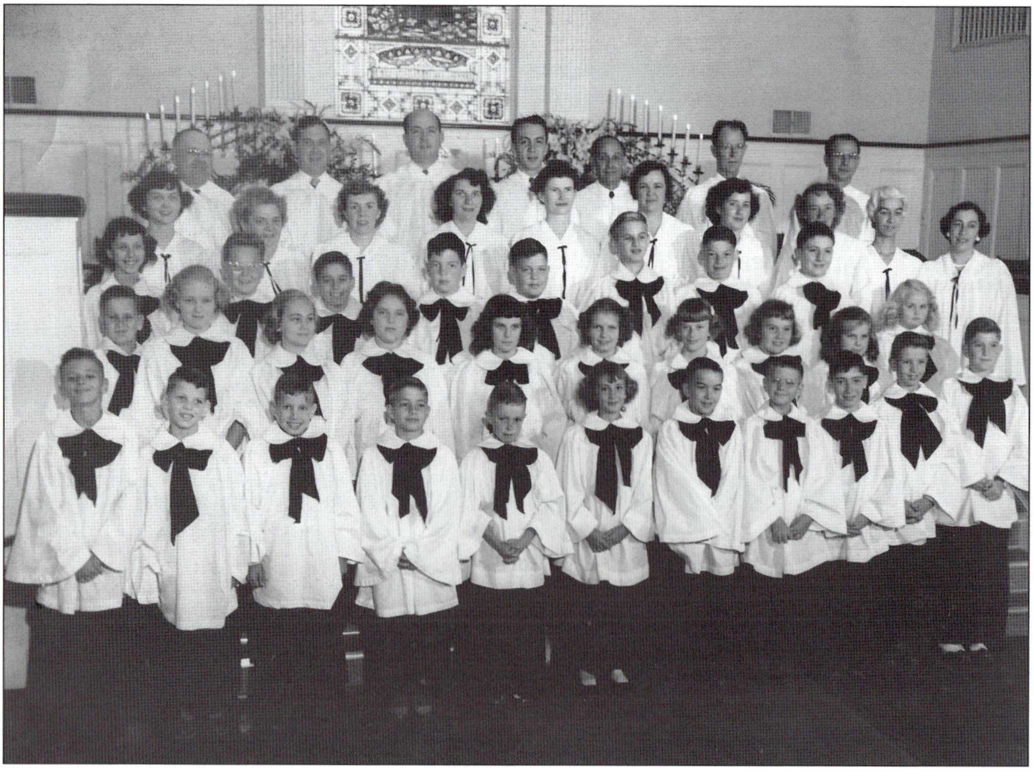

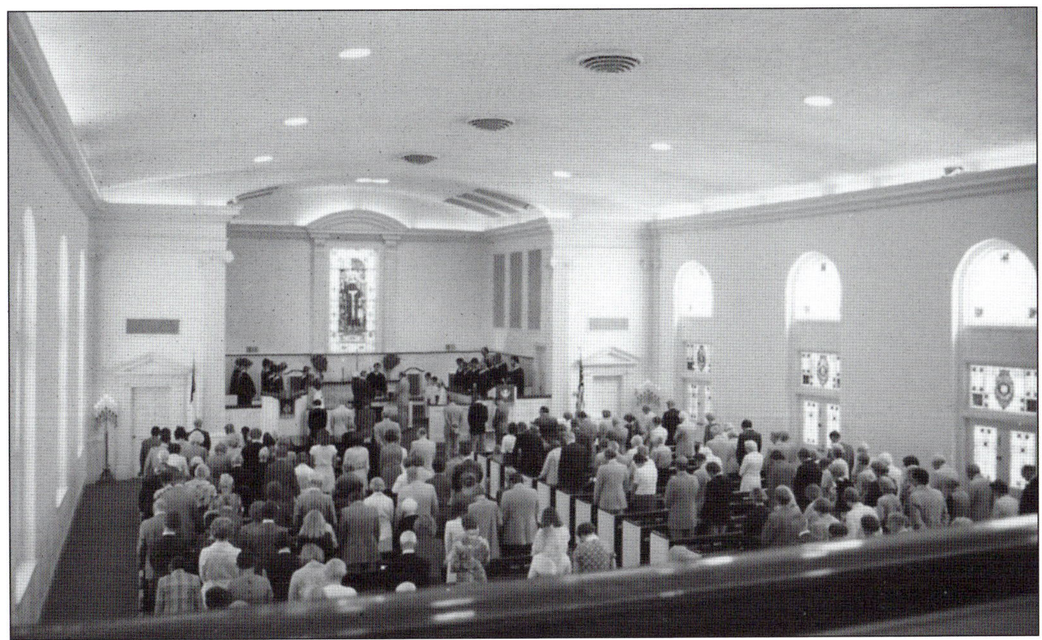

During the first church service in 1949, a total of 51 faithful were welcomed as new members, which increased membership to 843. The church plays an important role in community outreach, supporting many programs of assistance including Habitat for Humanity, Meals On Wheels, Metropolitan Ministries, Alpha House, Joshua House, Francis House, Abe Brown Prison Ministries, Lifepath Hospice, The Spring, Beth-El Presbyterian Mission, and many others. The new sanctuary is pictured above in 1975. The church youth group is seen below in 1974.

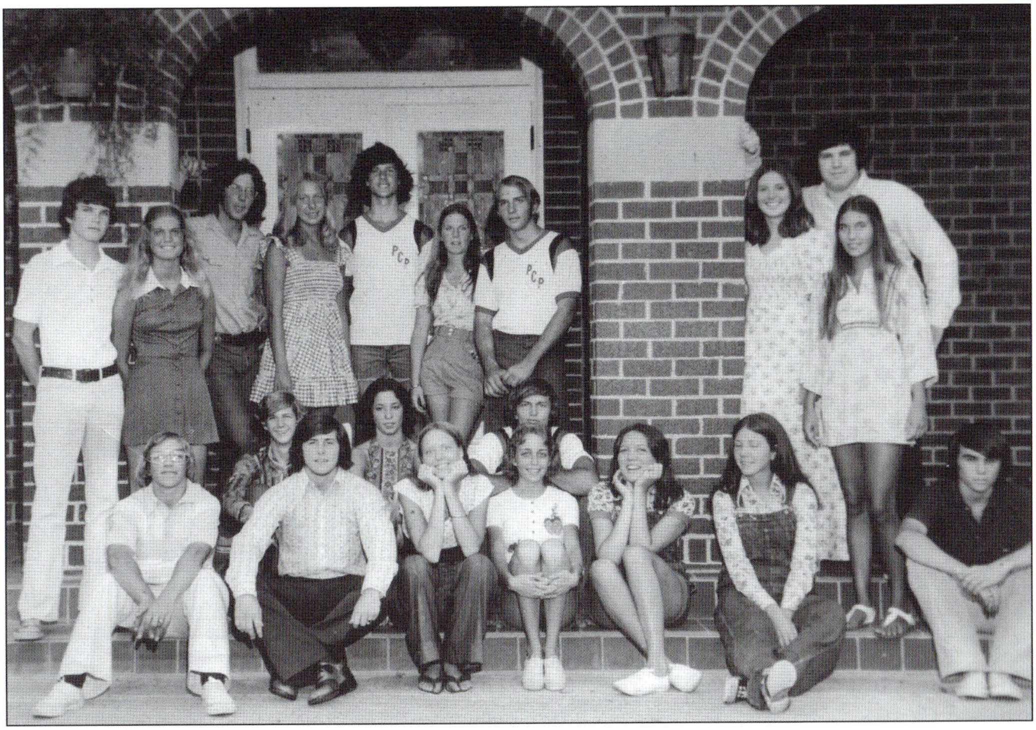

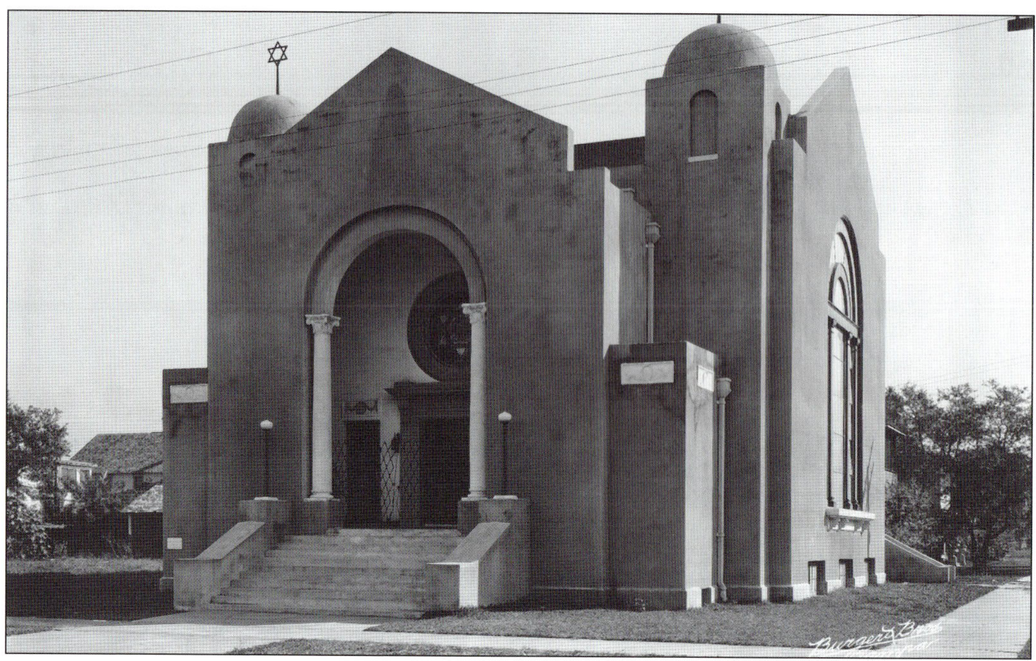

On October 14, 1894, a total of 31 congregants met in the home of M. Henry Cohen to form the first synagogue in Tampa, Schaarai Zedek (Gates of Righteousness). The corporate charter was granted on December 15, 1894, with Rabbi D. Jacobson as the first rabbi. In 1899, the first synagogue was erected at 1209 Florida Avenue. In 1902, dissension developed between the Reform and Orthodox members of the congregation. After a resolution was reached, Schaarai Zedek's constitution was changed to read: "The form of worship shall be in accordance with Reform Judaism." On December 19, 1924, a new synagogue was dedicated at the corner of Delaware and Deleon Streets, pictured above shortly after construction. The photograph below shows the children of the temple performing a mock wedding ceremony for the congregation in 1930.

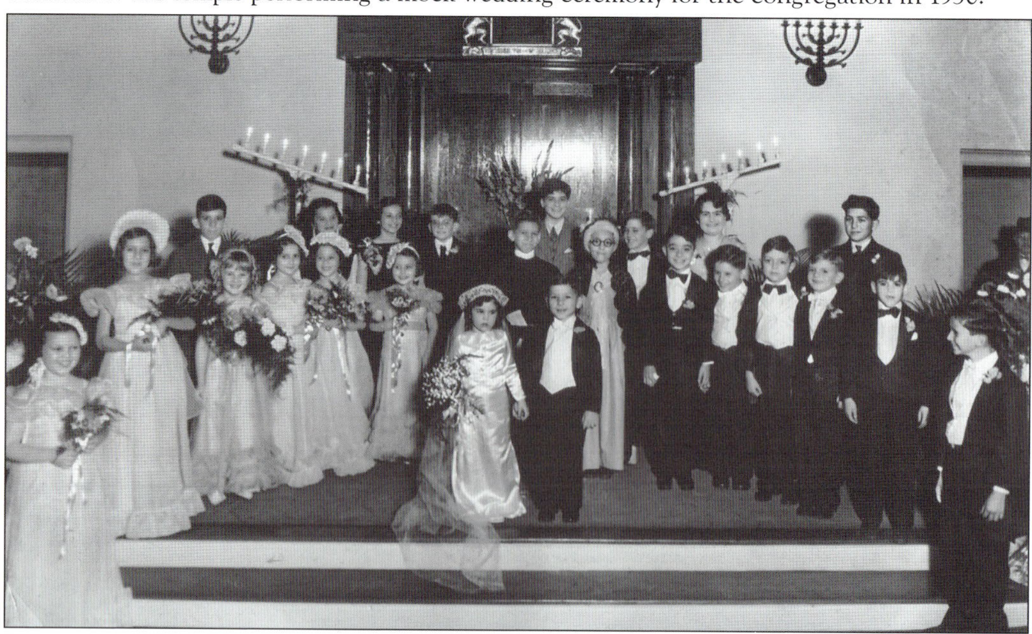

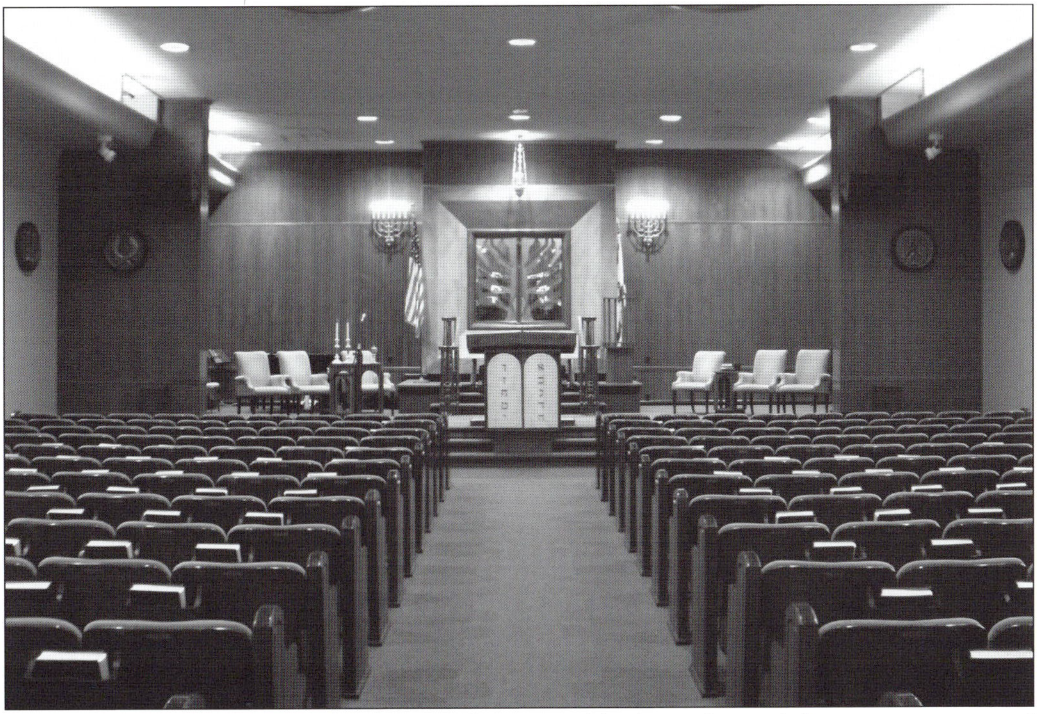

In 1930, Rabbi David L. Zielonka became the spiritual leader and served the congregation until his death in 1977. Ground breaking for the present temple, pictured here at the corner of Swann and Lincoln Avenues, was held on January 26, 1957. Rabbi Frank N. Sundheim became associate rabbi in 1967. He assumed the duties of senior rabbi in 1970. In 1986, Rabbi Richard J. Birnholz was named senior rabbi. The temple continues the mission of outreach and service to the community commissioned by those 31 founding members in 1894.

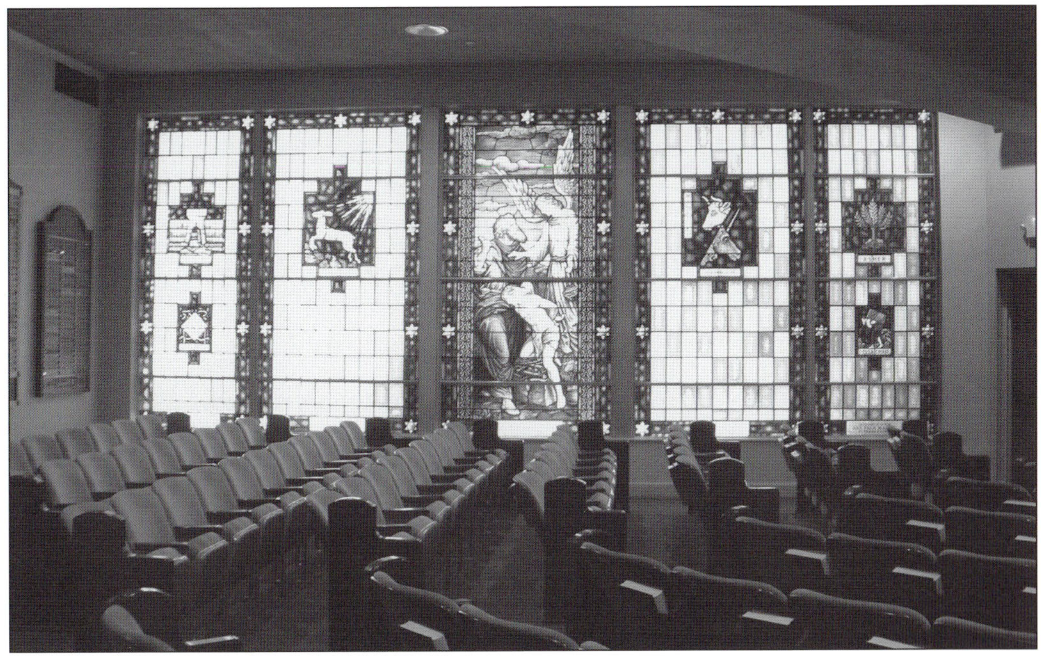

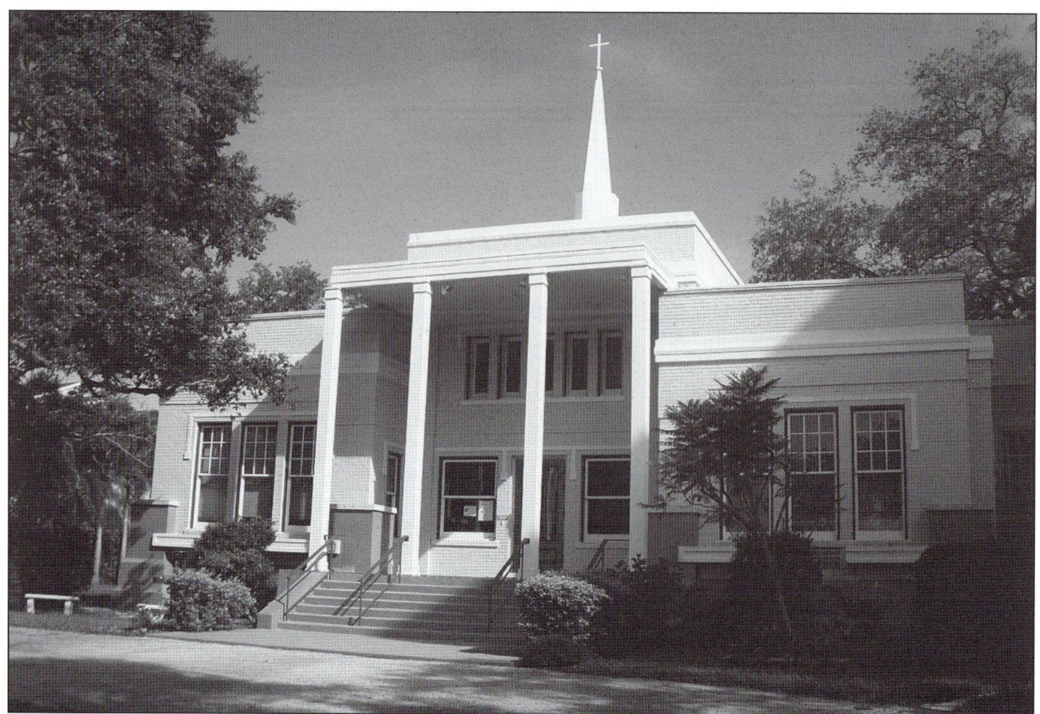

Bayshore Presbyterian Church is a success story for historic preservation, worshipping in a historic restored Bayshore Boulevard mansion. In 1967, the church moved from their Davis Island location since 1961 to a large parcel of property at 2515 Bayshore Boulevard. The church then renovated and restored the historic 1913 Hendry family mansion, repurposing the bedrooms into church offices. The project included adding on a two-story, 200-seat sanctuary to the back of the mansion and a columned portico and steeple to complete the transformation. The photograph below was taken in 1967 during the renovation project that converted the historic mansion into a church.

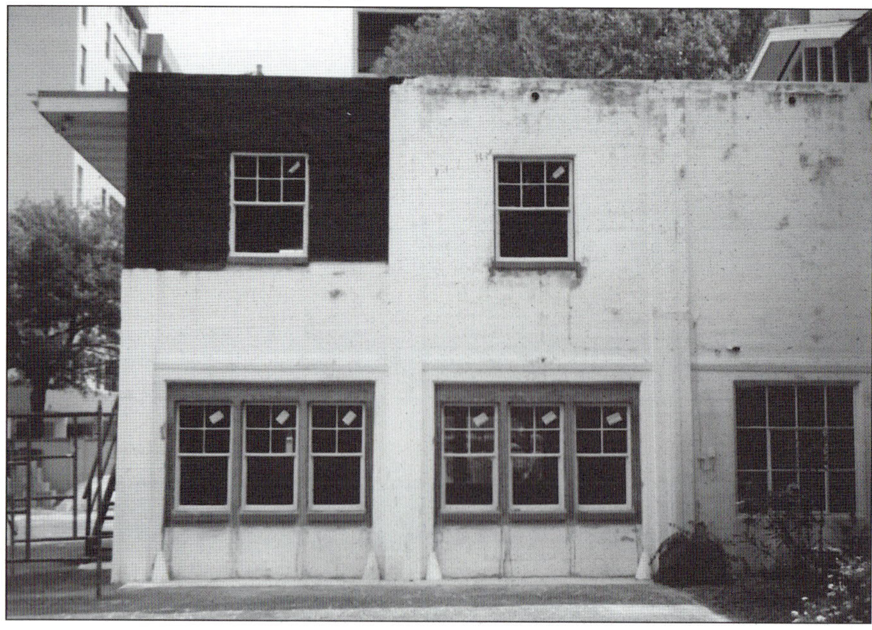

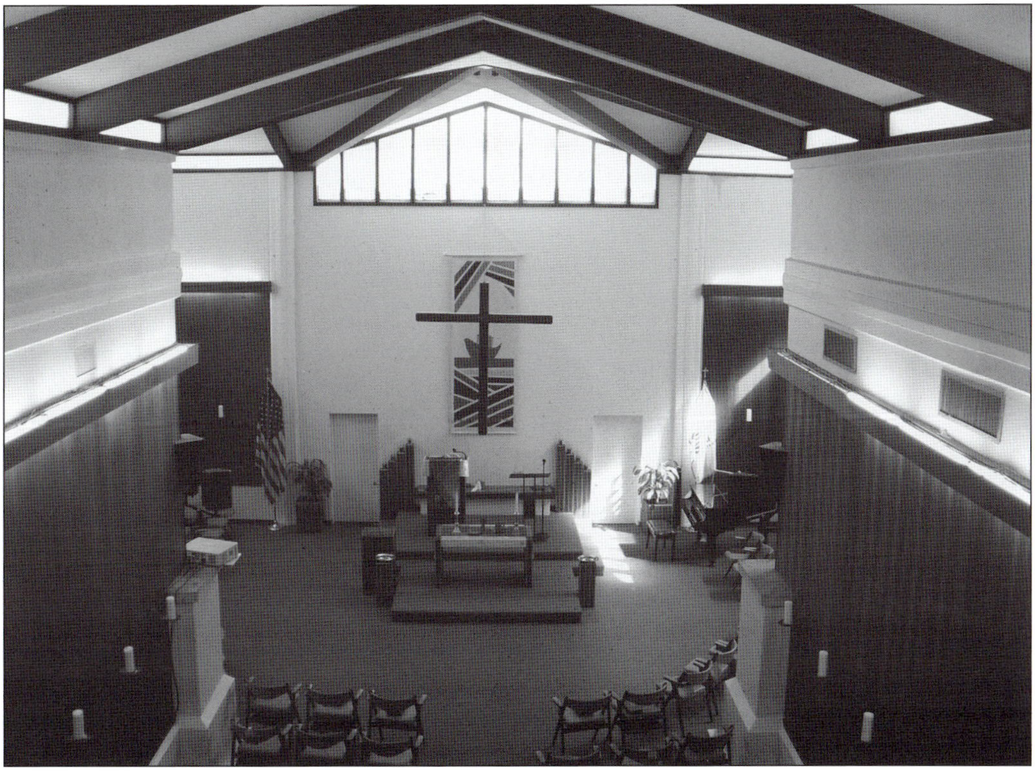

Pictured here is the sanctuary of Bayshore Presbyterian Church, which is actually a converted Bayshore Boulevard mansion, constructed in 1913. The church has a long history of community service, including ministries to assist the Beth-El Farmworkers Mission, Habitat for Humanity, addiction recovery programs, and Honduras Missionaries. The church also offers their fellowship hall to many groups in the community, including the local Boy Scouts and several 12-step programs.

St. Ignatius Catholic Church was established in 1896 and located at the corner of Fitzgerald and Chisholm Streets. The church was dedicated on May 14, 1899, and was staffed by the Jesuit Fathers and the Sisters of the Holy Names, who also operated a small school there. The church closed in 1942, when Christ the King Catholic Church became the primary parish for Catholics in South Tampa.

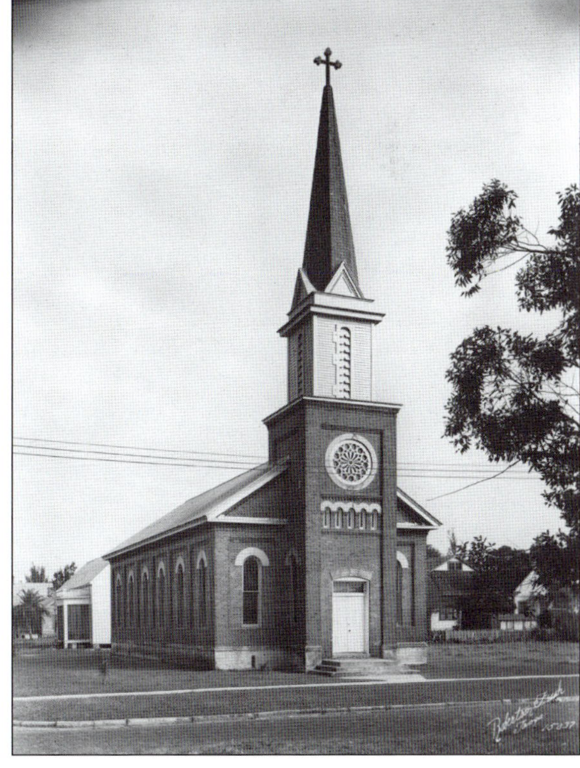

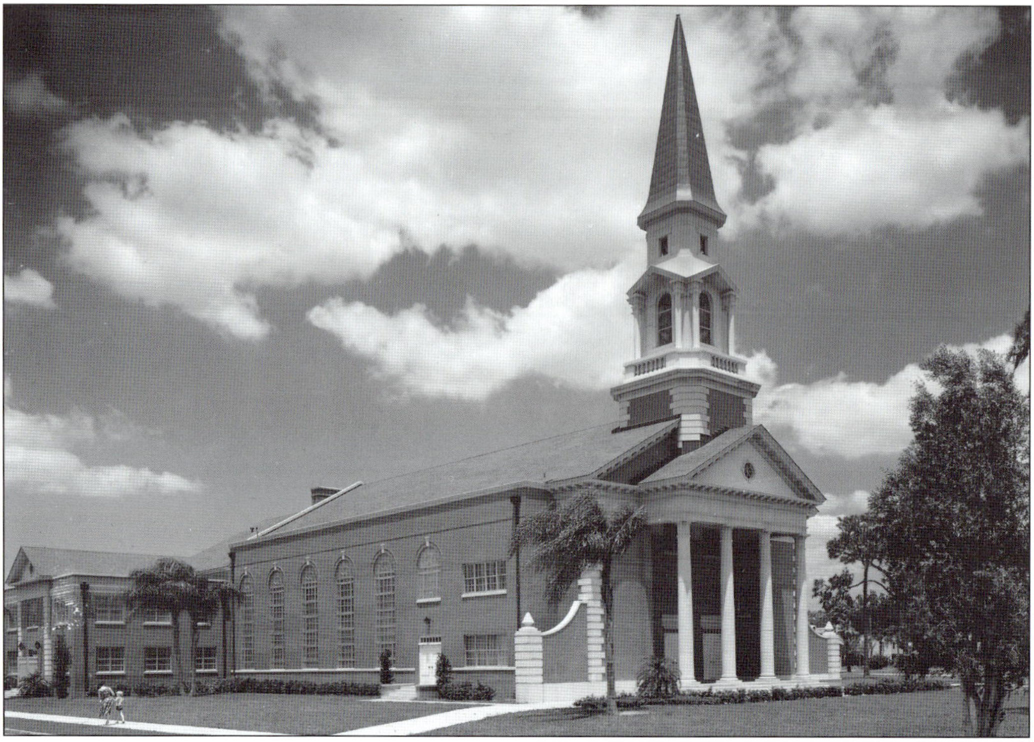

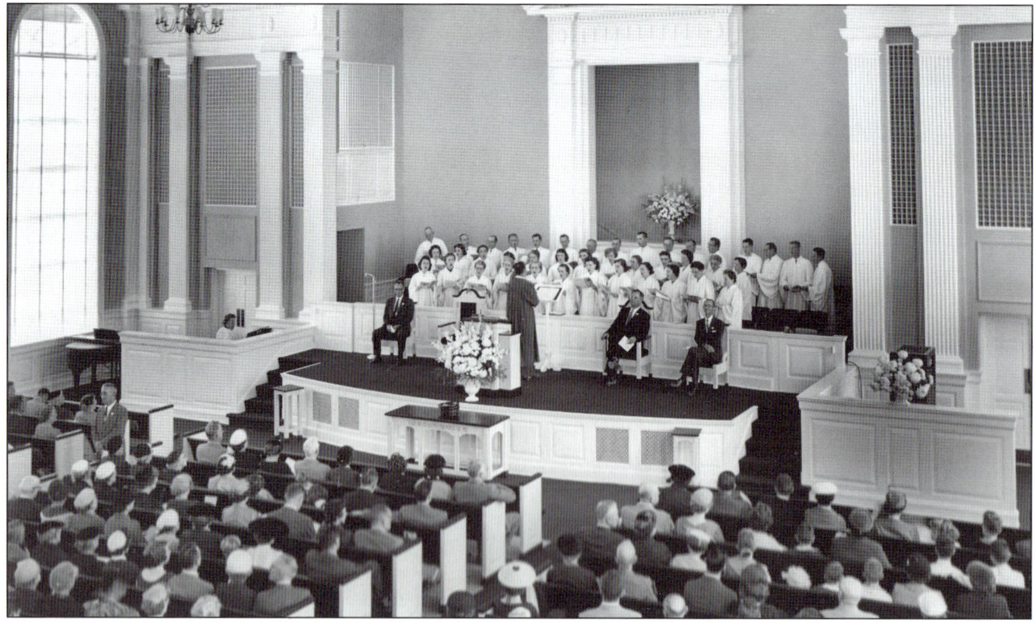

Bayshore Baptist Church is a familiar landmark on MacDill Avenue with a soaring steeple to remind all those passing by of her mission to lead the faithful into heaven. The history of this grand church begins in 1925 when the Tampa Baptist City Mission organized a new church in the southwest section of Tampa, which had no Baptist church. Dr. George Hyman, associate pastor at First Baptist Church, took the lead on development of the new congregation. These 1958 photographs show the new church at 3111 Morrison Avenue in 1956.

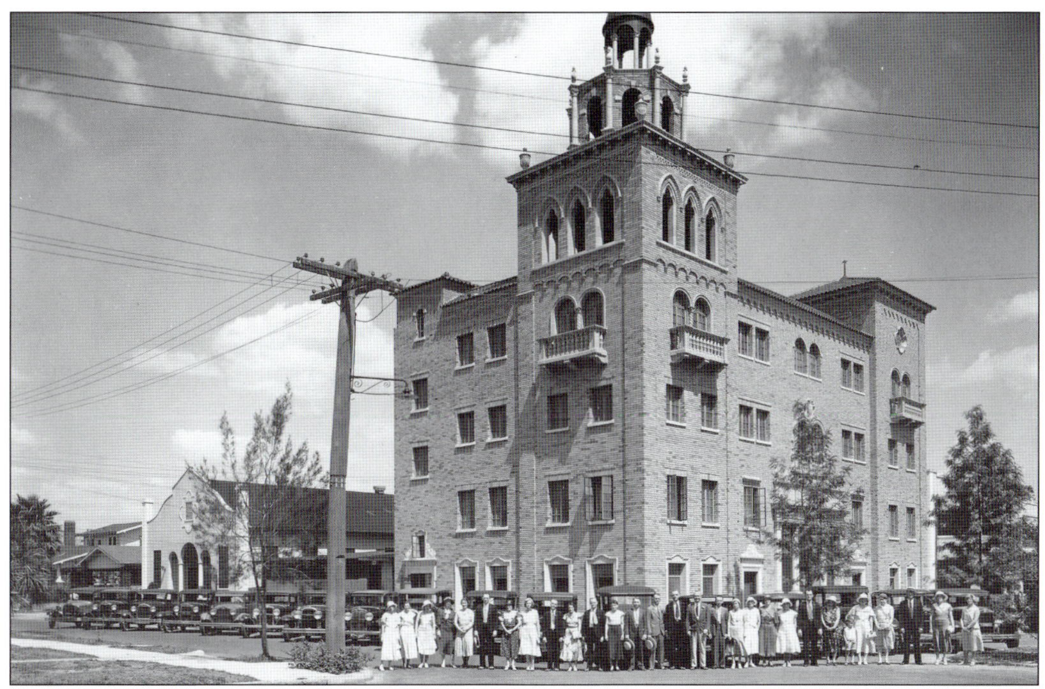

The first church was funded by First Baptist Church with $8,000 for the project. The original church was dedicated on March 21, 1926, at the corner of Dekle and Howard Avenues. On March 29, 1926, the church was constituted as Bayshore Baptist Church, with Dr. George Hyman appointed as the first pastor. In 1927, the church located a contractor who constructed the new four-story church at a cost of $35,000. The congregation celebrated the cornerstone ceremony on March 2, 1928, with Tampa mayor D.B. McKay in attendance. The above photograph was taken on May 8, 1932, with the congregation. The image below shows the Girls Auxiliary coronation in 1955.

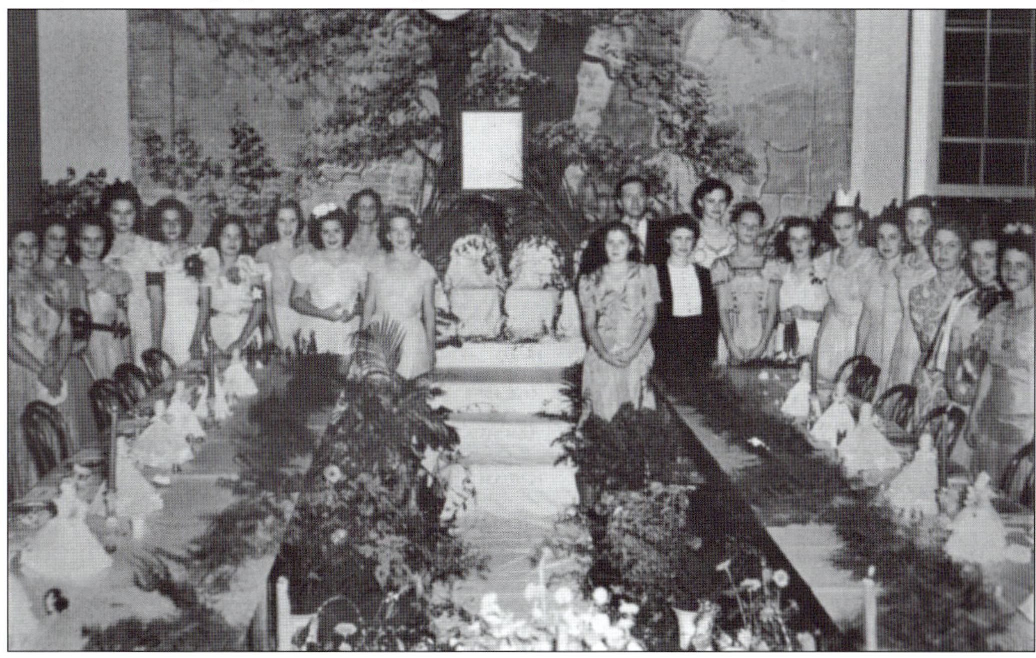

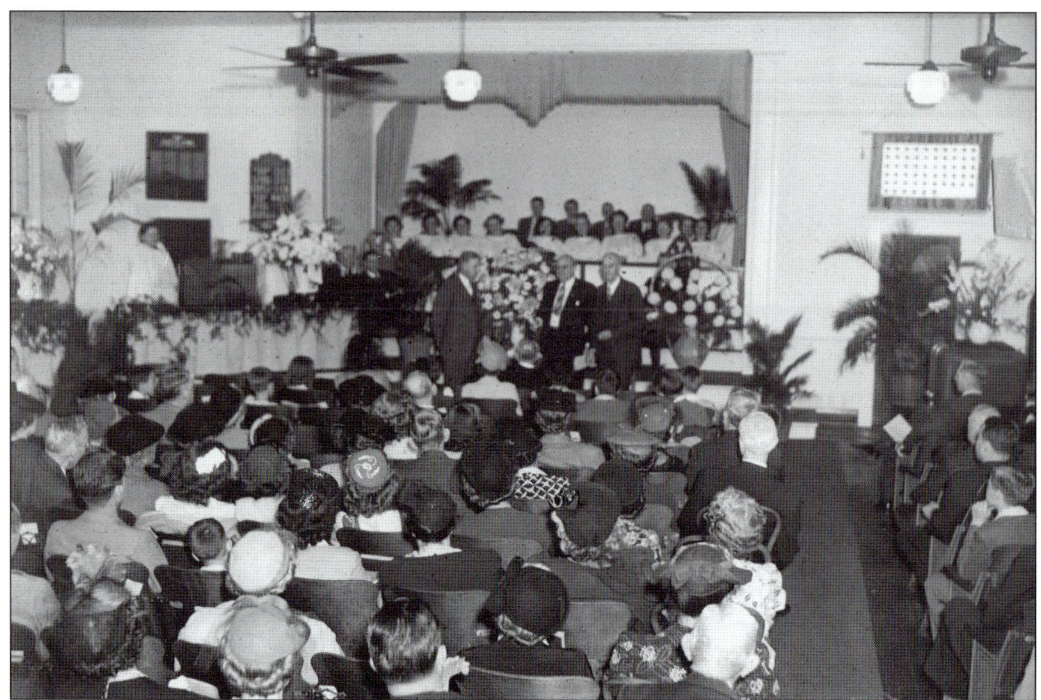

In 1945, the church began making plans for a new, larger church to accommodate the growth of the congregation. Three years later, with a gift from the estate of church benefactors Dr. John A. Gaines and his sister Addie C. Gaines, the church purchased property at the corner of South MacDill and Morrison Avenues. This parcel of land would suit the needs of a new church; however, there was an issue with zoning restrictions. For seven years, the church endured a series of court proceedings to permit construction. In 1953, the Florida state legislature supported a local bill that finally cleared the way for construction. Pictured above is a Veterans Day ceremony in the old church in 1944. The choir is seen below in the old church in 1944.

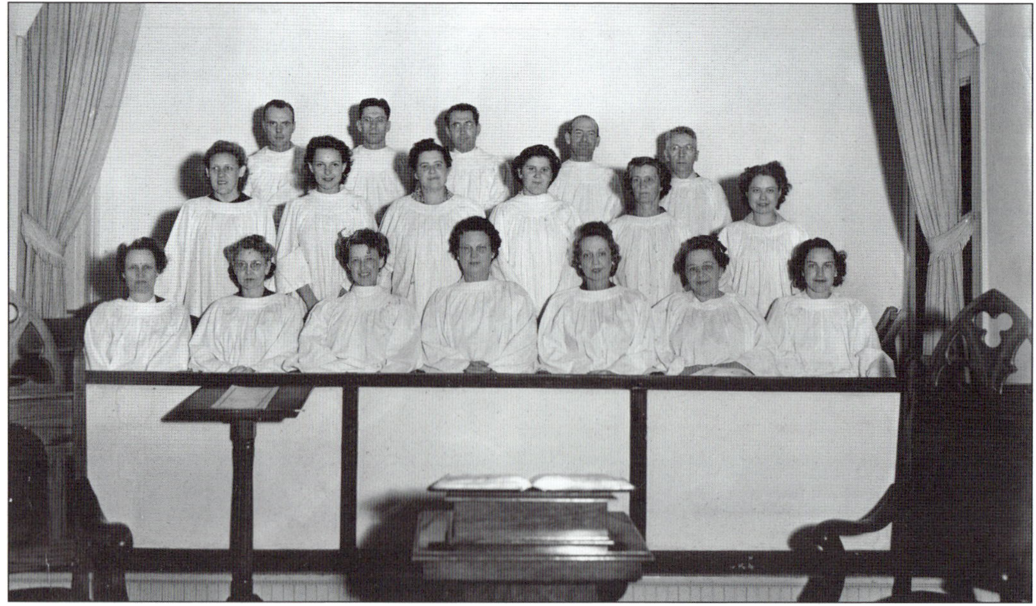

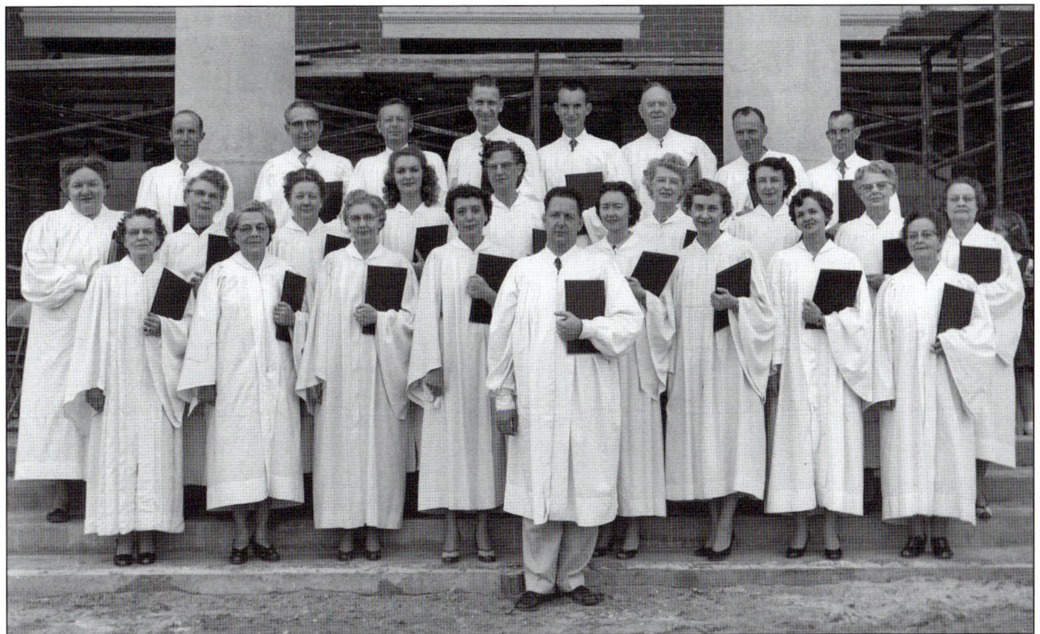

In 1955, Bayshore Baptist Church launched a campaign for the building fund and $200,000 was donated. The first service in the new church was celebrated on November 22, 1956, and the dedication ceremony was held on January 12, 1958. The church has served the community well, establishing four new churches and taking a lead role in the establishment of many charitable organizations, including Metropolitan Ministries, Meals On Wheels, the Judeo Christian Health Clinic, the Port Tampa Seafarers Ministry, Daystar Life Center, the Alafia Group Home, the Inner-City Mission Project, and the Dental Clinic. Pictured above is the choir in front of the church under construction in 1956. Below is the new sanctuary decorated for Christmas in 1969.

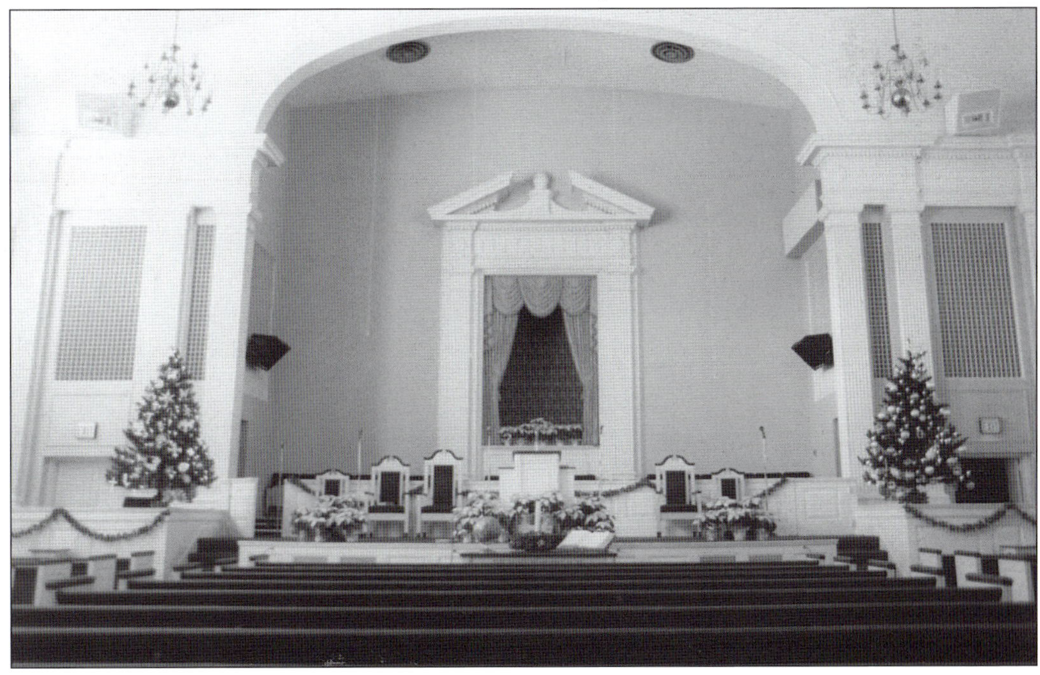

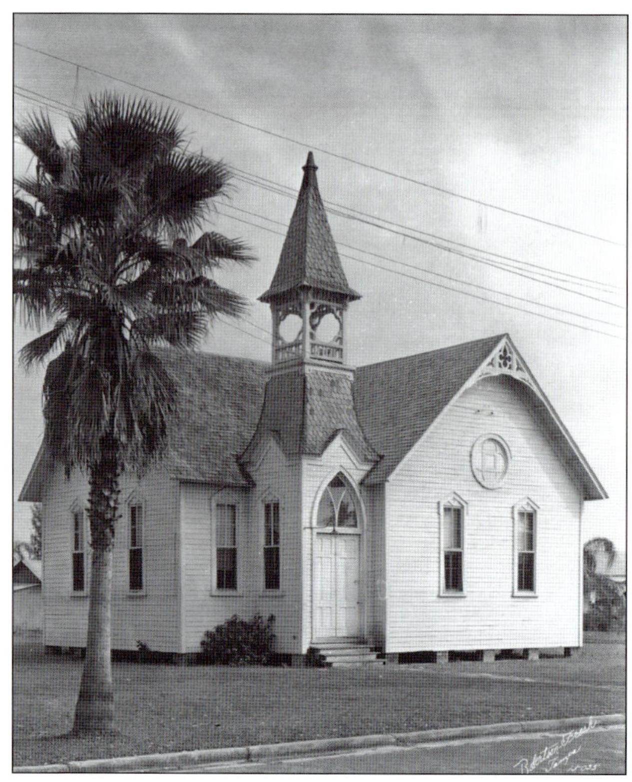

Pictured here in 1941 is the Port Tampa United Methodist Church, a landmark in Port Tampa established in 1894 at 6914 South DeSoto Street. In the formative years of the church's establishment, Baptists, Presbyterians, Episcopalians, and Methodists worshipped in the church building. Members included stevedores, dock workers, and some of Teddy Roosevelt's Rough Riders. The historic church was designed in the Queen Anne style and features the original church pews, stained-glass windows, and antique light fixtures. Pictured below is the congregation in 1925.

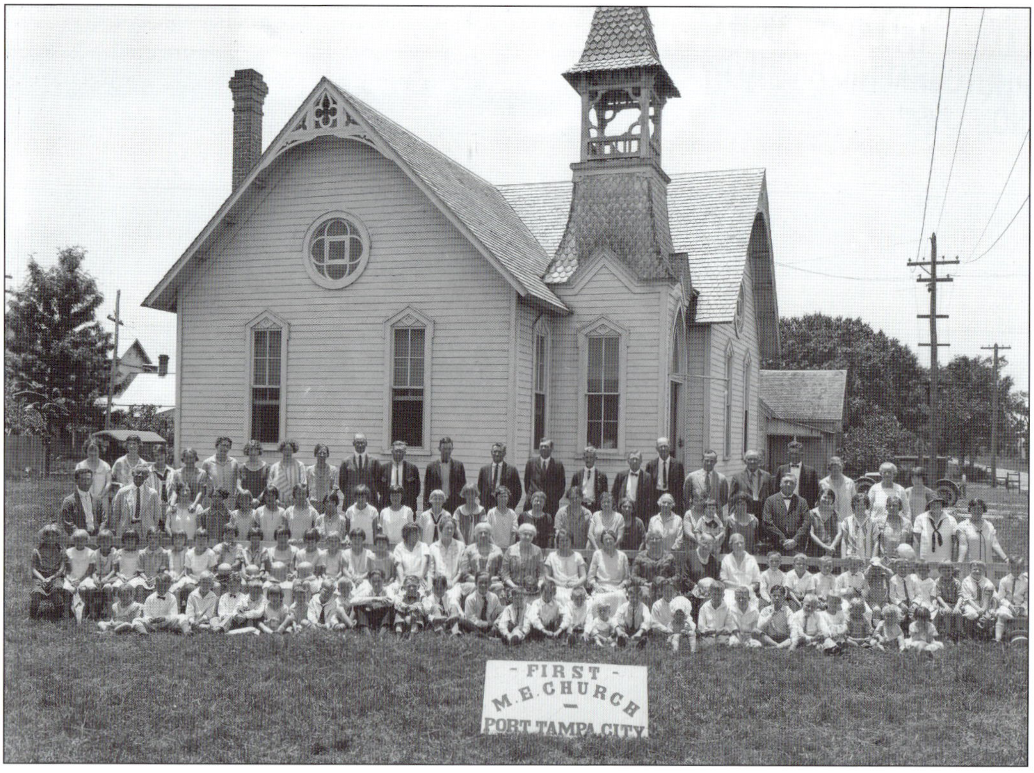

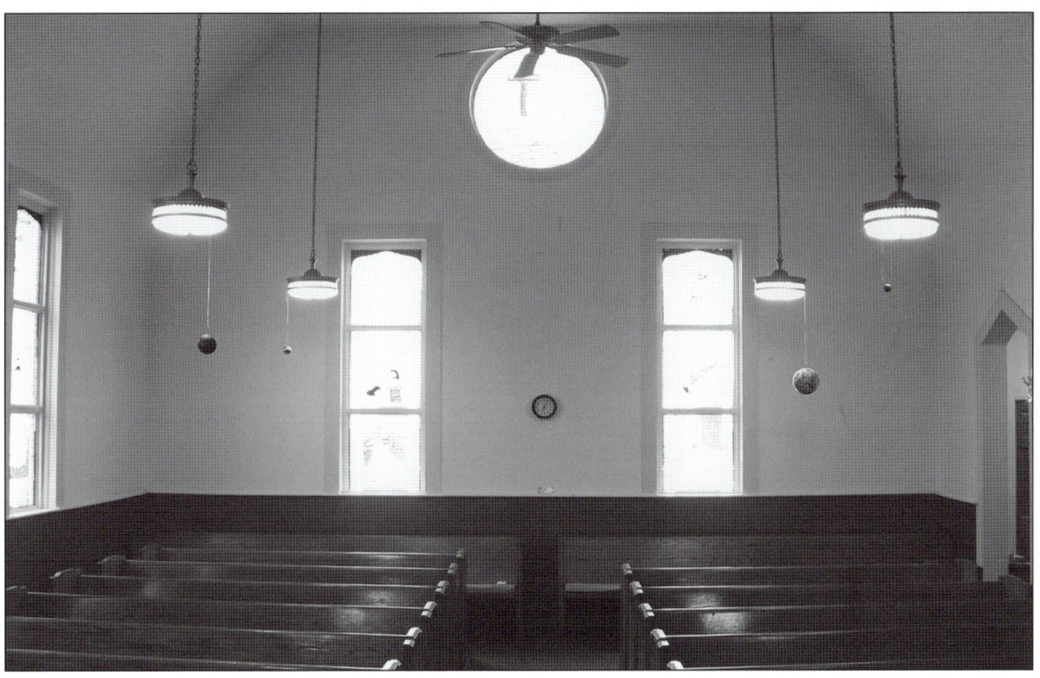

The first pastor assigned was Rev. J.H. Michler, who organized the congregation in August 1894. With the arrival of Henry Plant's railroad, Port Tampa City experienced steady growth during the 1880s, with more than 15,000 residents by 1898. Pictured below is the title transfer completed on March 27, 1902, when ownership of the property was transferred to the Southern Methodist Episcopal Conference. The original purchase price of the property was $500. The request was fulfilled by Mr. Peter O. Knight, who was one of the most prominent and entrepreneurial businessmen in the history of Tampa. He was one of the founders of the Exchange National Bank and the Tampa Electric Company.

PETER O. KNIGHT,
ATTORNEY,
EXCHANGE NATIONAL BANK BUILDING,
TAMPA, FLORIDA.

March 27th., 1902.

I have examined the foregoing abstract, and find the title to lot nine, block eighty six, of Port Tampa City, vested in the trustees of the M. E. Church, South, free from any and all incumbrances and liens, save and except a mortgage made to the Board of Church Extension, for five hundred dollars, on the 15th. of March, A.D., 1892.

I have also examined the mortgage and refunding bond, made by the trustees to the M. E. Church South, Port Tampa City, on the 24th. of March, A.D., 1902, and find the same executed in conformity with the laws of the state of Florida. Dated this 27th day of March, A.D., 1902.

Peter O. Knight

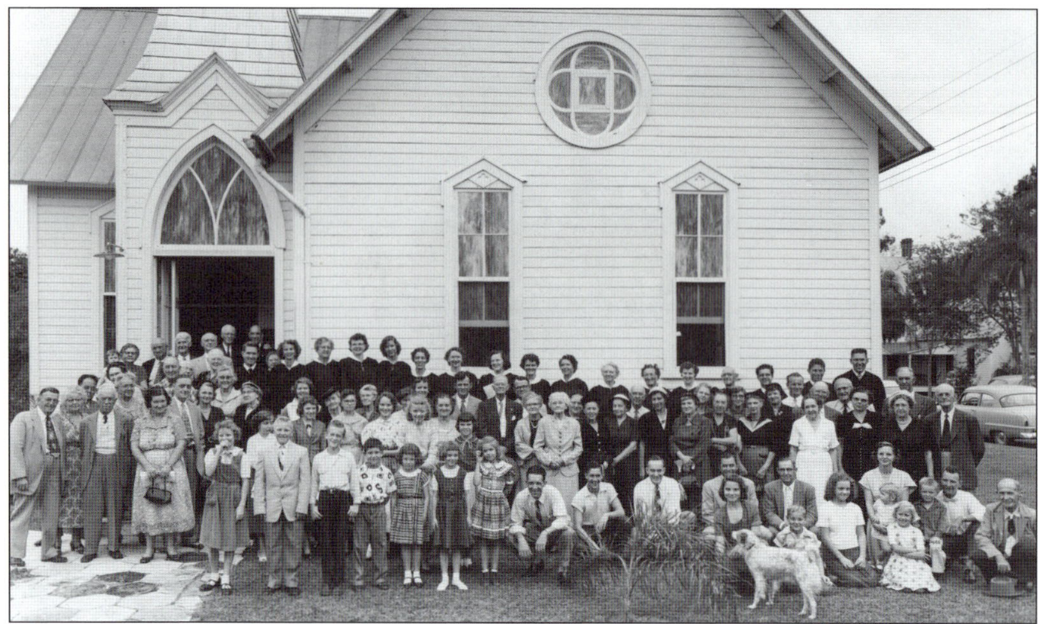

Port Tampa United Methodist Church has restored and preserved its historic church built in 1894, which has the original hardwood floors and steeple bell, acquired from the Atlantic Coastline Railroad in 1951 from one of its retired locomotives. The church is also home to the Port Tampa Players, presenting several stage shows and musical productions each year for the community. The congregation is pictured here in 1954.

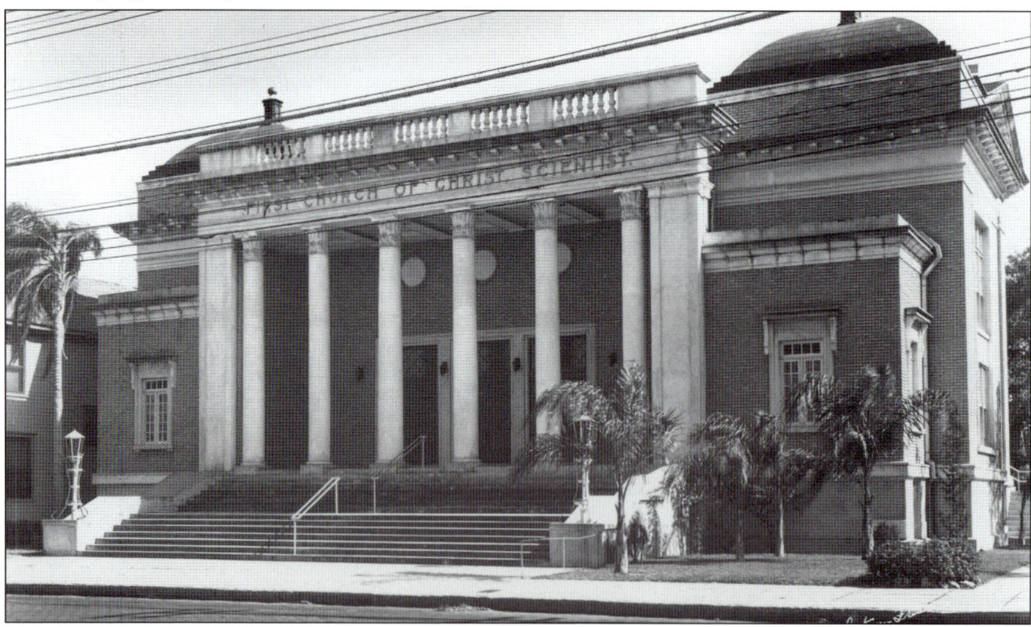

First Church of Christ Scientist is pictured here in 1944 at 408 Grand Central Avenue. This church was established in April 1908 and met at various locations until their church was completed in 1926. The church was dedicated on March 5, 1944, and features a unique blend of Greek Revival and Colonial Revival elements with an impressive columned portico and balustrading over the front entrance.

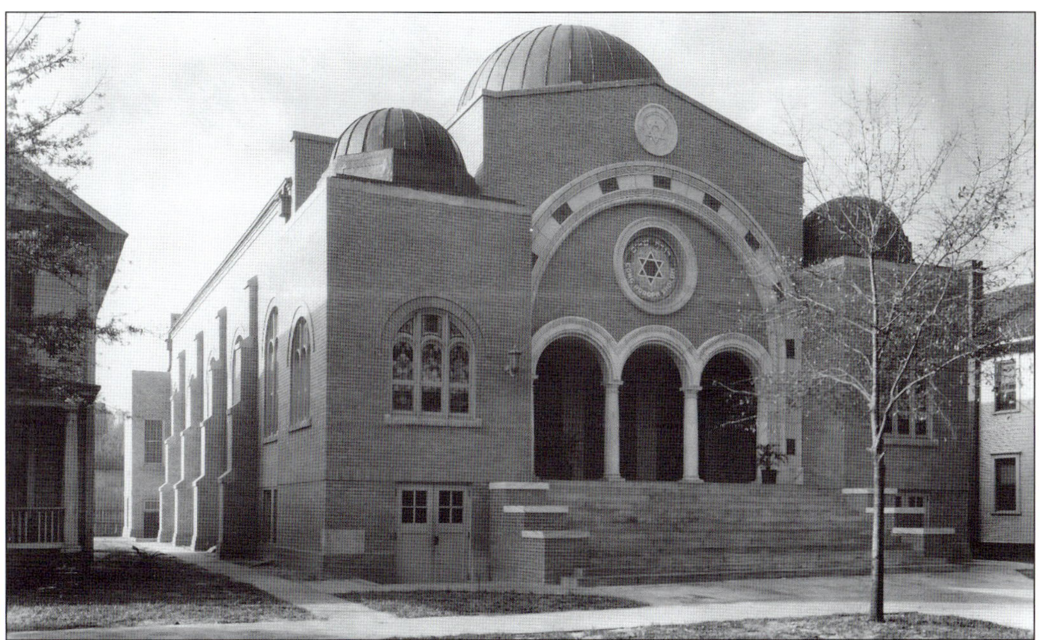

Congregation Rodeph Sholom is Tampa's oldest Conservative congregation, founded in 1903 with 26 families. In 1918, the religious school was organized. In 1925, the congregation dedicated their new temple at 309 Palm Avenue, pictured above in 1927. This building stood as a symbol of Conservative Judaism until 1968, when the new temple at 2713 Bayshore Boulevard was constructed, pictured below. In addition to regular religious school schedules and youth organizations, the congregation offers Torah study sessions, adult education programs, and adult Bar/Bat Mitzvah celebrations. With the merger of Beth Israel Synagogue in June 1980, Congregation Rodeph Sholom grew in members and spiritual strength. The leadership of Beth Israel gave the congregation new vigor and support.

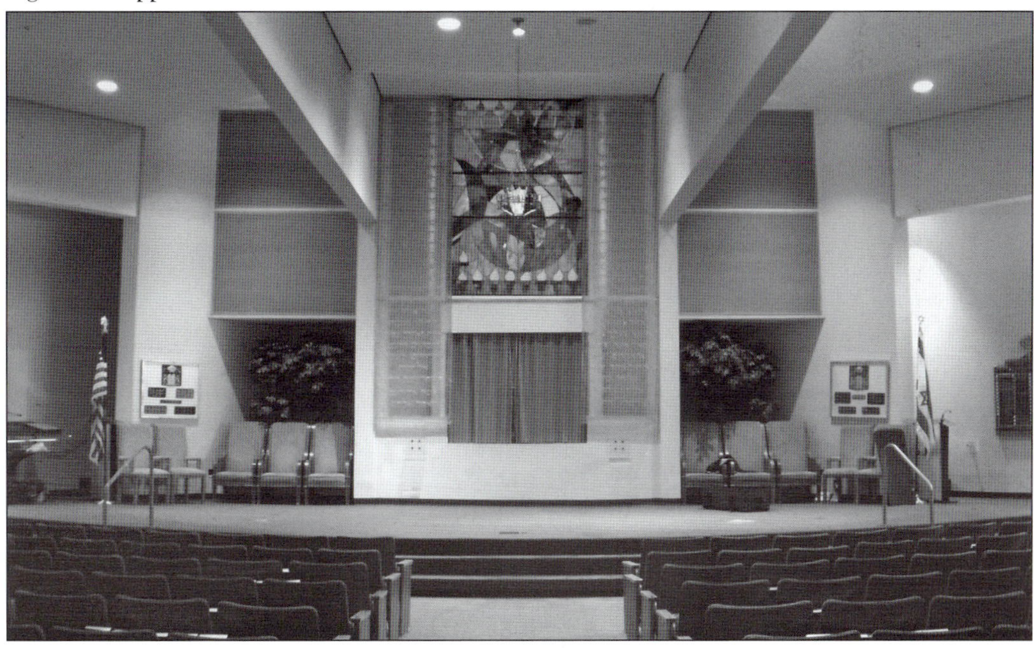

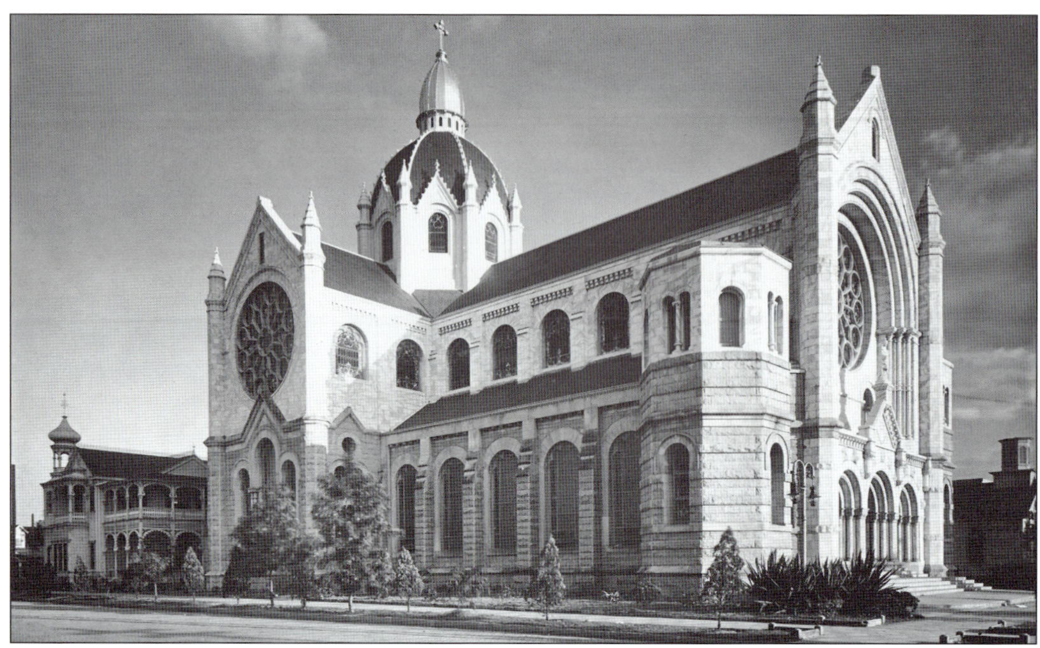

St. Louis Cemetery is the oldest Catholic cemetery on the west coast of Florida, established in 1874 for members of Tampa's first Catholic church, St. Louis Catholic Church (now Sacred Heart Catholic Church), pictured here in 1910. The cemetery is located at 606 Harrison Street, just north of the historic Oaklawn Cemetery. Among those at rest in the cemetery are Joseph Lancaster, first mayor of Tampa; patrolman John McCormick, the first Tampa policeman killed in the line of duty; Cecilia Morse, the founder of parochial education in the Tampa Bay area; five pioneer priests who established the first Catholic church in the city of Tampa; and Vicente Martinez-Ybor, founder of Ybor City. On the east side of the cemetery is a small brick building constructed in 1874 that was used for coffin storage.

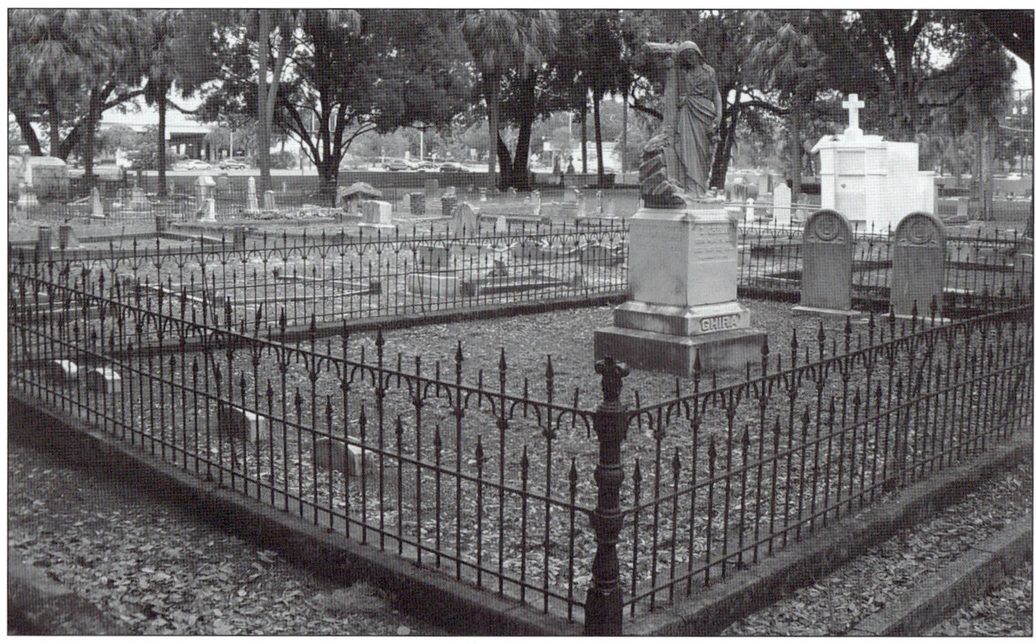

Two

TAMPA HEIGHTS, SEMINOLE HEIGHTS, AND NORTH TAMPA

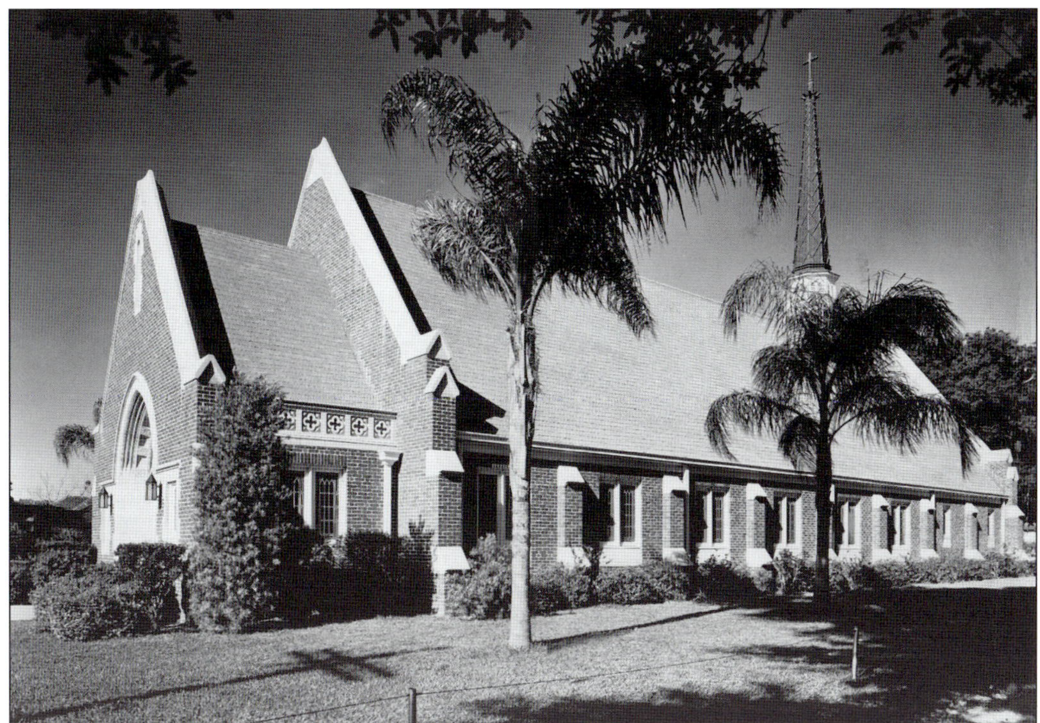

Pictured here in 1950 is St. Paul Lutheran Church at 5103 Central Avenue in Seminole Heights. The church was organized in 1927 and is the oldest Evangelical Lutheran Church in America church in Tampa, the "Mother Church" of the 11 others. The church originally met at the YMCA building in downtown Tampa with 65 faithful attending the first service on December 5, 1926. (HCPLC.)

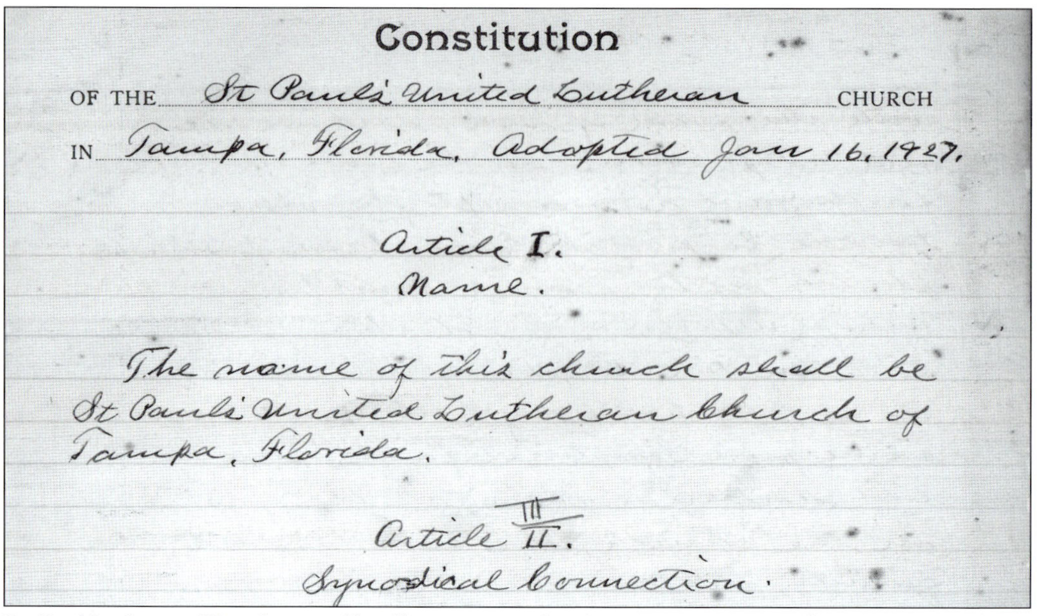

Constitution

OF THE _St Paul's United Lutheran_ CHURCH

IN _Tampa, Florida, Adopted Jan. 16, 1927._

Article I.
Name.

The name of this church shall be St Paul's United Lutheran Church of Tampa, Florida.

Article II.
Synodical Connection.

St. Paul Lutheran Church was officially constituted on January 16, 1927, with Rev. G.F. Snyder as the first pastor. On March 4, 1930, church leaders purchased a lot in Seminole Heights across the street from Hillsborough High School at 5103 Central Avenue for $9,009. The property included a two-story farmhouse that was converted to a church. The first service held at the church was on Pentecost Sunday, June 8, 1930. Pictured above is the original hand-written constitution of St. Paul Lutheran Church dated January 16, 1927, by Reverend Snyder. The below photograph was taken in the original church building during a fund-raising event in 1947.

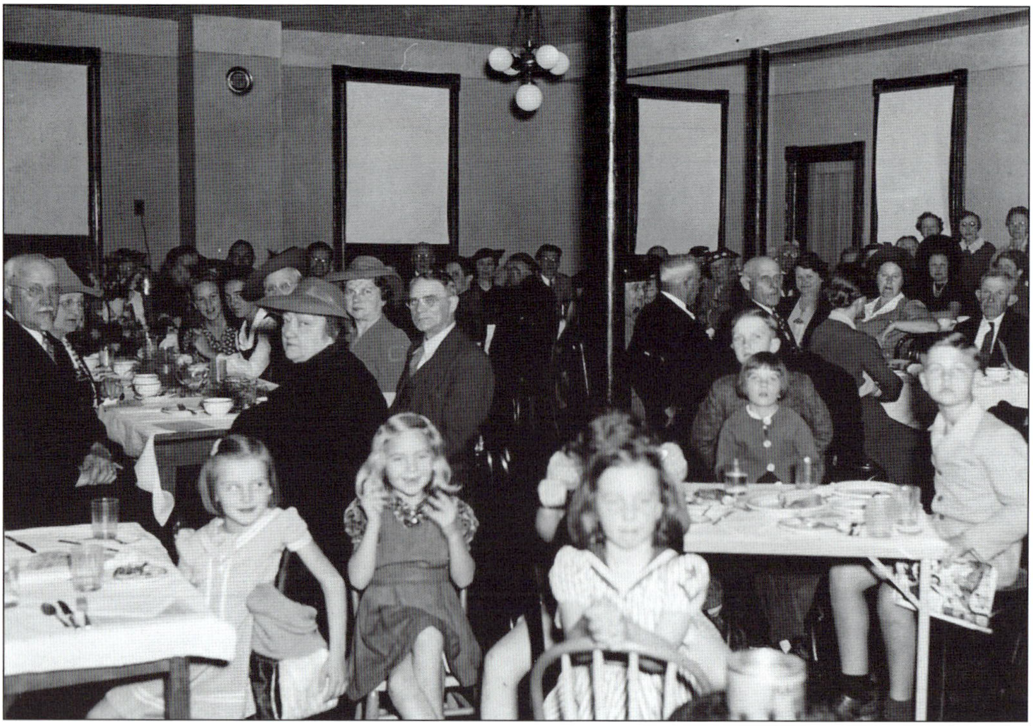

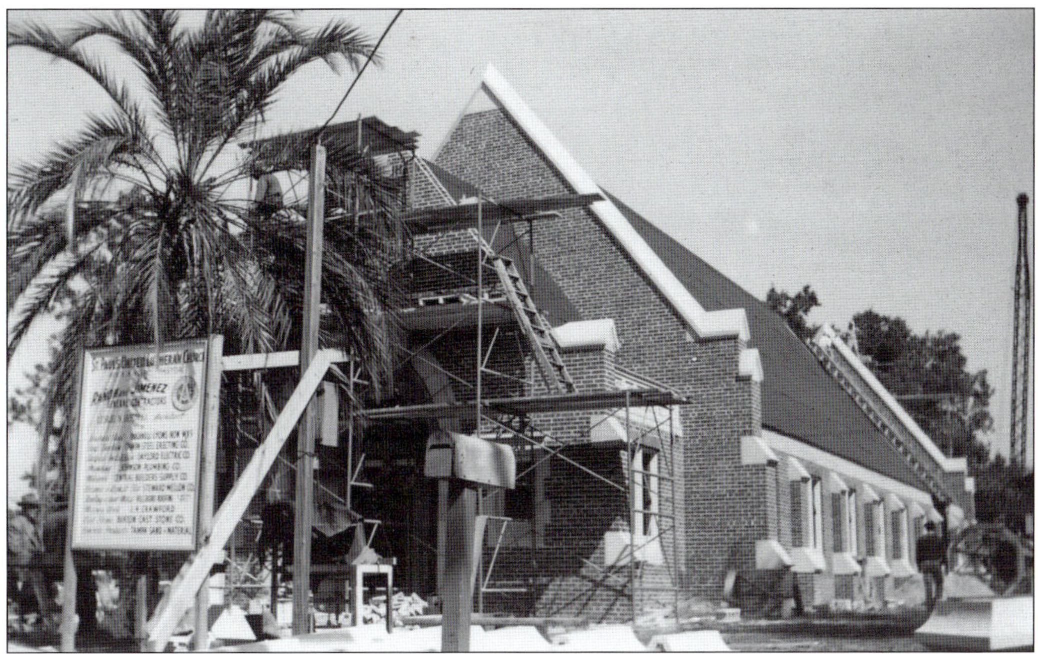

In 1942, the church started a building fund with a Buy-A-Brick campaign to raise funds for a larger permanent church building. During the war years, the church sponsored a Thursday evening social night for soldiers at the USO. By the end of 1942, church membership had grown to 181. In 1948, a building committee was established to begin plans for a new larger church to accommodate the growth of the community. In June 1949, the church accepted bids for construction and awarded the contract to Ranon and Jimenez Contractors for a cost of $51,925. These 1949 photographs show the church under construction.

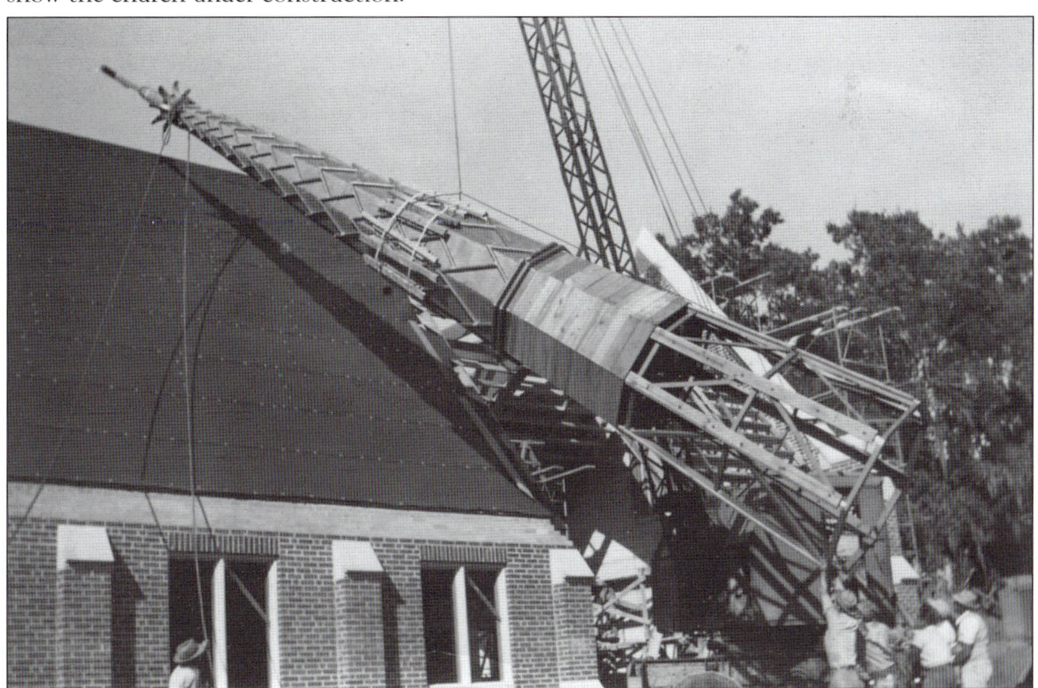

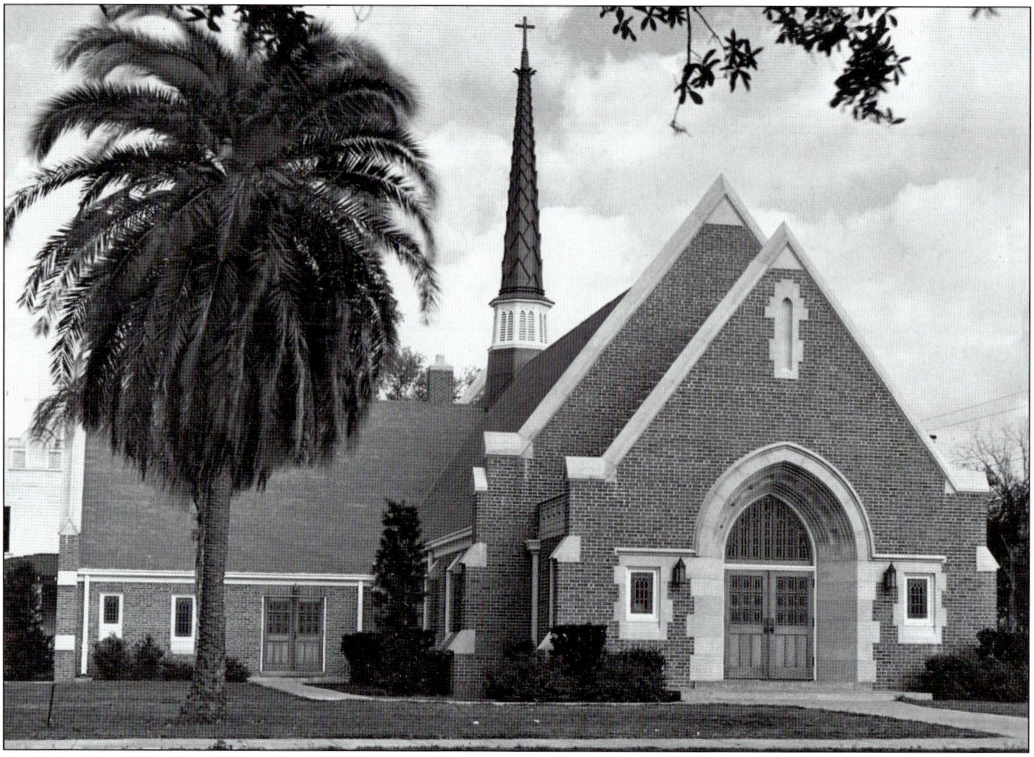

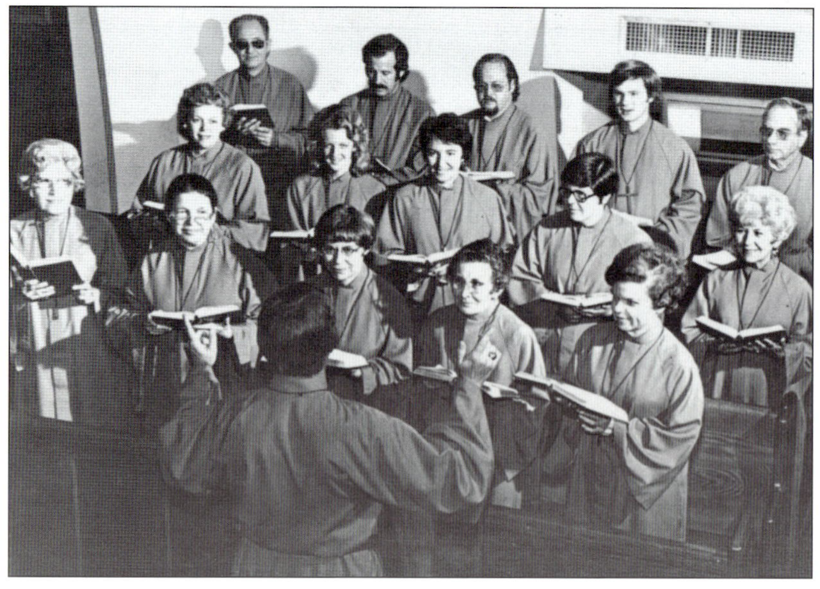

On January 22, 1950, the cornerstone ceremony was held, and on September 3, 1950, St. Paul Lutheran Church was dedicated. The church has assisted in the establishment of many new churches, including Good Shepherd Lutheran Church in 1952, Faith Lutheran Church in 1956, Lutheran Church of Our Savior in 1963, Grace Lutheran Church in 1970, and St. Timothy Lutheran Church in 1985. The church also helped to establish Metropolitan Ministries and took a lead role in establishing the Francis House Ministry. The photograph above shows the new church in 1950, with the original church just behind it. The choir is pictured below in the sanctuary in 1976.

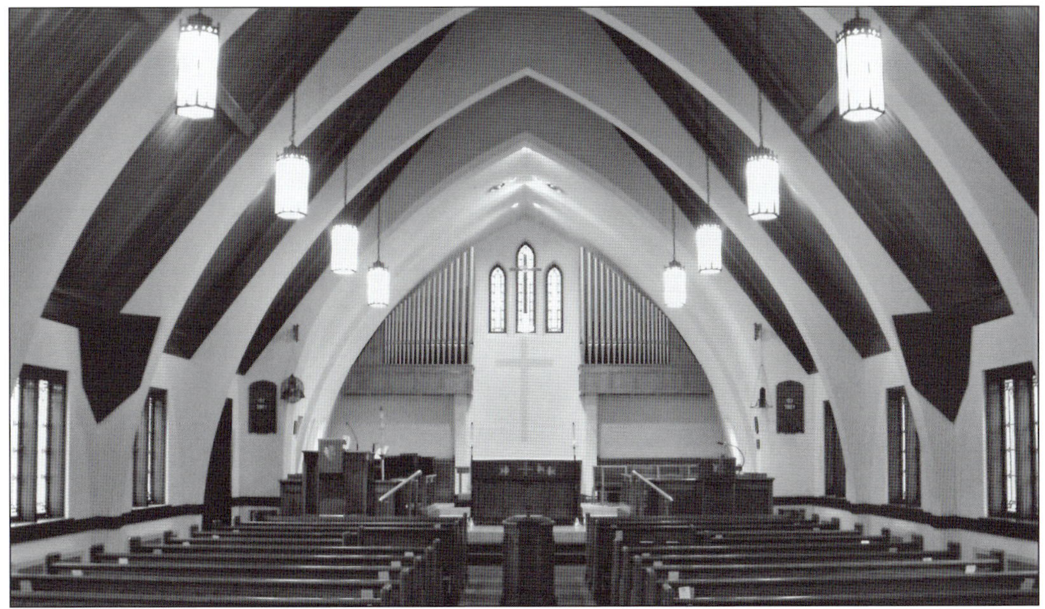

An annual event at the church called Throwback Sunday celebrates the heritage of the church and is extended to members of the community. On this particular Sunday, the church welcomes visitors to join them in vintage 1950s attire, with ladies wearing hats and gloves and gentlemen wearing suits and ties. The service often features 1950s-style gospel music and an old-fashioned ice cream social fellowship. In 2010, the church dedicated the Memorial Garden, a beautifully landscaped area next to the church, to remember departed loved ones. Pictured below is the church youth group in 1975.

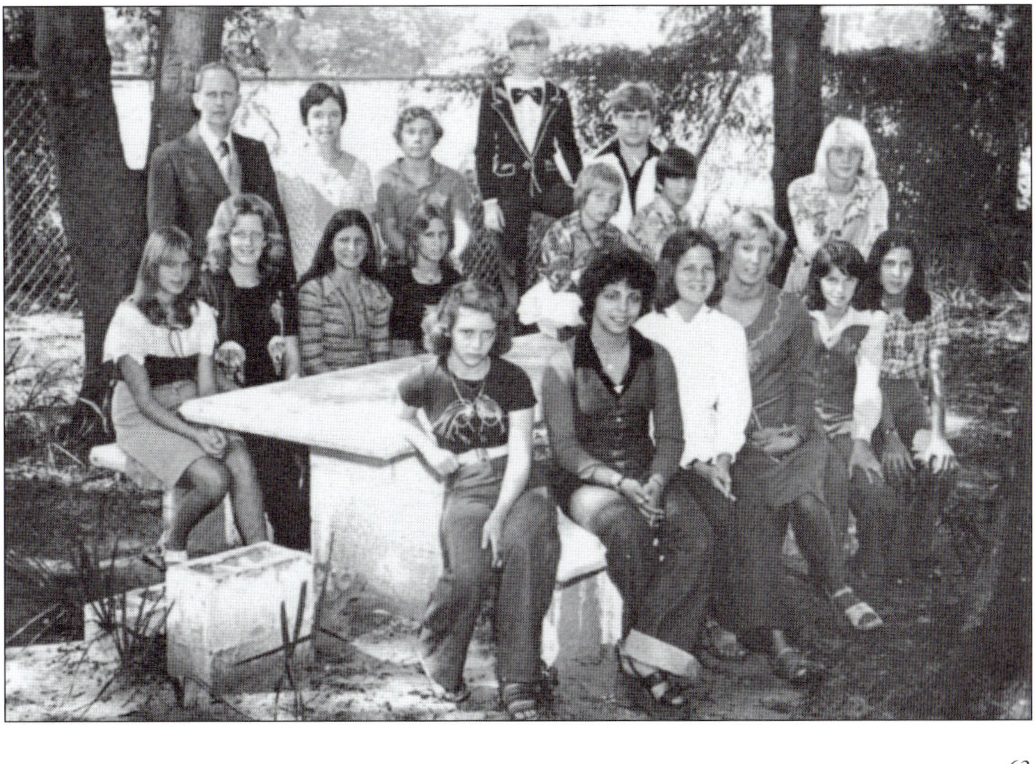

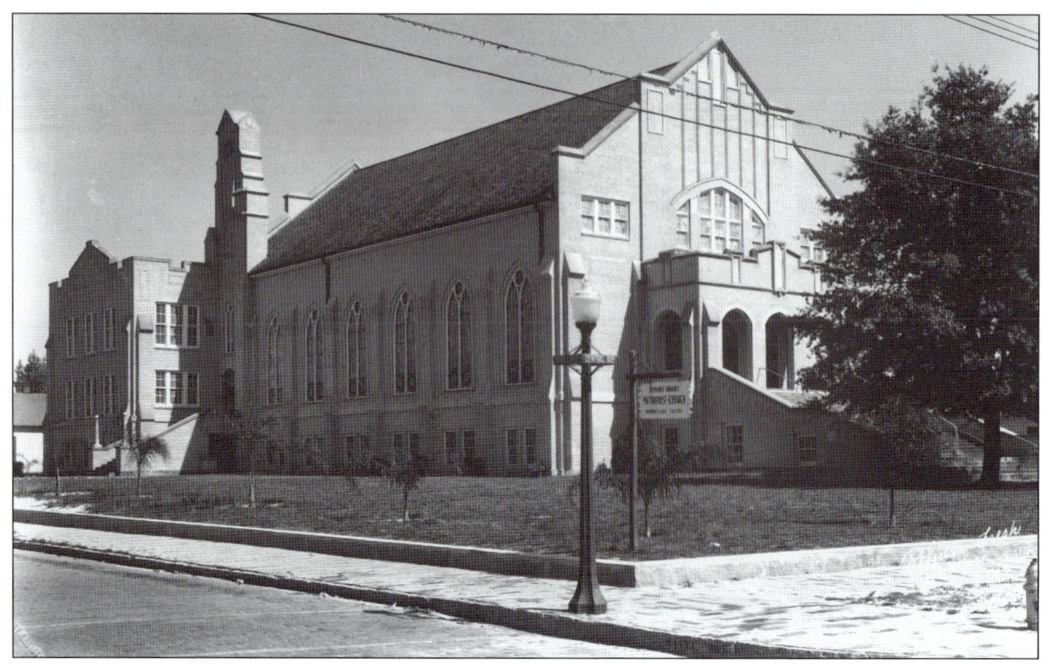

One of the most beautiful historic churches in Tampa is Seminole Heights United Methodist Church, pictured here in 1939 at 6111 Central Avenue. Established in 1921 by Rev. Robert Allen, the congregation of 110 charter members originally met in the former Seminole Heights Elementary School on this same property. The school was relocated to its present campus directly across Hanna Avenue, which cleared the way for construction of the church. In 1922, the church built a wood-frame structure on this site. The congregation quickly outgrew their small church. On March 11, 1928, the community celebrated the dedication of the new church, a large three-story Gothic cream-hued brick structure. Pictured below is the Sunday school group in front of the original church buildings in 1921.

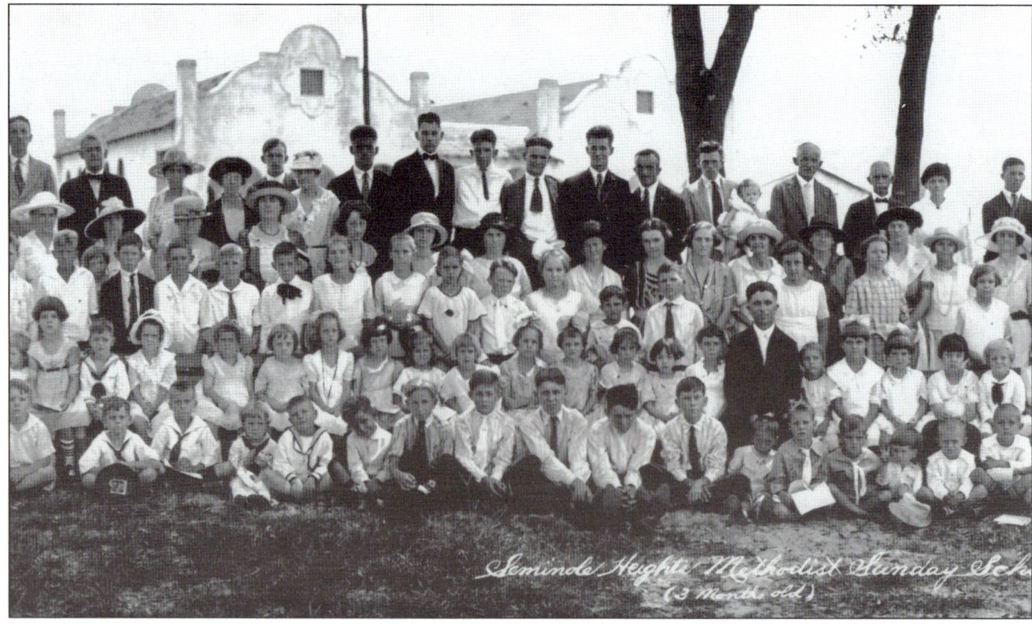

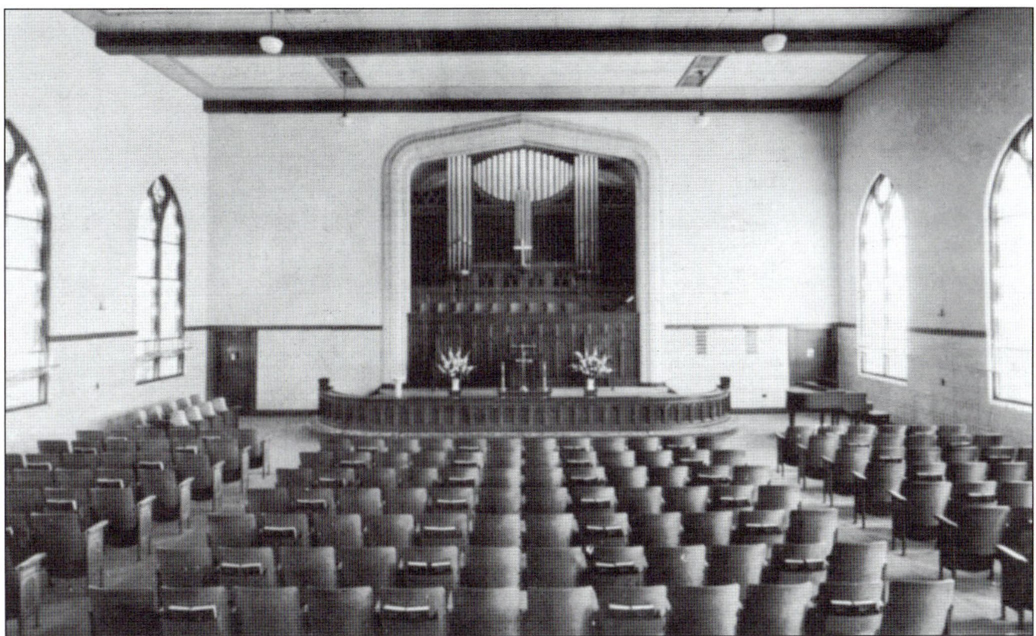

Pictured above is the sanctuary of the church in 1960. That same year, the church constructed an education building and kindergarten school named in honor of teacher Ione Schell for her many years of dedicated service. The church later opened a preschool and day-care center in this building. Pictured below is the Sunday school staff in 1958.

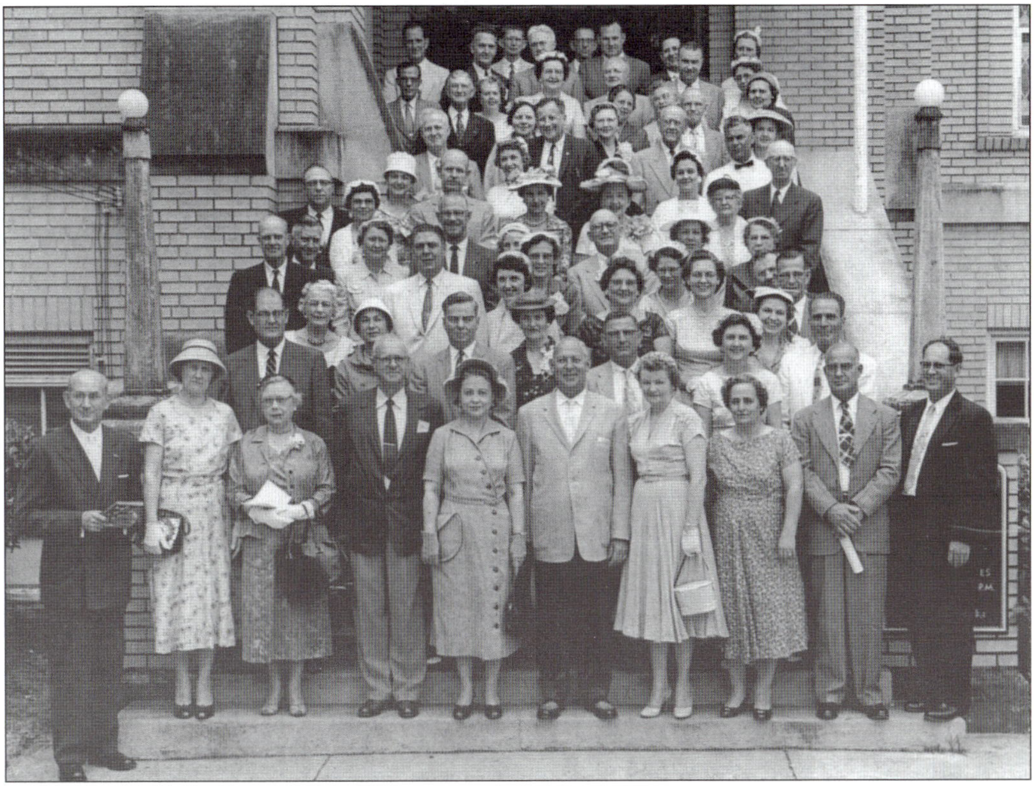

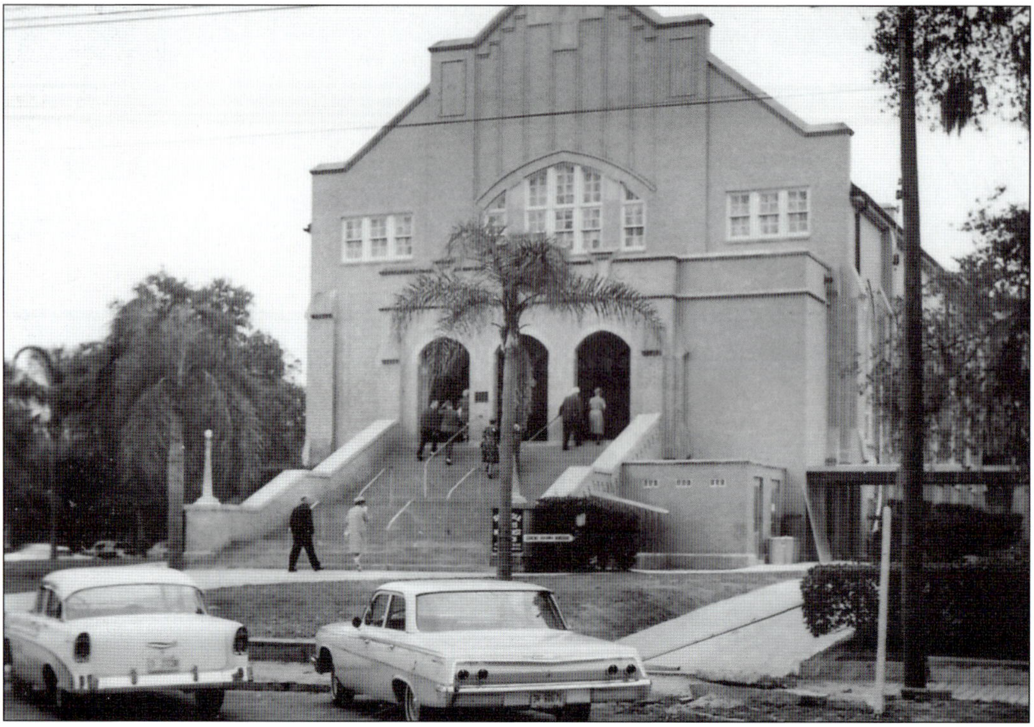

The three-story church, pictured here in 1962, features English Gothic elements including 12 towering stained-glass windows and an arched portico spanning the front entrance. It is one of the few structures in Tampa with a full basement, which serves as the fellowship hall. The church was designed by one of Tampa's most highly regarded architects, Frank A. Winn Jr., who designed several other historic landmarks, including the Ballast Point Park Pier.

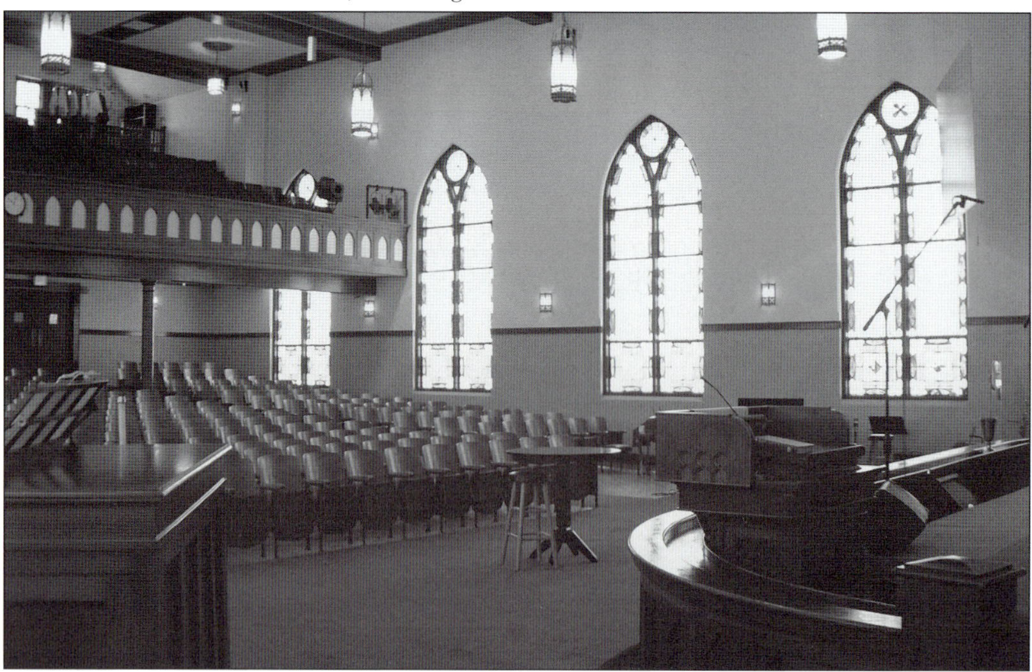

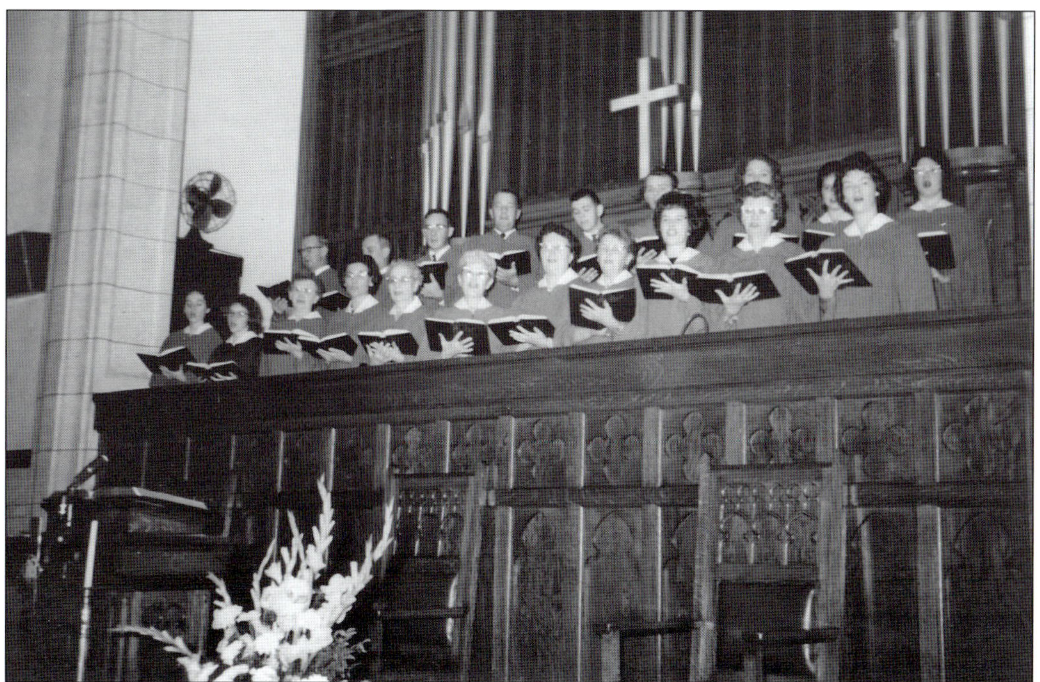

Music ministry has always been an important part of the community at Seminole Heights United Methodist Church. Pictured above is the choir in 1959. The historical pipe organ above the choir loft is a 1928 Kilgen model very similar to theater organs used during the silent-film era of the 1920s. The organ cost of $10,000 was raised by the ladies of the church through various fundraisers, and it was considered to be one of the finest pipe organs on the west coast of Florida when it was installed. Pictured below is the congregation in 1962.

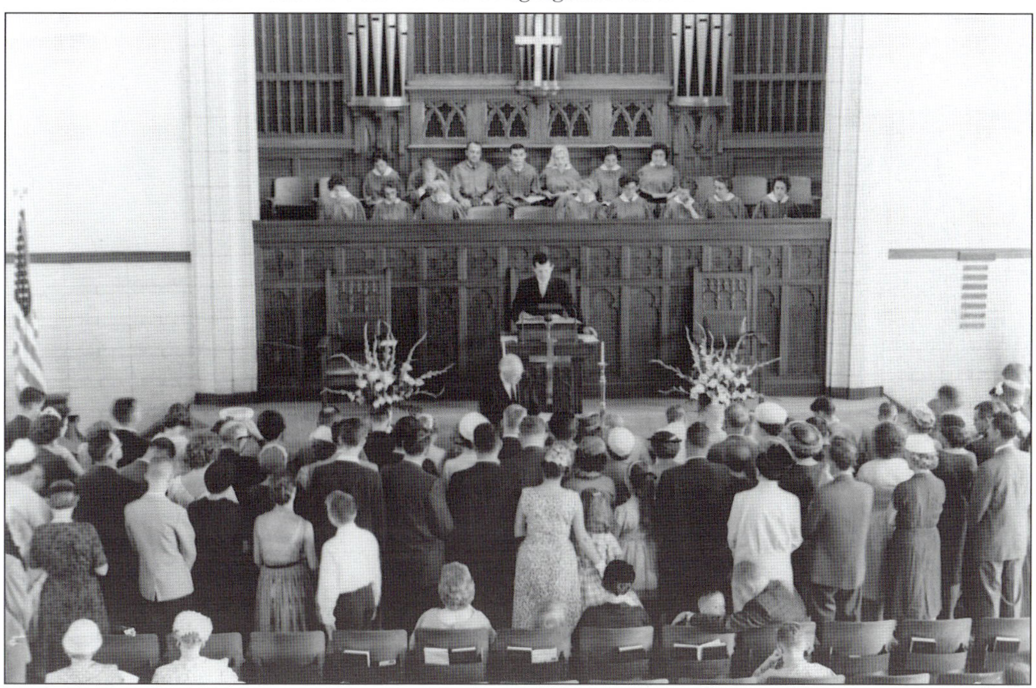

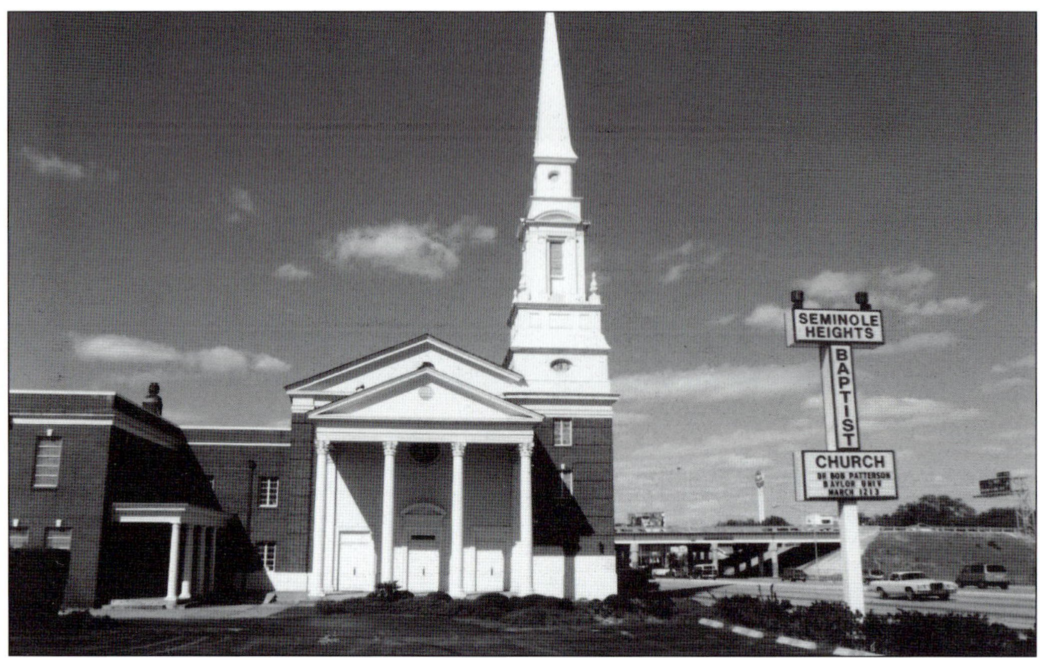

Seminole Heights Baptist Church was established on December 18, 1921, with Dr. J.H. Snow as the first pastor. At the opening service, 42 new congregants were listed as charter members. The first church was a small wood-frame building at 611 East Hillsborough Avenue, pictured below in 1938. The congregation later moved two blocks east to property at the corner of Hillsborough and Nebraska Avenues. On Sunday, June 25, 1922, the church observed the Lord's Supper for the first time. In 1928, the men of the church built an addition for Sunday school classes. The ladies of the church prepared meals on work nights so the men could come directly from their jobs to work on the construction project.

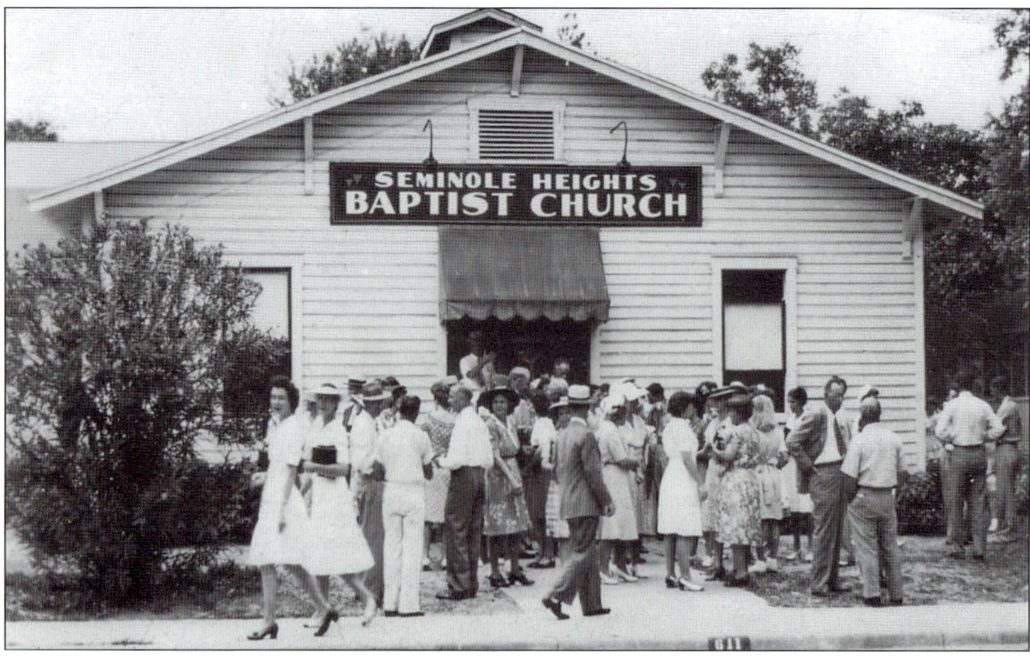

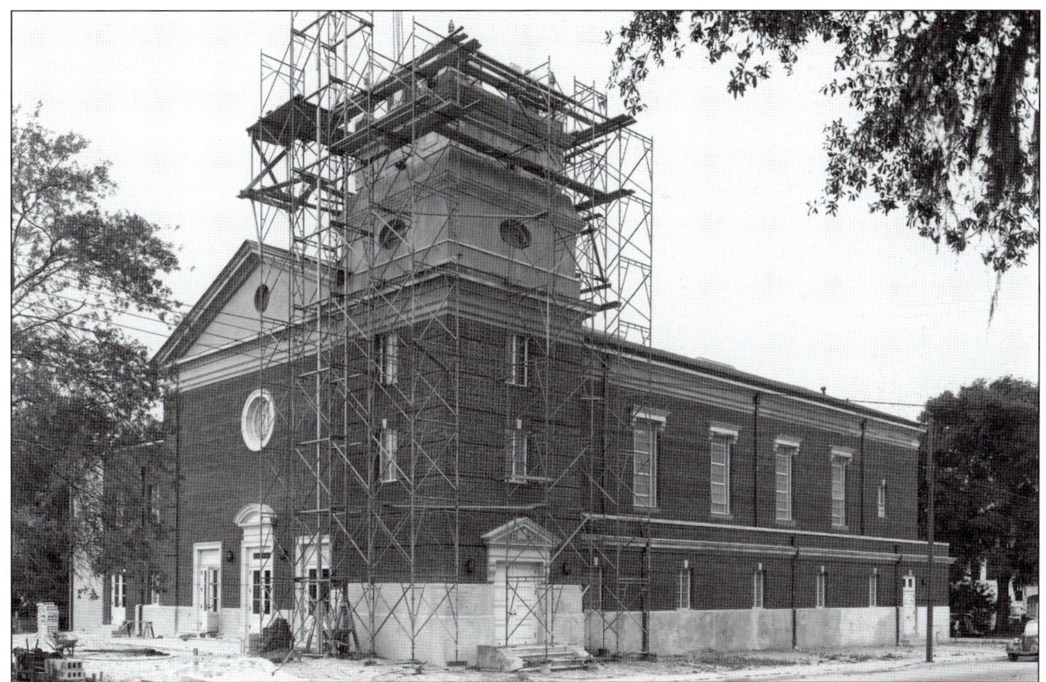

In 1947, Pastor A.W. Mathis began making plans for a new, larger church to accommodate the growth of the community. On November 15, 1947, ground-breaking ceremonies were held and construction commenced at a cost of $213,000. The cornerstone was laid on January 1, 1948, and the congregation celebrated the dedication ceremony of their new Colonial Revival–style church on May 6, 1949, pictured below. The photograph above shows construction of the new church in 1949. Through the efforts of Pastor Mathis, during his tenure, the church would grow from 253 members to over 1,400.

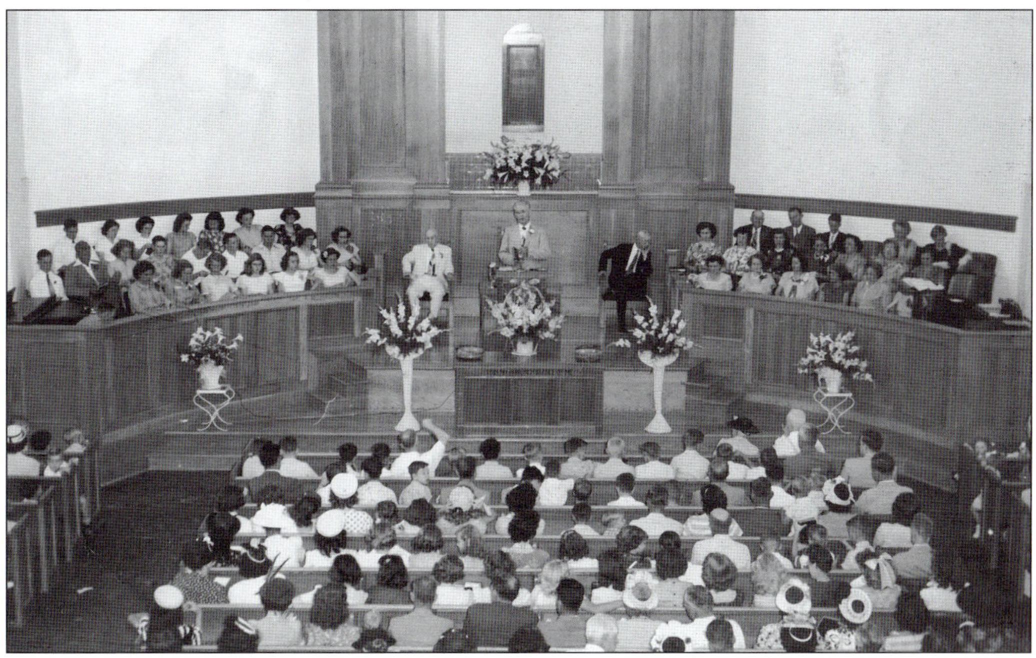

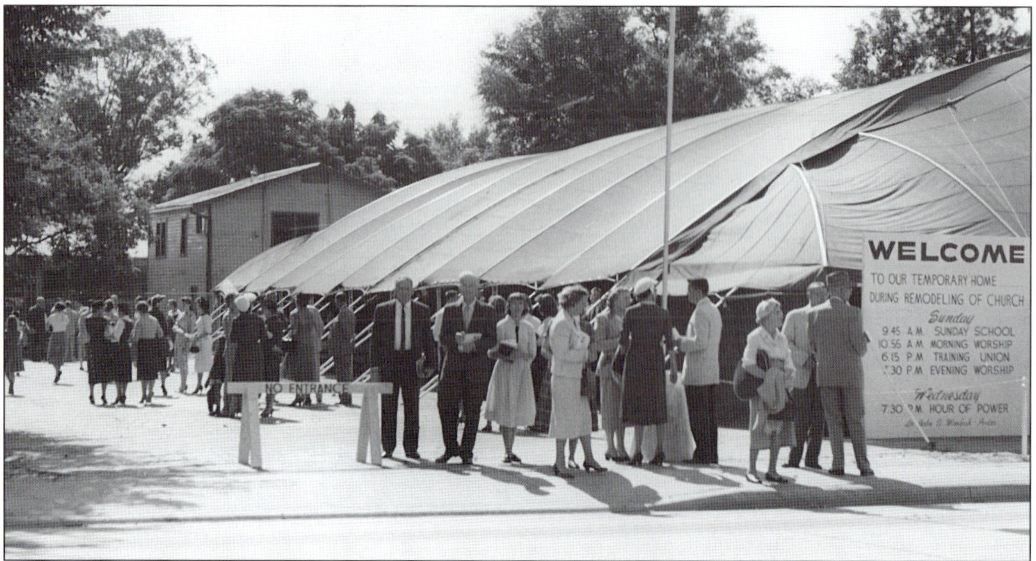

In the fall of 1958, the church erected a large tent in the parking lot and named it the Canvas Cathedral, pictured above. This would become the temporary worship center while the church underwent a major expansion project that included construction of an education building, remodeling of the sanctuary, addition of the portico, and installation of the needle-point steeple atop the bell tower. The new steeple would become the tallest of any church in the city. On February 1, 1959, the renovation project was completed. Pictured below is the construction project underway in 1958.

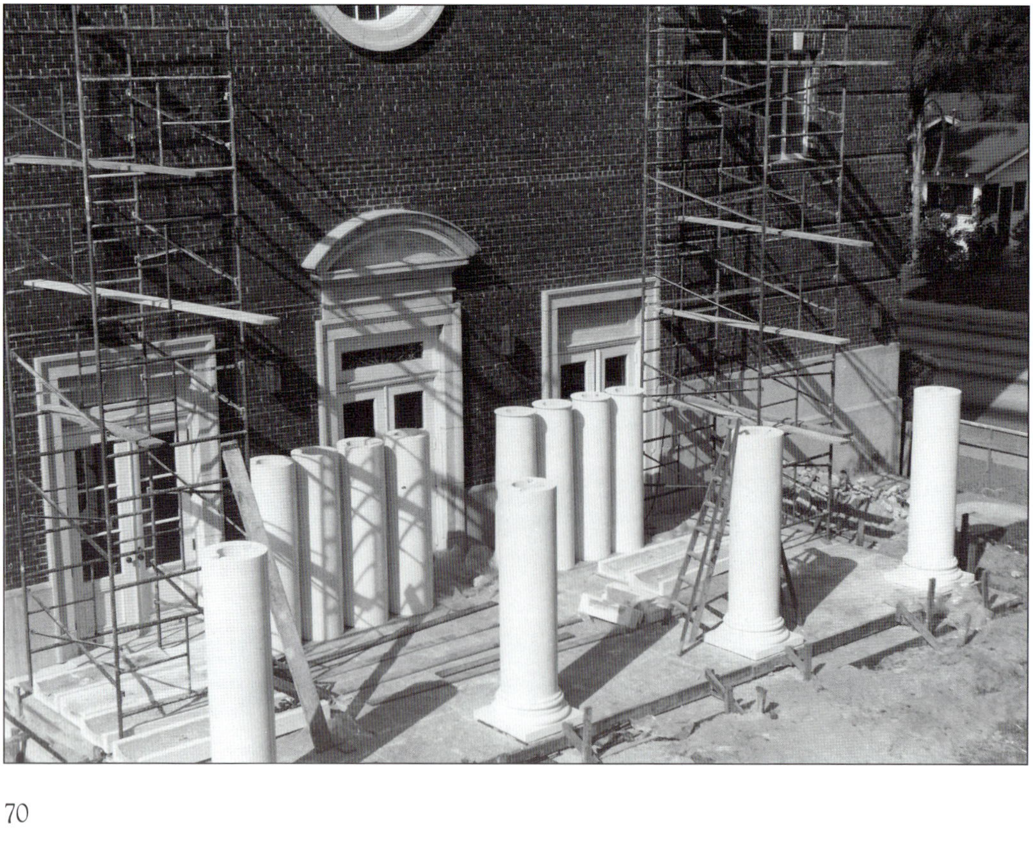

Throughout the long history of Seminole Heights Baptist Church, the community has been dedicated to outreach programs. In 1927, the first mission sponsored was Spencer Memorial Baptist Church, followed by Idlewild Baptist Church in 1934, North Rome Baptist Church in 1944, Hubert Avenue Baptist Church in 1952, and Salem Baptist Church in 1970. In 1958, the congregation established one of the first church day-care centers in Tampa, called Babyland. Pictured at right is the raising of the new steeple in 1958, and below is the church choir in 1959.

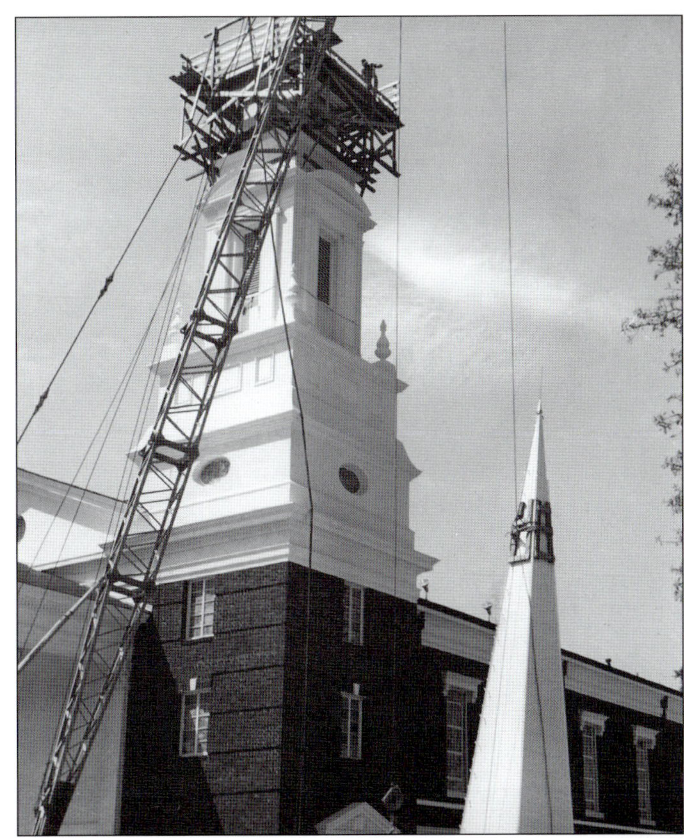

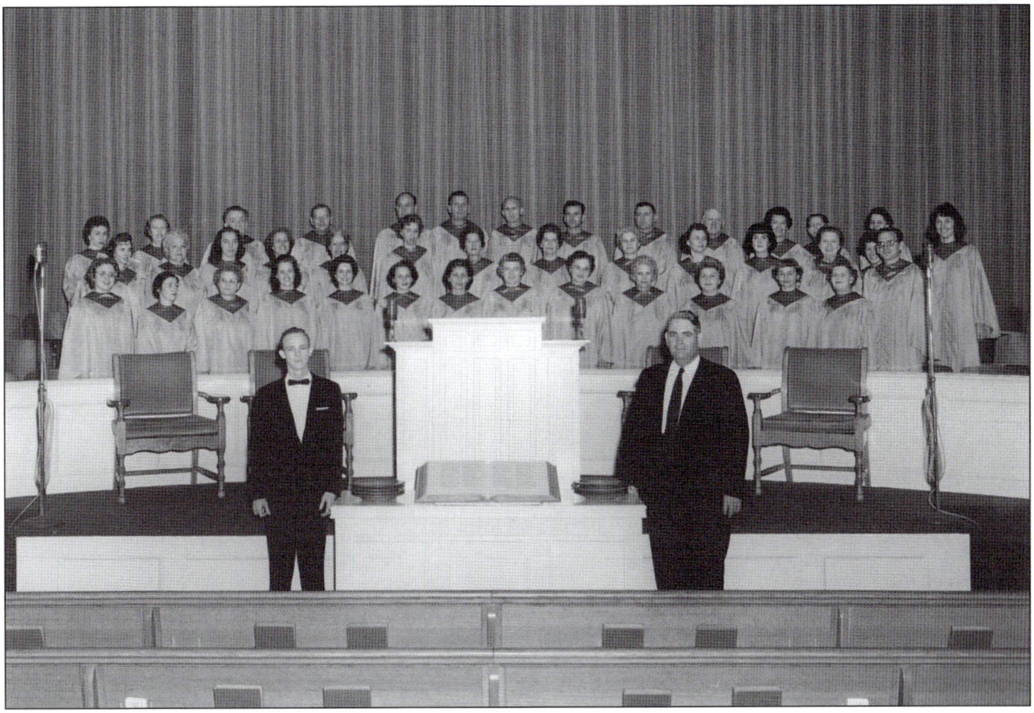

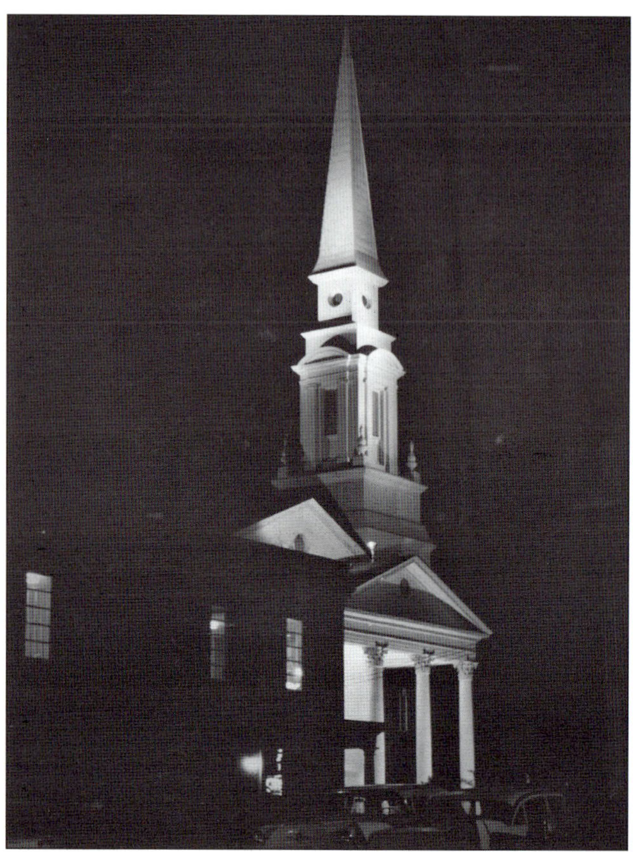

Seminole Heights Baptist Church, pictured in 1959, was a pioneer in Christian television broadcasting. In 1962, the church produced one of the first local Christian television shows, called *Good News*, which was broadcast on weekday mornings. In 1974, the church established another television show called *Steeple Time* airing on Sunday mornings. In 1985, the church established a new program called *Bringing Tampa to Life*.

Lake Magdalene United Methodist Church was established in 1895 by Rev. Isaac Ward Bearss in a chapel on the shore of Lake Carroll. In 1925, the church dedicated a new building at 2900 Fletcher Avenue, pictured here in 1945 with the congregation. During World War II, the bell tower of the church was used as a lookout post for German planes. In 2002, the church dedicated its current sanctuary.

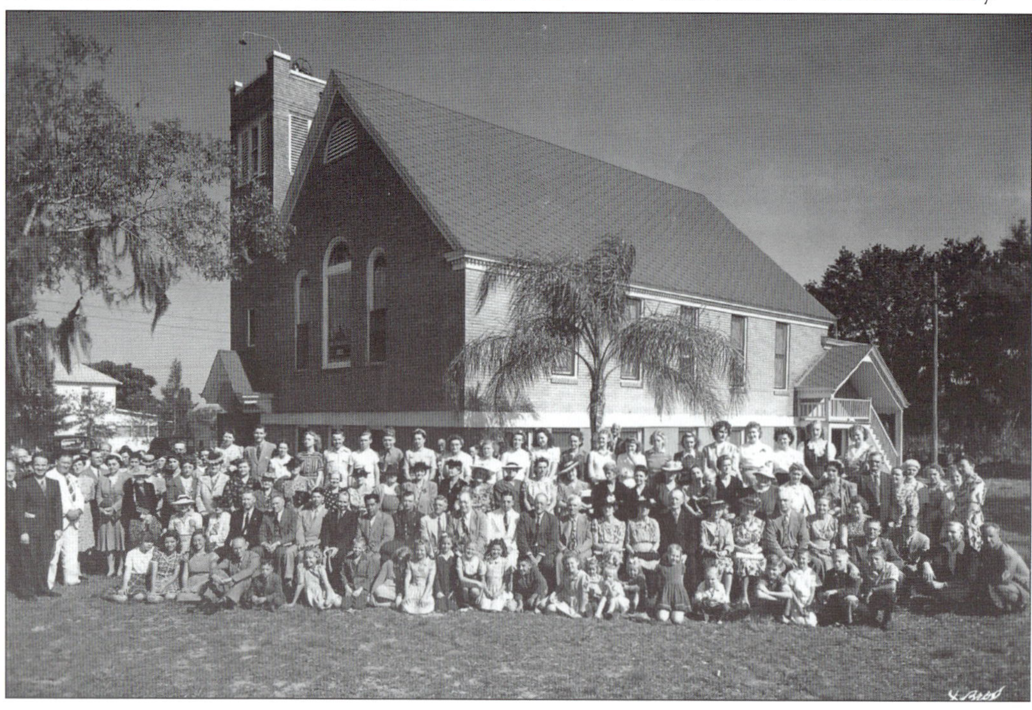

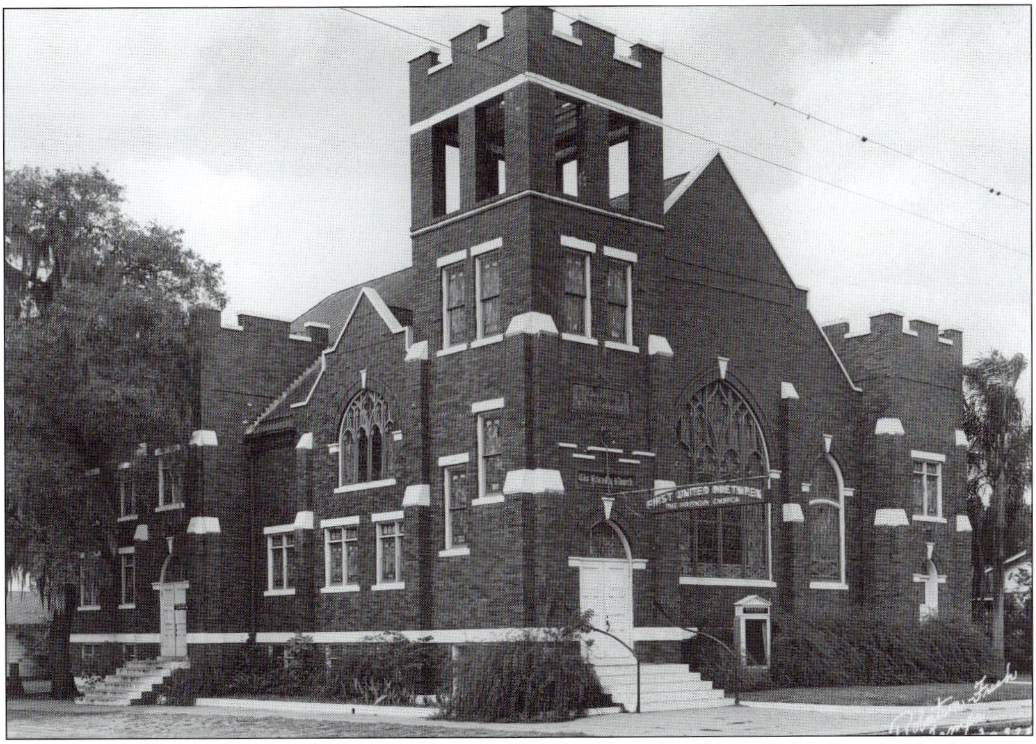

Pictured here in 1939 is the First United Brethren in Christ Church, located at 3300 Nebraska Avenue and constituted in 1911. In 1916, the church completed construction of this Gothic Revival structure featuring 38 stained-glass windows, a bell tower, and pipe organ. On the church sign, the congregation advertises itself as "The Friendly Church." Today, Deeper Life Christian Church worships here and ministers to the community.

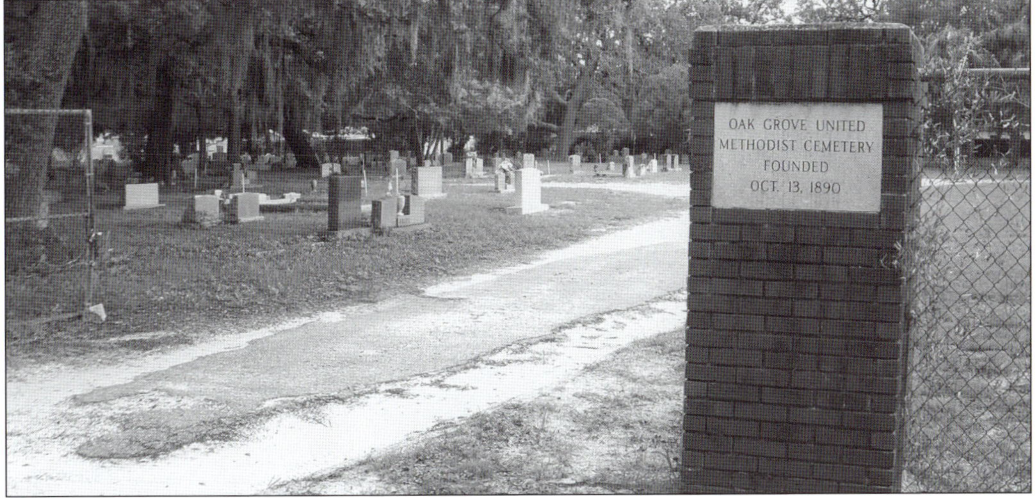

Pictured here is the Oak Grove United Methodist Church Cemetery, established in 1890. It is one of the few church cemeteries in Tampa. From 1880 to 1920, the church was located on this property. Many of Tampa's pioneer families are buried here along with nearly 150 members of the armed forces. On July 24, 2007, the cemetery was honored with a historic landmark designation by the Hillsborough County Commission.

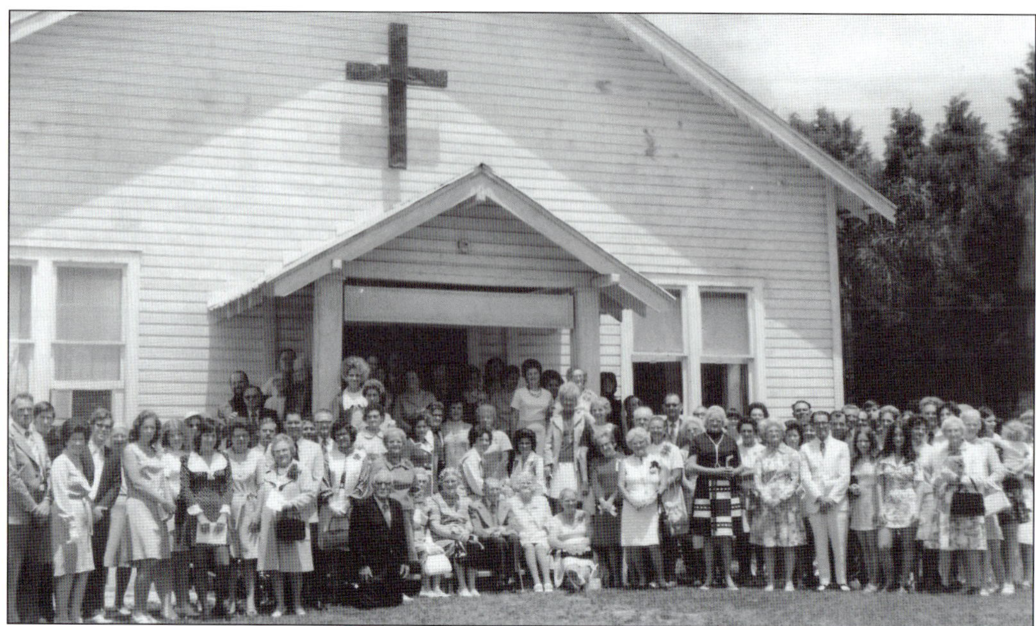

Oak Grove United Methodist Church is one of the oldest churches in Tampa, established in 1880 by Rev. Jason Gant. The congregation originally met on land that was donated to the church by the Florida Central & Peninsular Railroad Company in the 3000 block of Sitka Street. The first church was a one-room log cabin. In 1890, a cemetery was established next to the church. In 1920, the congregation moved to a small chapel on the corner of Habana and Waters Avenues and later constructed a larger church in 1926, pictured above with the congregation in 1966. Pictured below in 1965 is the sanctuary of the new church, constructed in 1956.

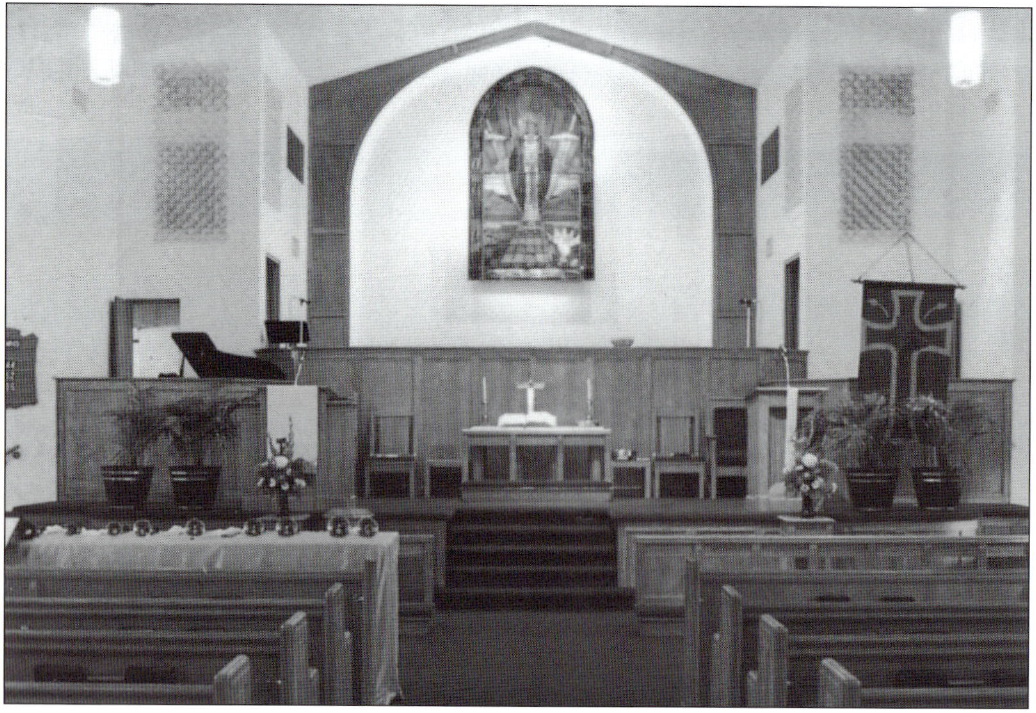

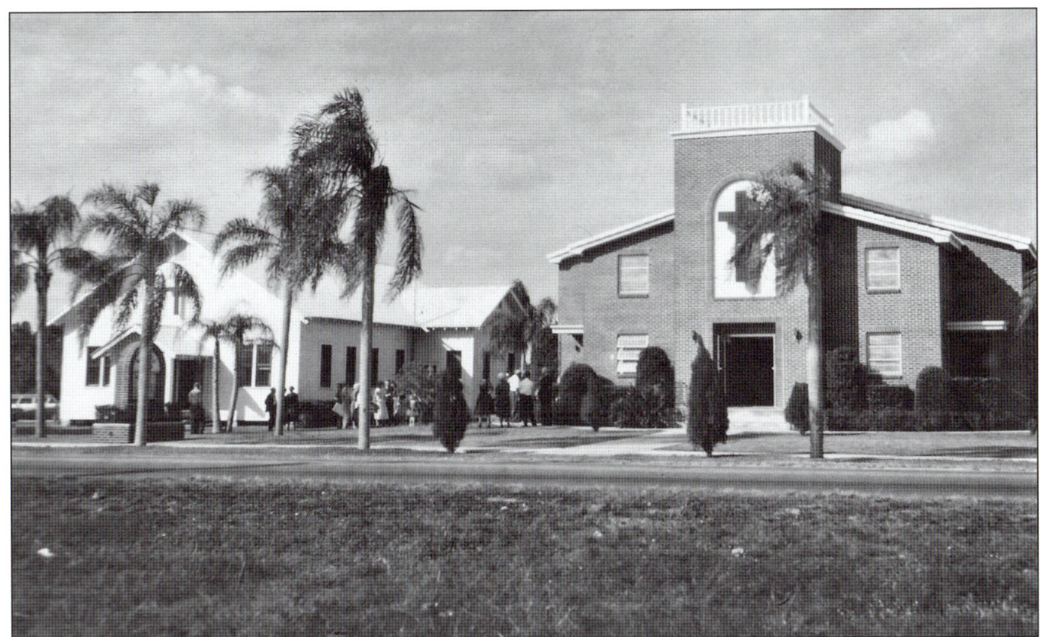

In 1949, the church began making plans for a new church to accommodate the growing congregation. That same year a new education building was completed. With a donation of land received from a church benefactor, the congregation moved forward with plans for a new church. In 1954, ground-breaking ceremonies were held. Construction began shortly thereafter, and the new church was completed in 1956. The first service held in the new 700-seat church was on February 26, 1956. The above photograph shows the old church and the new church in 1956. The photograph below from 1983 shows the congregation in the new church.

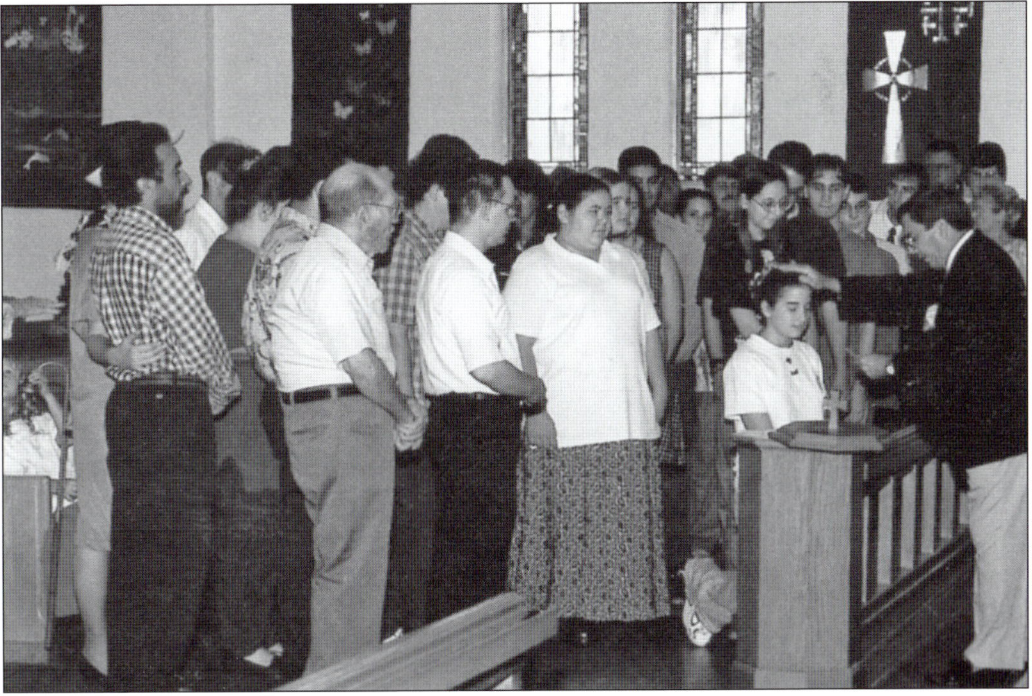

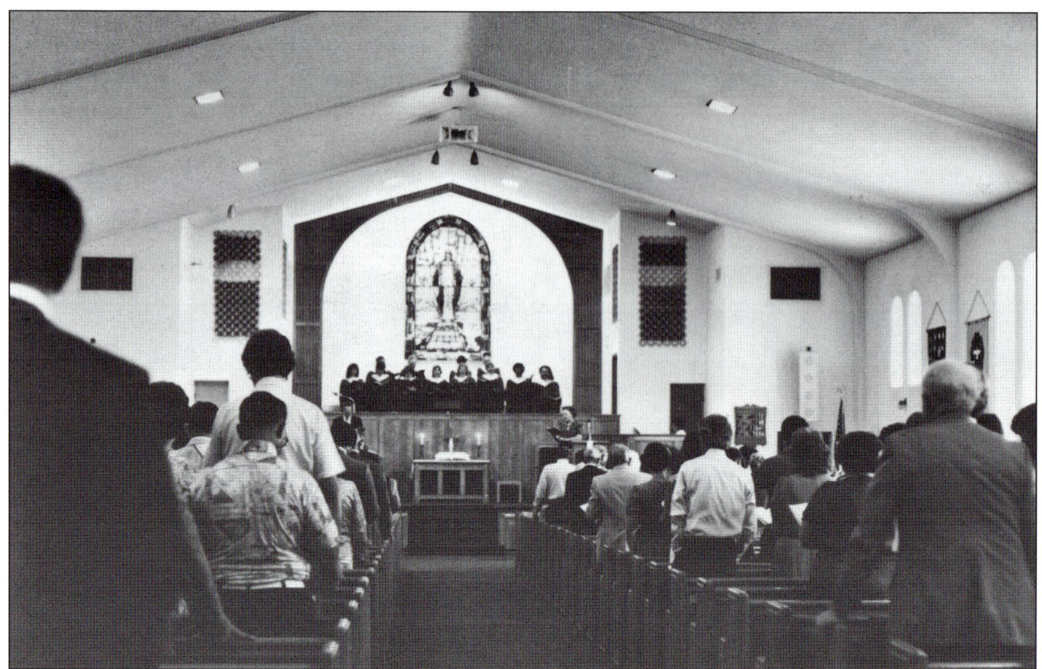

The new Oak Grove United Methodist Church was dedicated on November 13, 1960, by Bishop James Henley and Rev. Melton Ware, district superintendent. In 1965, the church established the Oak Grove Kindergarten School. That same year, the church celebrated the installation of the new stained-glass chancel window. Pictured above is the sanctuary in 1969. Below is the choir at their Christmas Cantata presentation in 1997.

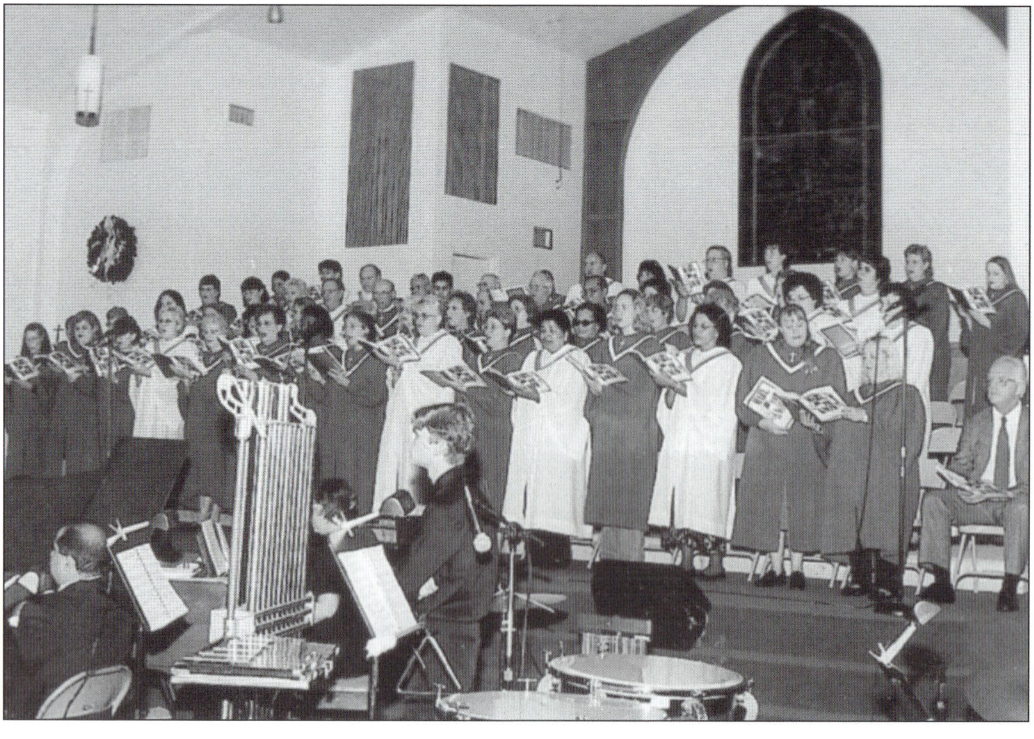

In 1969, the church proudly celebrated the crowning of its new house of worship with a steeple, pictured here shortly after the installation. The original church building has been converted into offices, with the sanctuary preserved as a chapel for small gatherings. The church continues the mission of their founding faithful who met in a simple log cabin, by offering many special ministries of outreach and service to the community. Pictured below is the church choir in 1983.

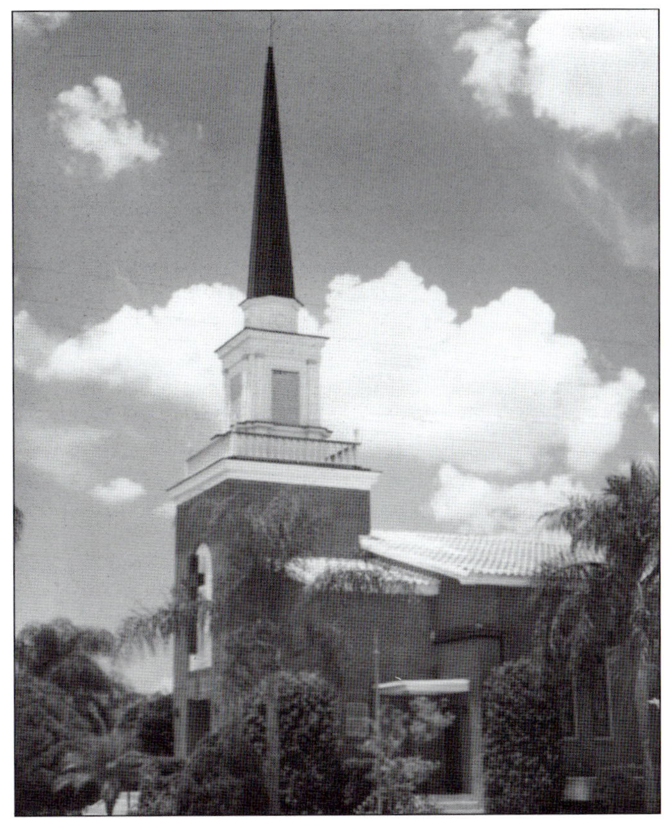

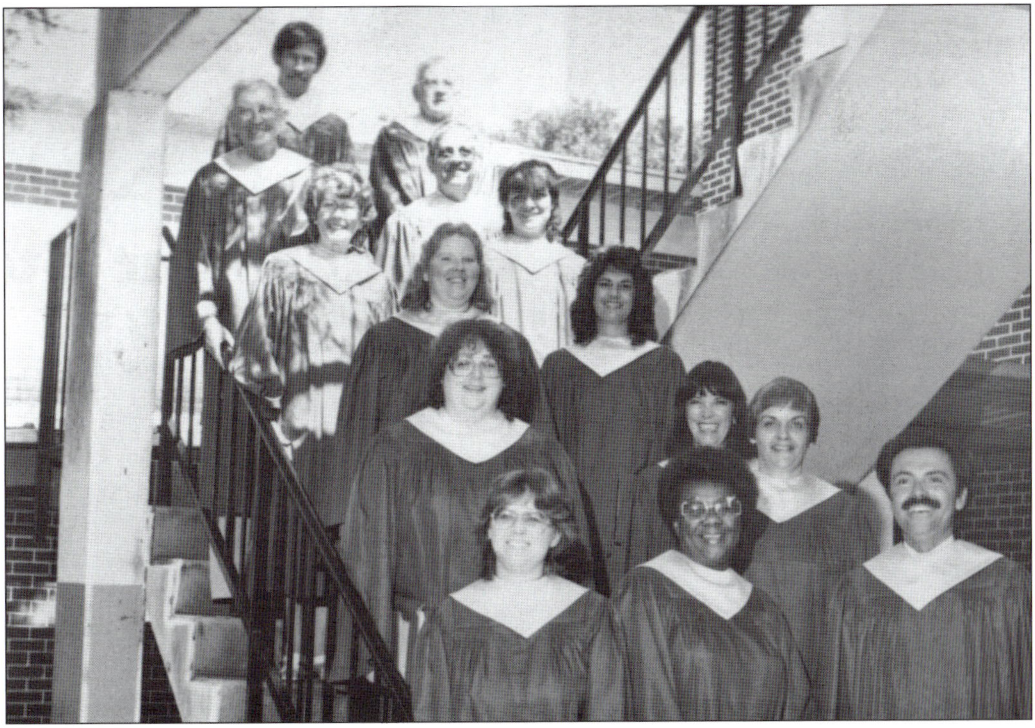

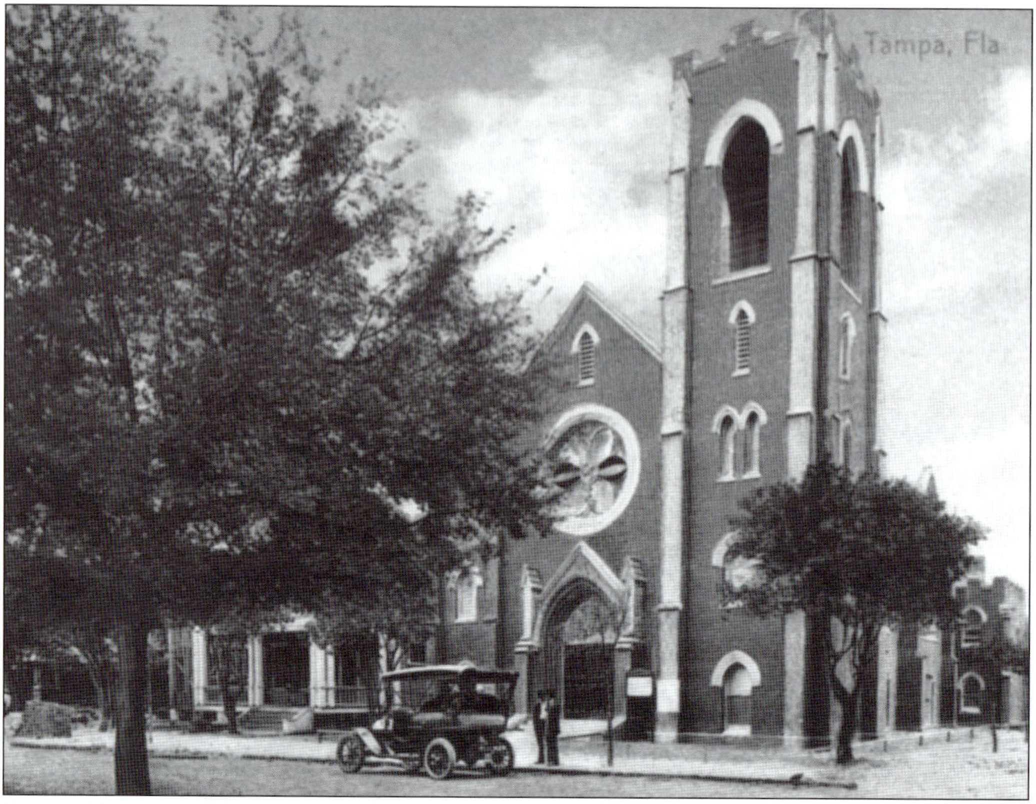

Pictured here in 1919 is the First Congregational Church at the corner of Florida and Frances Avenues in Tampa Heights. Constituted in 1885, the congregation originally gathered at the Palmetto Hotel in downtown Tampa and later constructed a chapel at Florida Avenue and Royal Street, where they worshipped until this new church was consecrated in 1906. The first pastor was Rev. Sidney Crawford. The new stately Gothic Revival church was constructed at a cost of $16,350 and featured a five-story bell tower, stained-glass windows, choir loft, and pipe organ.

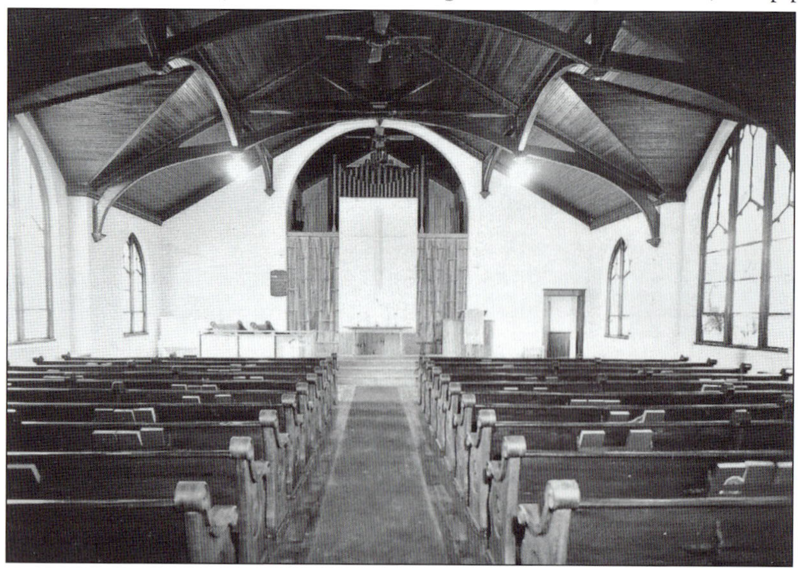

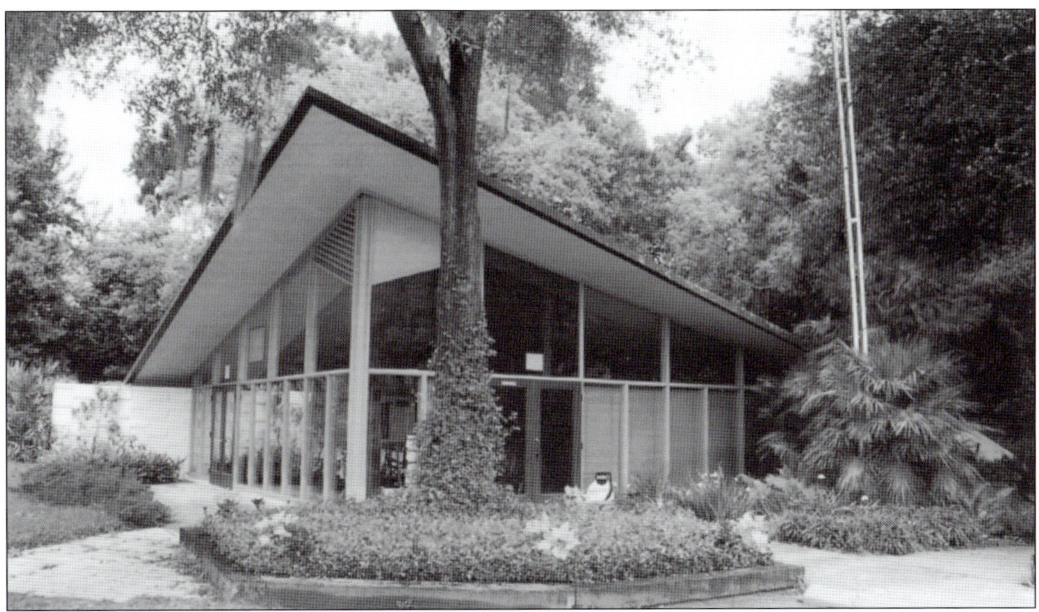

In 1957, the Congregational Church merged with the Evangelical and Reformed Church and became the First United Church of Christ. In 1958, the congregation decided to move to a developing area of North Tampa at 7308 Fowler Avenue. On Thanksgiving Day 1959, the church held its ground-breaking ceremony. During construction of the new church, pictured here, a powerful windstorm came through the area and tore the entire roof off. Despite this setback, construction resumed, and the dedication ceremony was held on April 3, 1960. The design of the new church was inspired by the image of a dove in flight, the ancient Christian symbol of the Holy Spirit. The church features glass walls throughout the sanctuary, with a magnificent view of the foliage along the Hillsborough River.

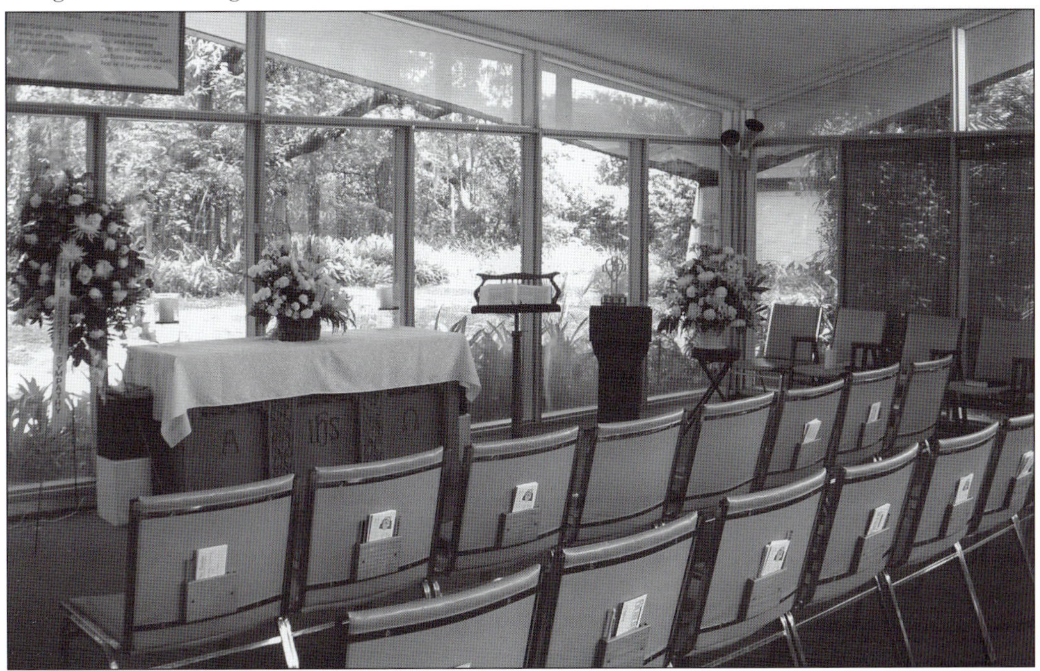

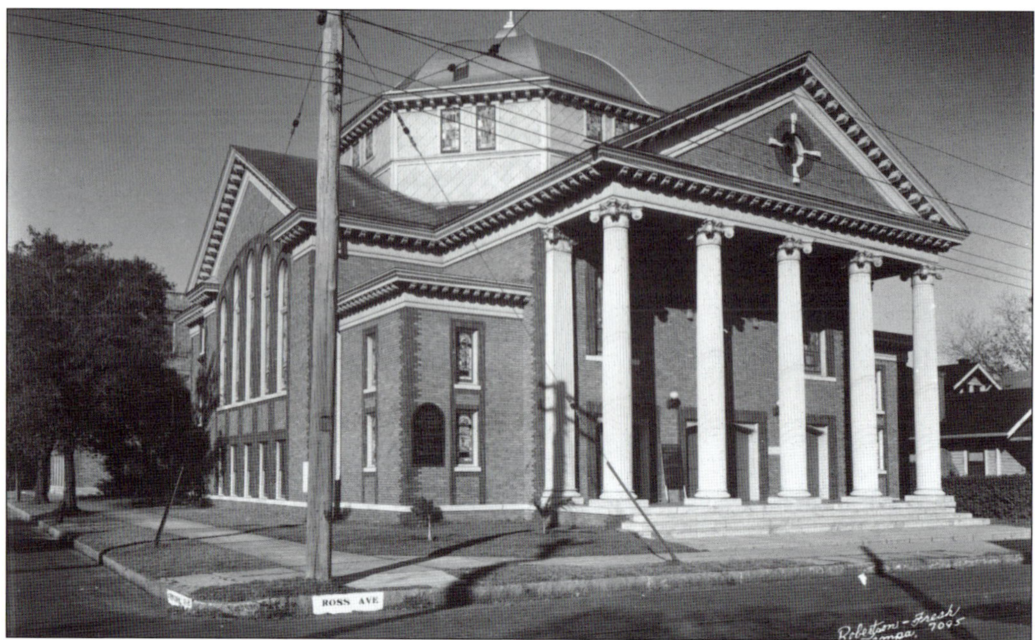

Tampa Heights Methodist Episcopal Church was constituted in 1899, with Rev. Henry Rice as pastor. The congregation completed construction of the church pictured here in 1913 at 502 Ross Avenue. This large Greek Revival–style church featured 32 stained-glass windows and a pipe organ. When these pictures were taken in 1940, the church records reflected membership of 710. In later years, the church was renamed Tyer Temple United Methodist Church. Today, the church has been preserved and is now the Sanctuary Lofts, a unique apartment community. It is considered to be one of the few surviving outstanding examples of turn of the century Greek Revival architecture and is another success story for historic preservation. (Both, USFSCL.)

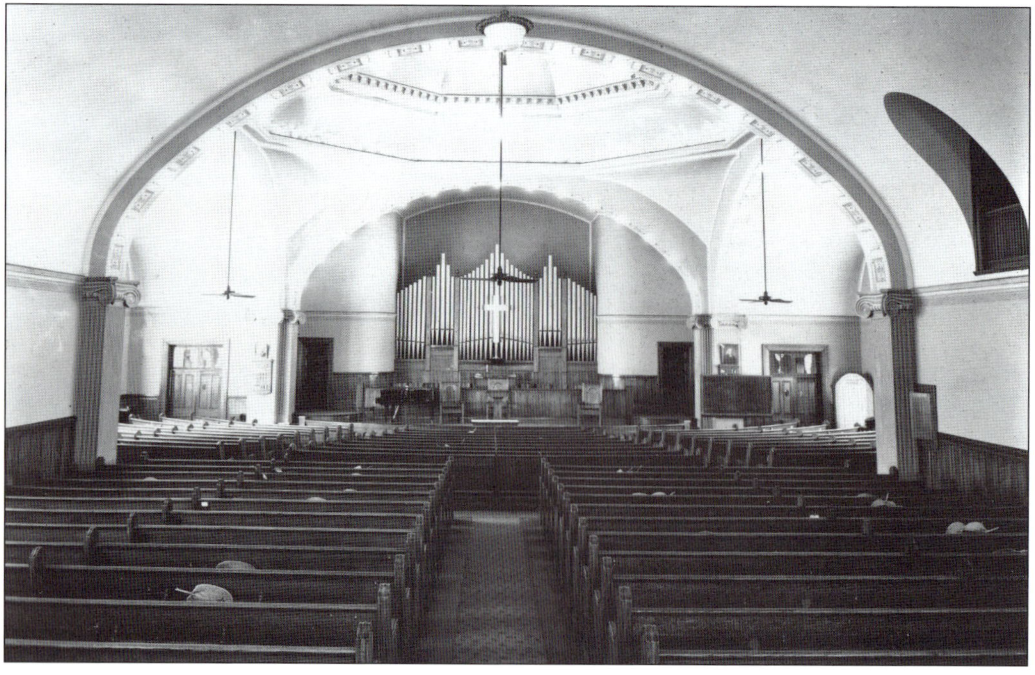

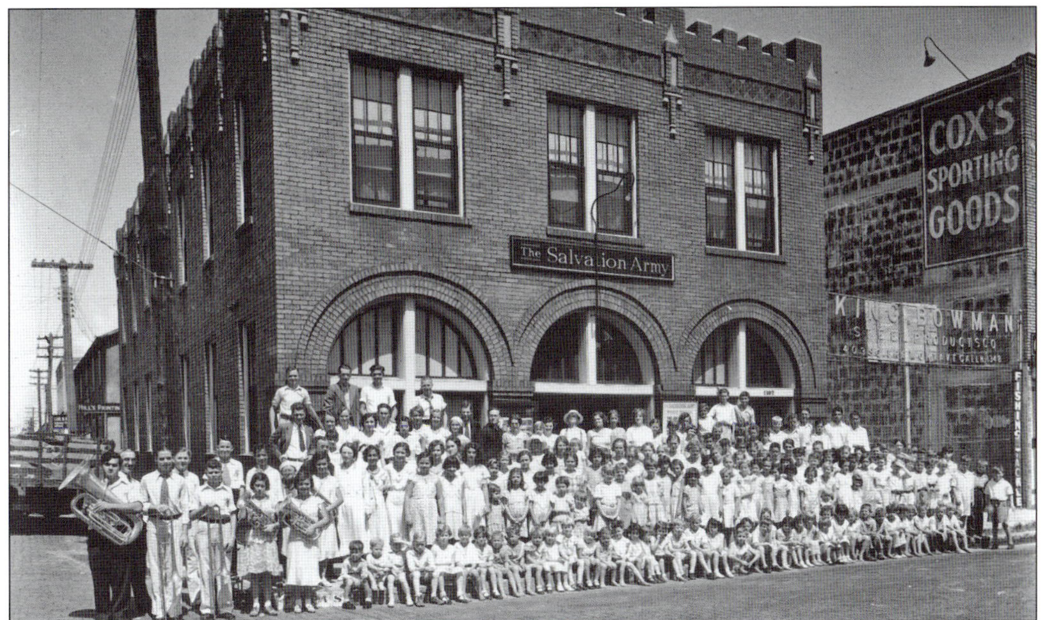

Since 1893, the Salvation Army Church has been serving the needs of the community, helping Tampa families recover from hardships, feeding the poor, and sheltering the homeless. Another ministry is the Angel Tree program, providing Christmas gifts for underprivileged children of Tampa. Pictured above in 1923 is the congregation in front of the original church at 1102 North Tampa Street. The church later relocated to 1100 Sligh Avenue.

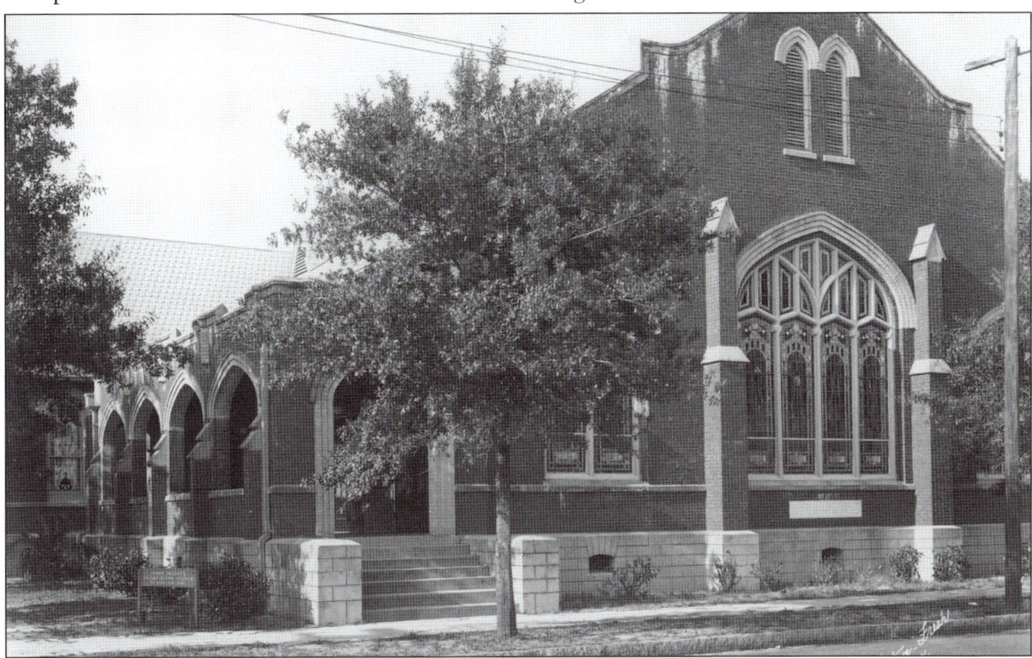

Tampa Heights Presbyterian Church was established in 1905 and originally met in a small chapel constructed in 1908. This Gothic Revival structure at 602 Palm Avenue was completed in 1923 and featured 22 stained-glass windows and a pipe organ. The church was officially dedicated in 1937. It has been preserved and serves the community as the Tampa Heights Junior Civic Association.

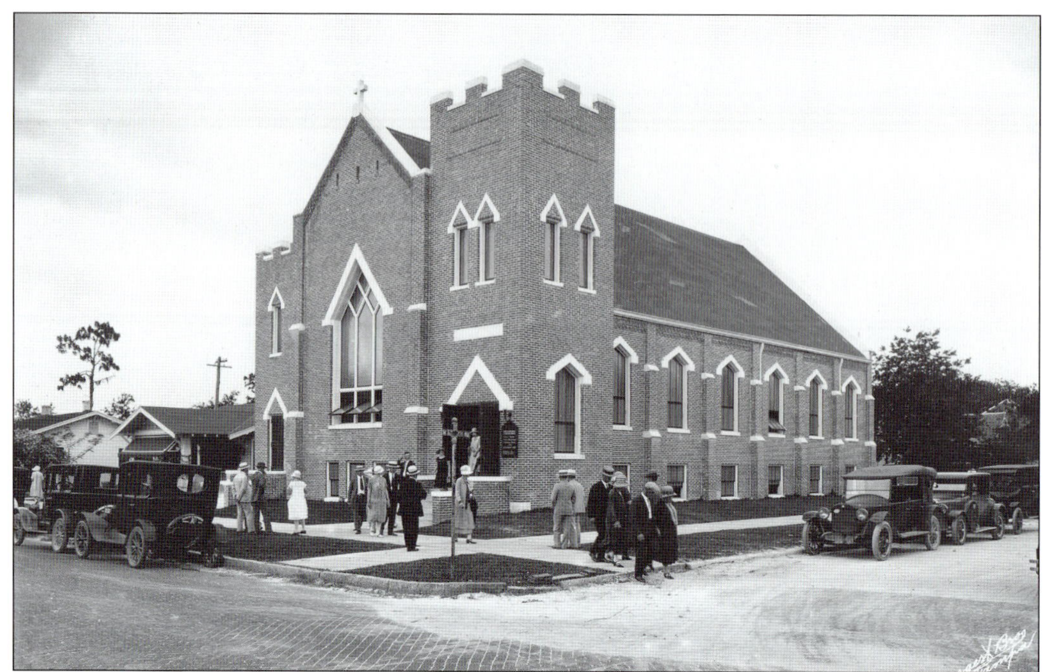

Zion Lutheran Church is a hidden treasure tucked away in an old Tampa Heights neighborhood. This beautiful church dates to 1893, when it was formally organized by Rev. C.F. Broomer, the first pastor. The first church building was completed in 1894 at the corner of Tyler and Marion Streets in downtown Tampa. By 1924, the congregation had outgrown the small chapel and plans were made for the construction of a larger church at 2901 Highland Avenue. The new Gothic Revival redbrick sanctuary was dedicated in 1925. Pictured above is the church one Sunday morning in 1928. Below is the 1937 confirmation class with Rev. P.G. Heckel. (Both, HCPLC.)

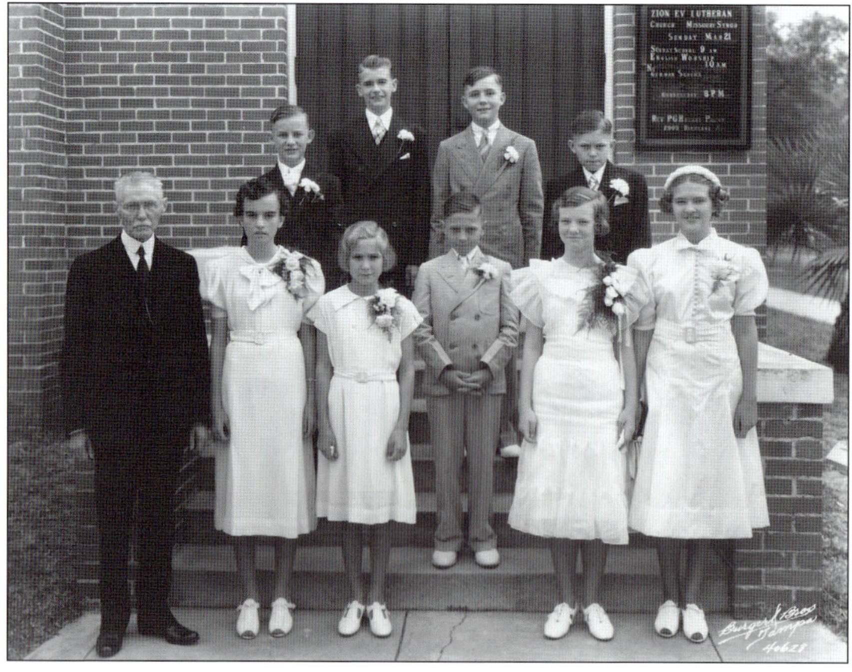

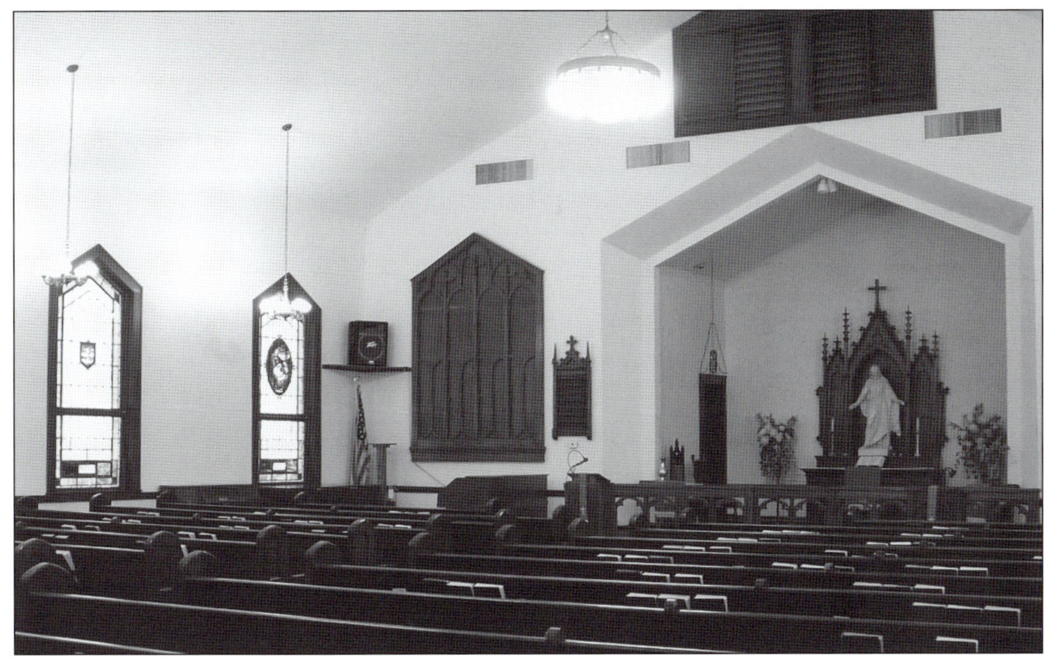

Zion Lutheran Church is considered the "Mother Congregation" of the Gulf Coast and Central Ridge region for the German Evangelical Lutheran Synod of Missouri. During World War II, German POWs at Tampa's Drew Field were escorted to the church on Sundays to worship in the church of their native country. The church features vintage light fixtures from 1925, along with extraordinary stained-glass windows and the original pews, all lovingly restored and maintained by the congregation. The church also has a full basement, a rare feature in Tampa, which is used for fellowship dinners and prayer meetings. One of the most distinguishing features of the historic sanctuary is the inspiring Gothic altar, handcrafted in fine detail. This church is another success story for historic preservation.

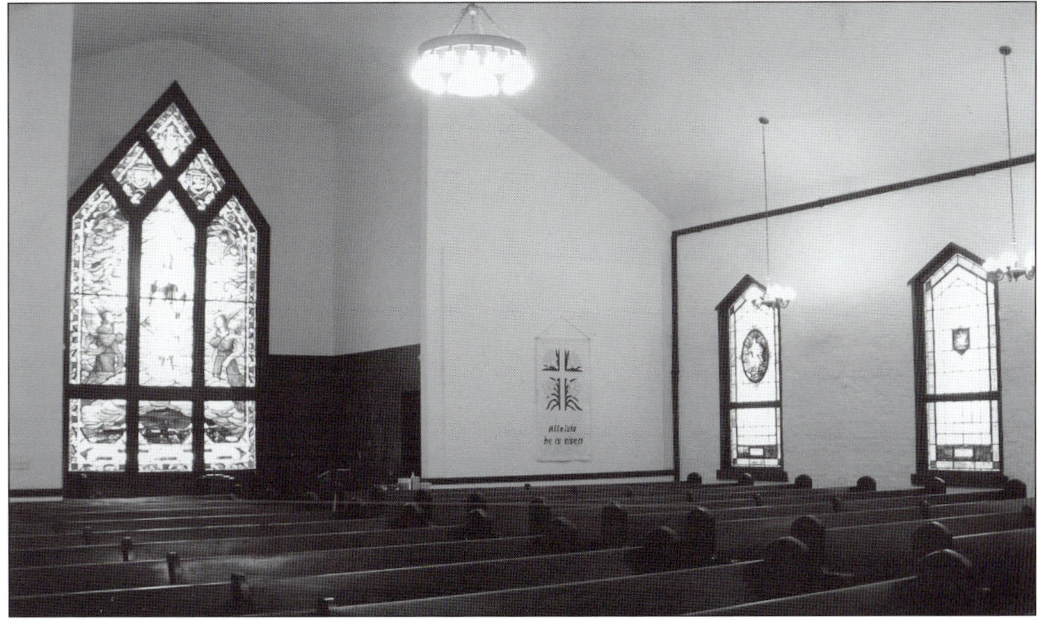

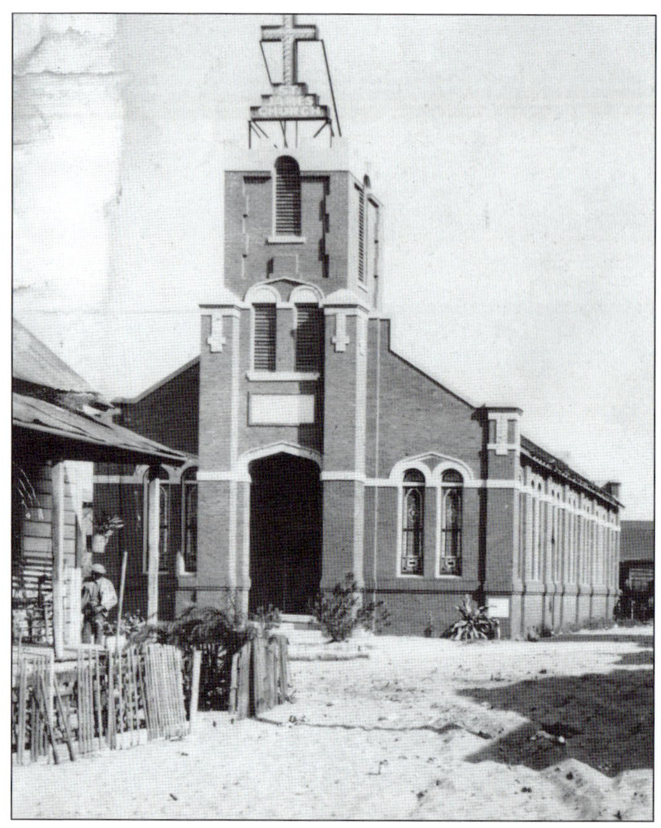

St. James Episcopal Church was established in 1891 and constituted in 1895 by a group of Bahamian, Cuban, and Spanish cigar workers who moved to Ybor City from Key West in the late 1880s. At that time, there was no Episcopal church in Tampa for the African American community. In 1893, Rev. Matthew McDuffie was appointed the first pastor and coordinated the building of a church. He later established St. James School. In 1919, the parish began construction of a larger church, dedicated in 1921 at the corner of Scott Street and Lamar Avenue. The beautiful new church, pictured here shortly after construction, featured a three-story bell tower and stained-glass windows. In 1997, the congregation merged with the Episcopal House of Prayer in Tampa Heights to form St. James House of Prayer Episcopal Church.

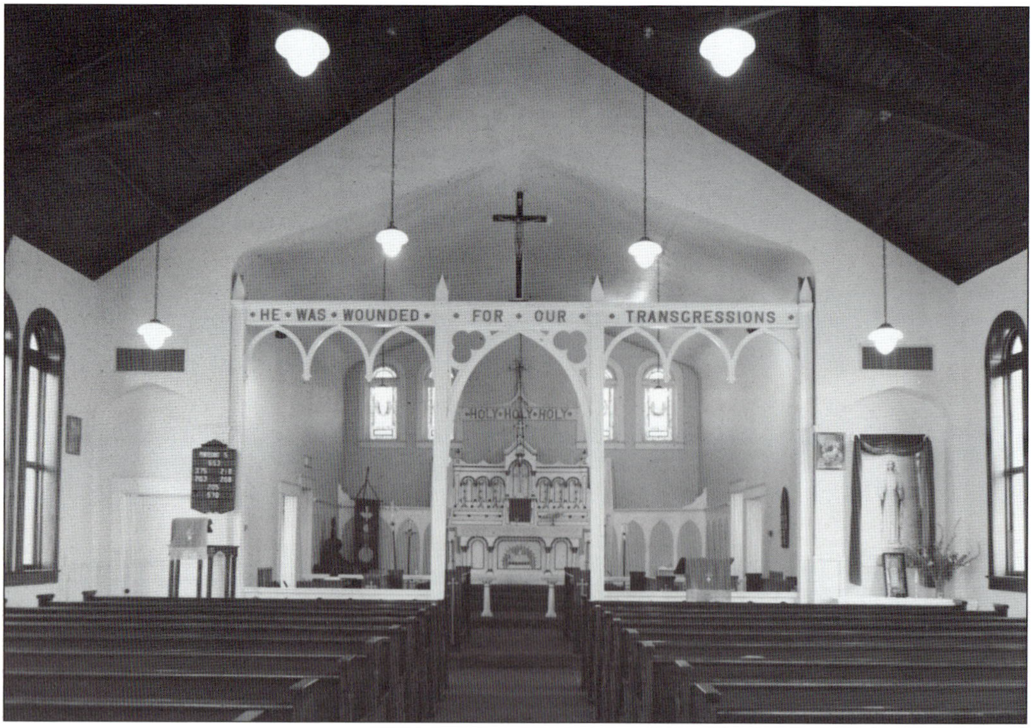

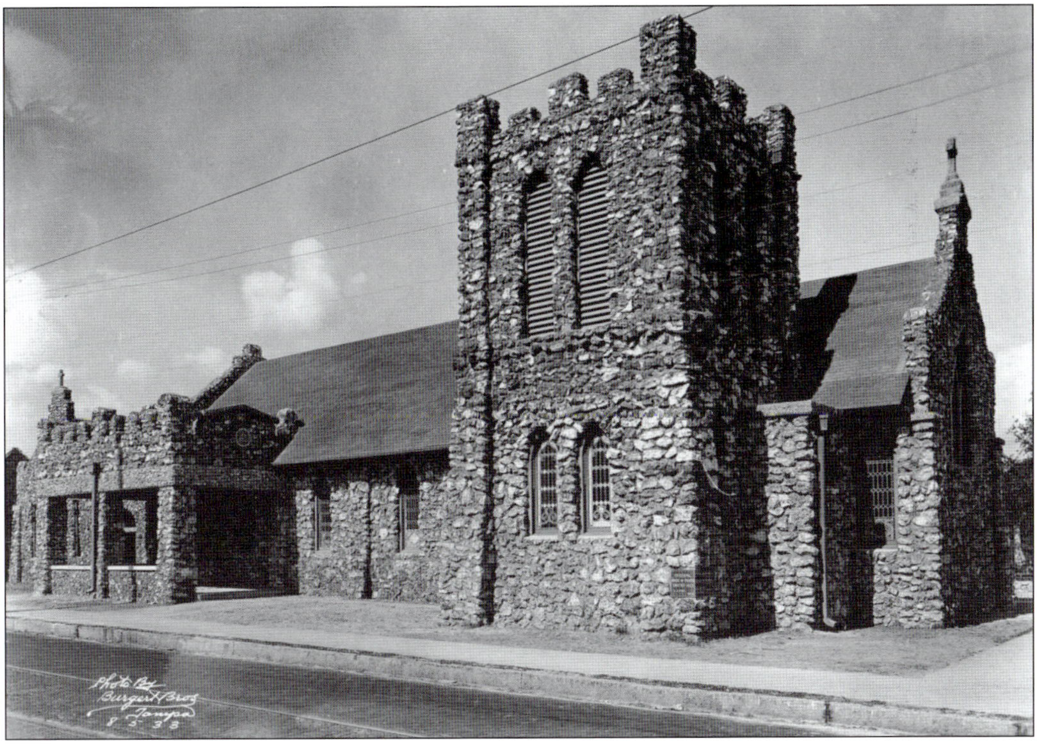

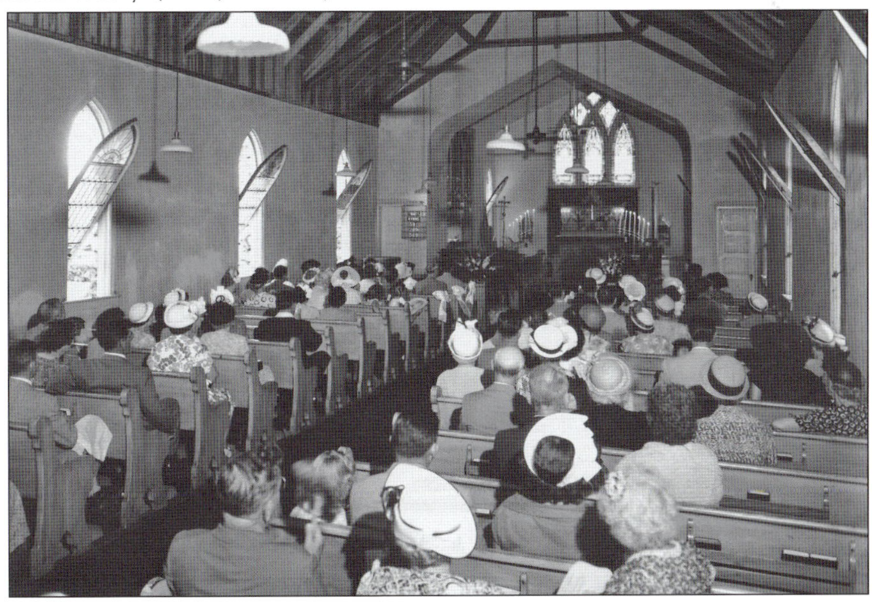

One of the most unique churches in Tampa is the St. James House of Prayer Episcopal Church, constructed in 1922 on the corner of Columbus Drive and Central Avenue. The church was established in 1907 as the Episcopal House of Prayer and merged in 1997 with St. James Episcopal Church. The church, pictured above in 1923, features Gothic Revival elements and was constructed using rocks collected from the bottom of the Hillsborough River. In 1991, the church was listed in the National Register of Historic Places. The below photograph from 1957 shows the congregation inside the sanctuary. (Both, HCPLC.)

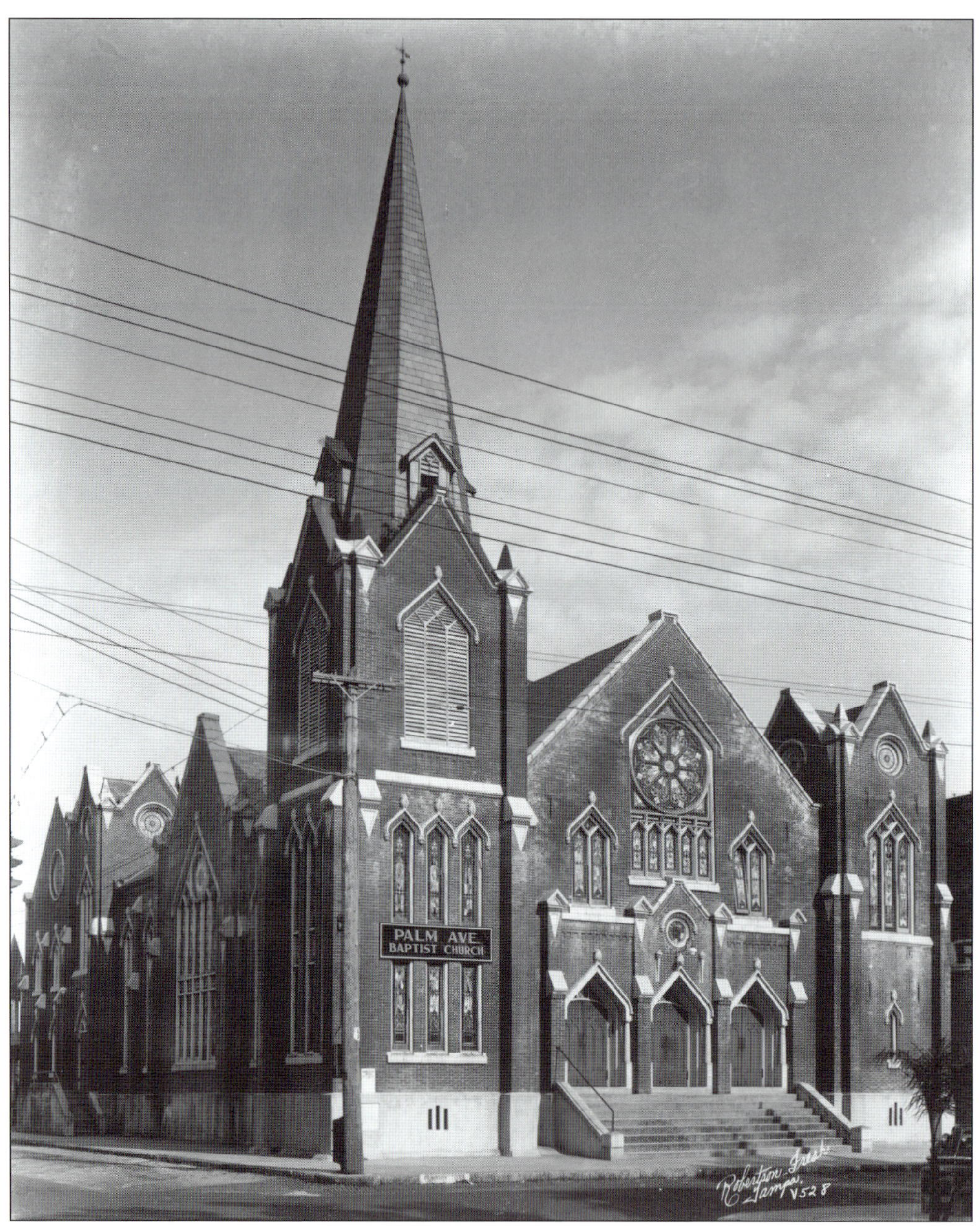

One of the most beautiful churches in Tampa Heights is Palm Avenue Baptist Church, located at the southeast corner of Florida and Palm Avenues and pictured here in 1939. Established in 1900 as a mission of First Baptist Church, the congregation originally met in a small wood-frame building on this property, which was sold to a nearby Jewish congregation and moved to allow for construction of a new, larger church. This Early American Ecclesiastical–style church was completed in four phases of construction beginning in 1901 and was dedicated in 1912 under the direction of Rev. C.H. Nash, the first pastor. It is the oldest church building in the Tampa Heights historic neighborhood. In 1974, the church built a 16-story apartment building next to the church dedicated as the Palm Avenue Baptist Tower, to provide housing for senior citizens and disabled residents of Tampa Heights. (USFSCL.)

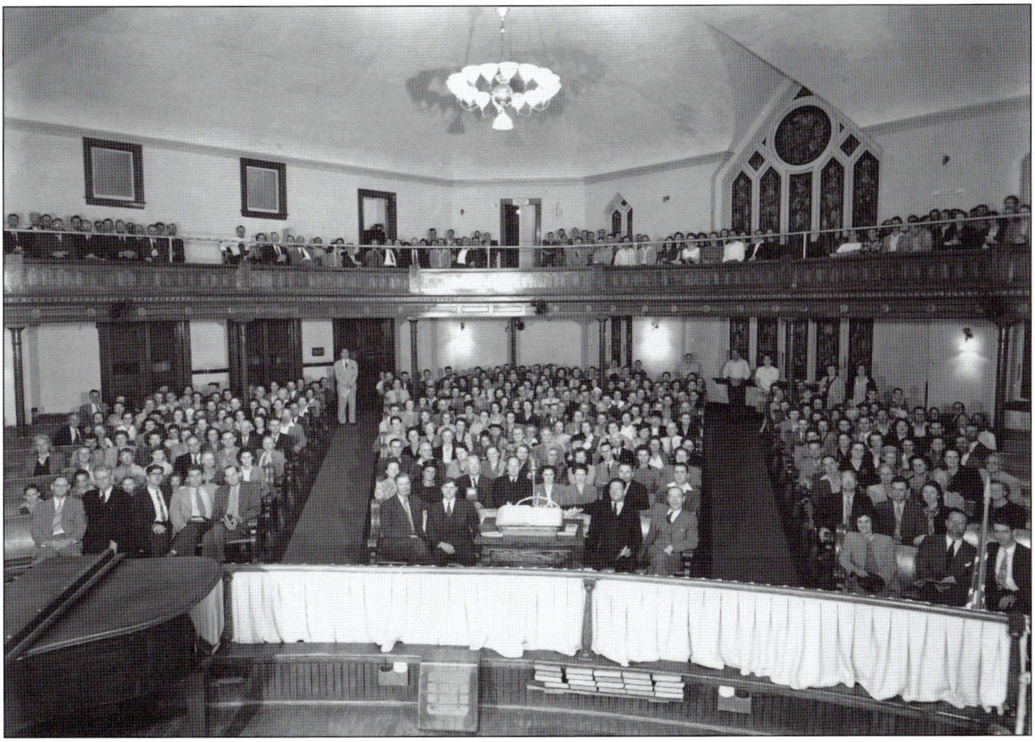

Pictured above in 1939 is the congregation of Palm Avenue Baptist Church in their sanctuary at 1805 Florida Avenue. On February 27, 1907, Palm Avenue Baptist Church established a mission that originally met in the vicinity of Nebraska and Buffalo Avenues. This mission was constituted as Buffalo Avenue Baptist Church in 1916 at 802 East Buffalo Avenue. In 1932, Buffalo Avenue Baptist Church dedicated their new church, pictured below shortly after construction. It was Tampa's first air-conditioned church. In 1962, Buffalo Avenue Baptist Church moved to a larger facility to accommodate the growth of their church community, on the corner of Church Street and Henry Avenue; it was dedicated as the new Hillsdale Baptist Church.

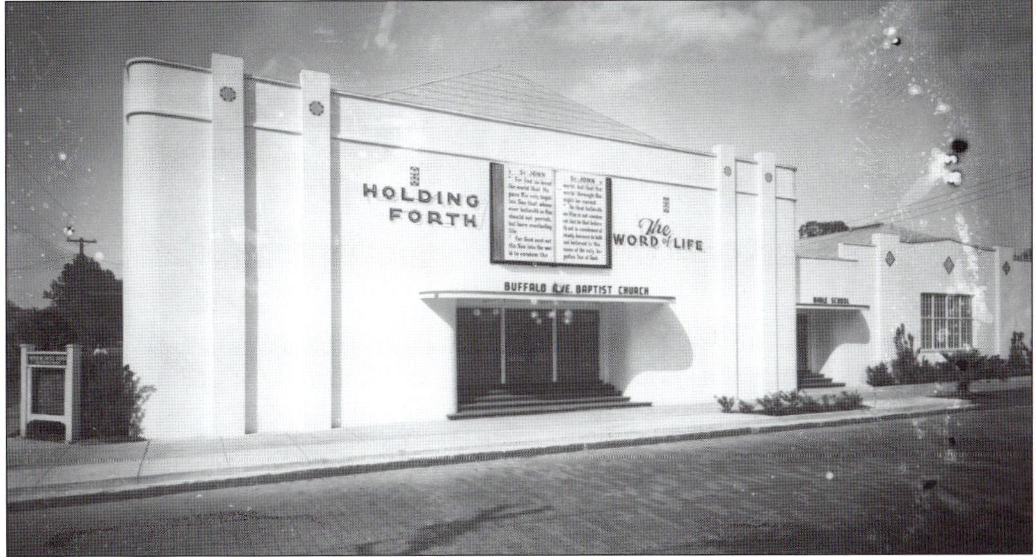

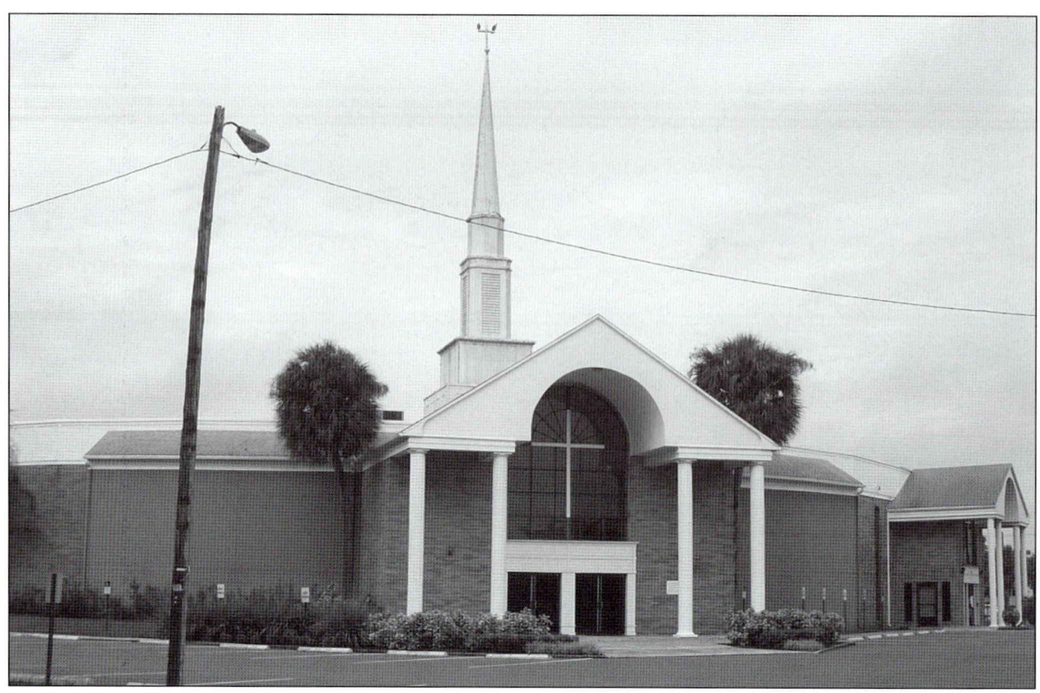

Bethel Temple Assembly of God is a familiar landmark on West Hillsborough Avenue. The church was constituted in 1926 by Rev. and Mrs. J.L. Webb, who served as the first pastors. The congregation originally met in a tent for their entire first year at Ross Avenue and Tampa Street in the Tampa Heights neighborhood. The first church was a small chapel constructed in 1927 at 2208 Highland Avenue named Highland Park Tabernacle. In 1941, the church was formally received into the General Council Fellowship, changing its name to Bethel Temple Assembly of God. In 1956, Rev. and Mrs. Percy King were appointed pastors of the church and would lead the community of faithful through a period of tremendous growth. Pictured below is the choir shortly after the new church was constructed in 1977.

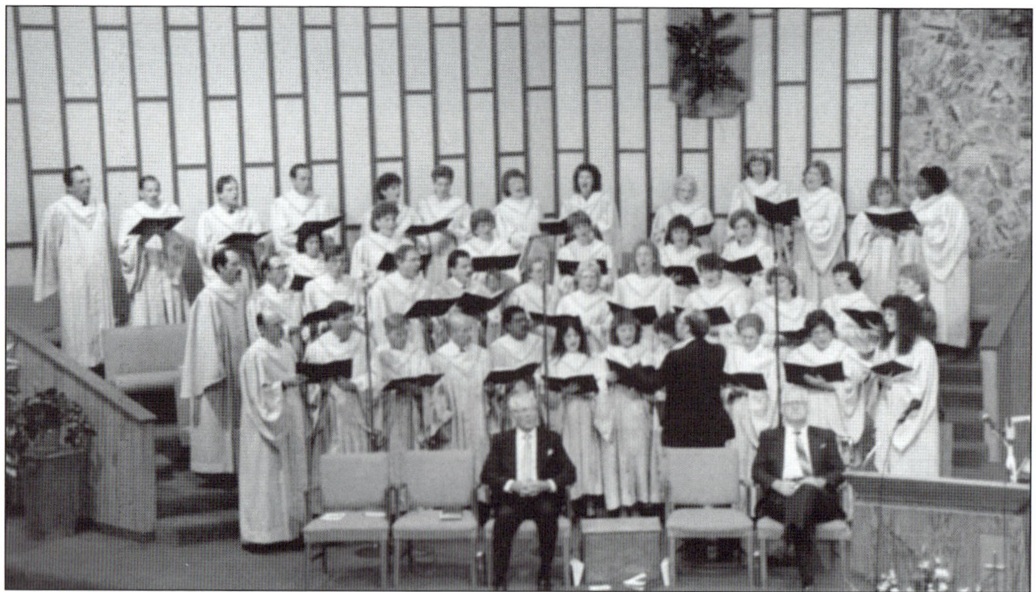

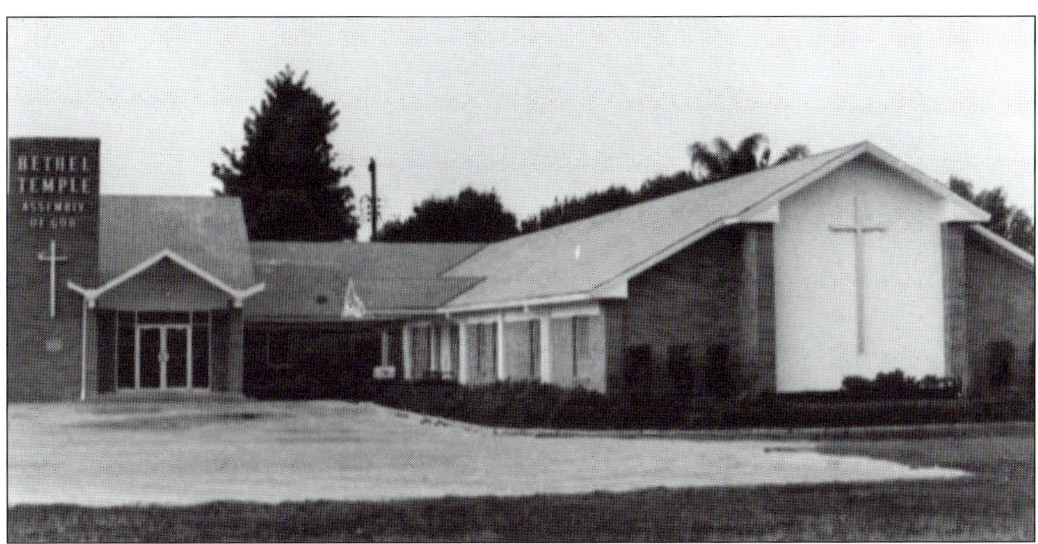

In November 1965, the old church on Highland Avenue was sold and the church moved to their new church pictured above at 1510 West Hillsborough Avenue shortly after completion. On September 6, 1970, Rev. Gordon Matheny was appointed pastor and would lead the church through its most expansive building projects. In 1977, the church celebrated the completion of their beautiful new church, which featured a columned portico and seating for 1,000. Bethel Temple Assembly of God continues the mission of those founding pastors who led the faithful in a simple tent on a street corner, by offering many community outreach programs to the underprivileged. The church also has a long history of inspiring musical presentations. The below photograph shows the music ministry's 1978 living Christmas tree at the Christmas Eve service in the newly constructed church.

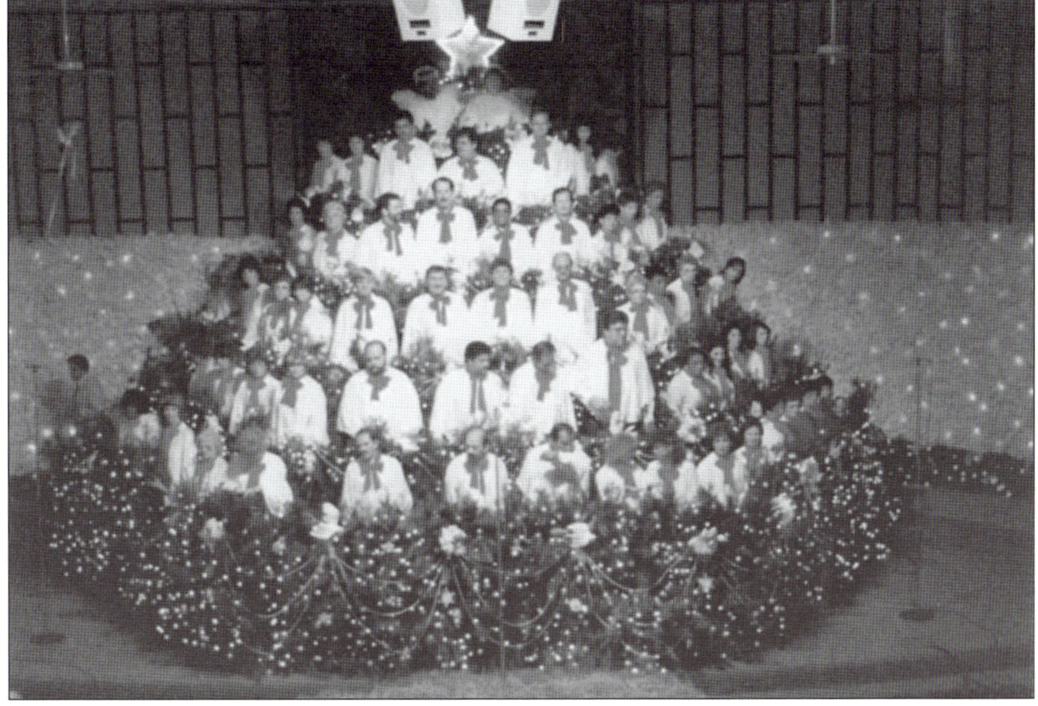

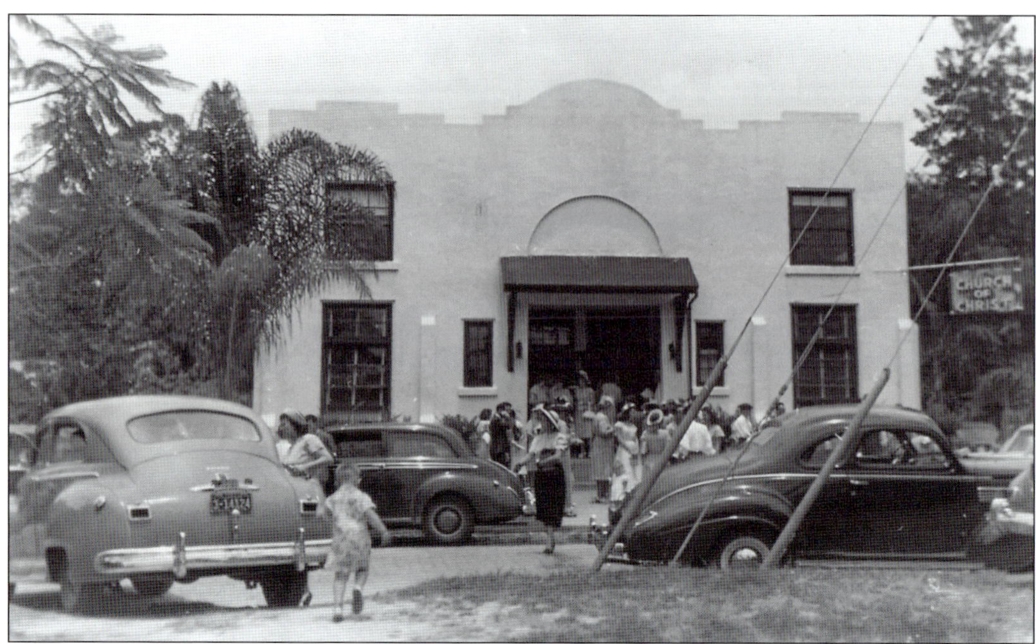

Seminole Church of Christ was established in 1925, when a group of Christians was organized by brother S.F. Morrow in a tent on the corner of Central Avenue and North Street. In 1926, the congregation completed their first church at 610 North Street, pictured above in 1947. In March 1957, the church celebrated the ground-breaking ceremony for a new church to accommodate their growing congregation at 4740 Wishart Boulevard. On February 9, 1958, the new church was dedicated. The new church is pictured below shortly after construction in 1957. After the congregation moved into the new church, there was a small group of members who did not want to leave their beloved Seminole Heights neighborhood, so the church established North Street Church of Christ in their old building, where this group of faithful remained.

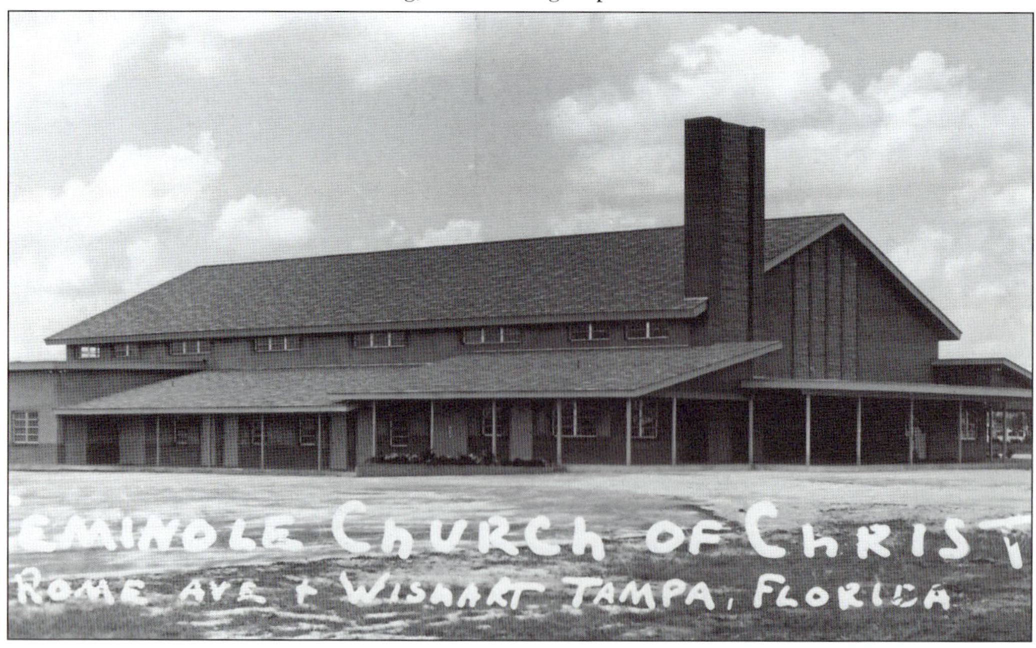

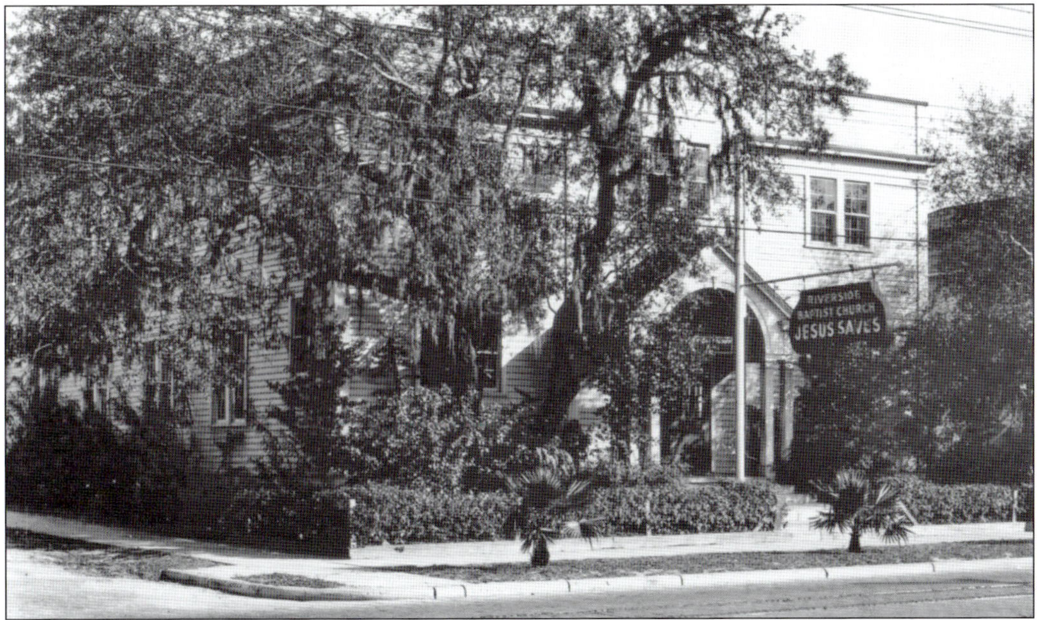

Riverside Baptist Church is pictured here in 1939 at 2923 Tampa Street. This church was established in 1927 as a mission of Palm Avenue Baptist Church with Rev. W.L. Head as the first pastor, and services at B.C. Graham School. The church pictured here was dedicated in 1928. Today, the church site is home to Central Tampa Baptist Church.

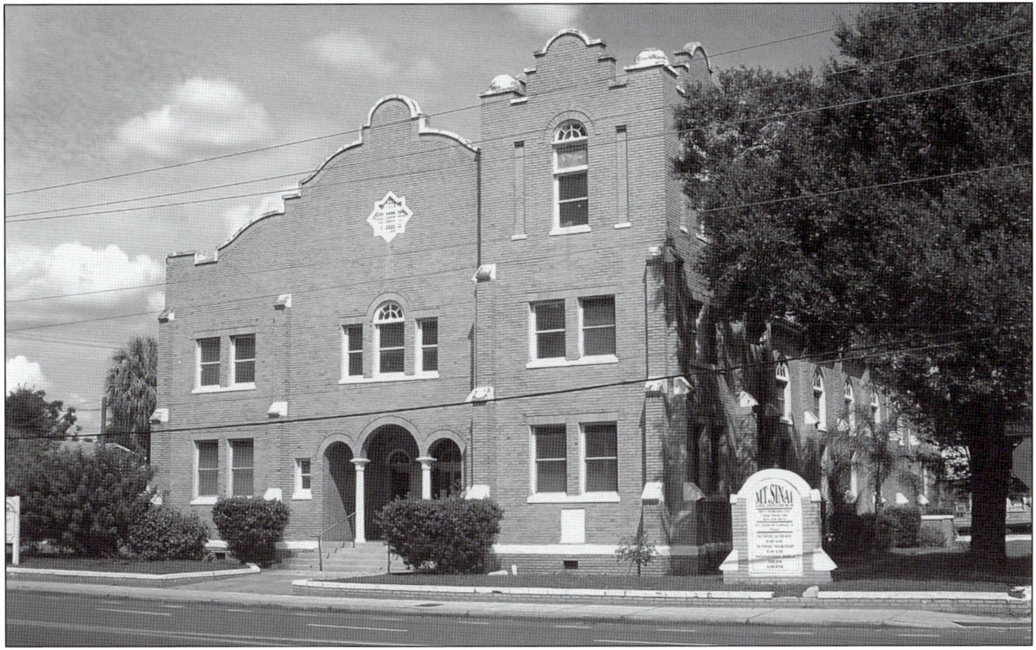

Mount Sinai AME Zion Church at 2909 Nebraska Avenue was founded in 1863 by newly freed men and women seeking to worship God in spirit and in truth. The first pastor was Rev. G.W. Maize. The AME Zion Church is known as the Freedom Church. One of the most notable members includes civil rights leader Harriett Tubman. The church continues the work of their founding members, ministering to inner-city residents.

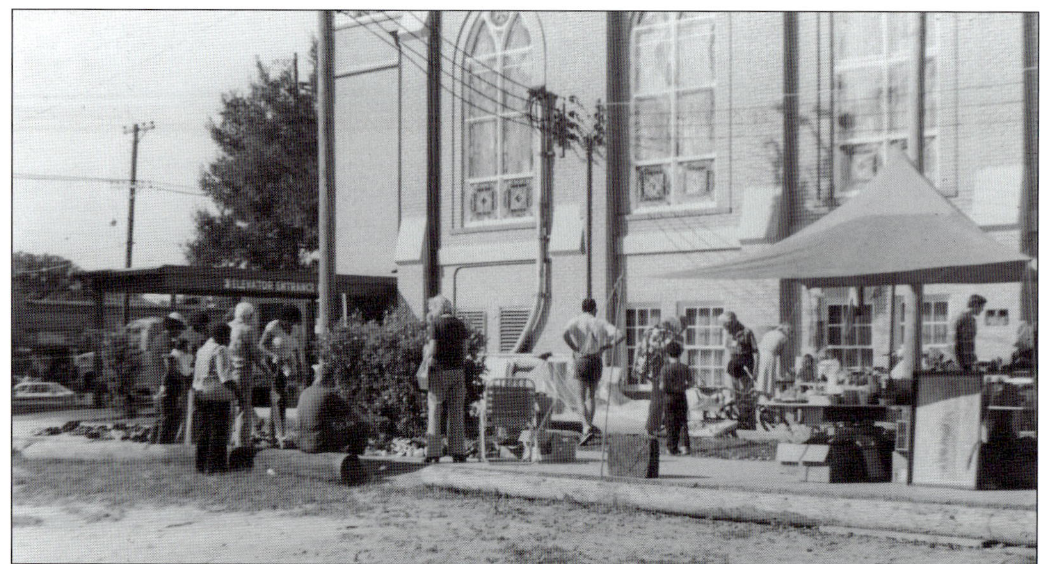

Seminole Heights United Methodist Church sponsors many special events each year for local residents and church members, such as movie nights, flea markets, and craft bazaars. One of the annual events at the church is their fall bazaar, which has become a popular community-wide event for the neighborhood. Pictured here is the 1972 fall bazaar.

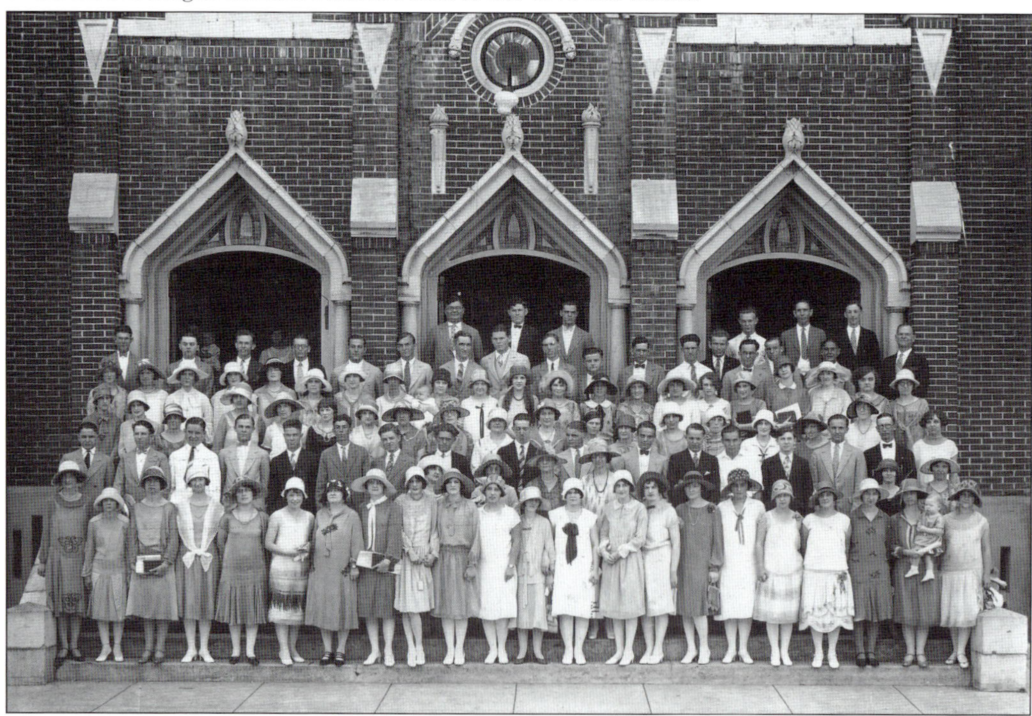

Pictured here in 1928 is the congregation of Palm Avenue Baptist Church at 1805 Florida Avenue. In 1945, church member Susan Porterfield donated her property on Lake Platt in North Tampa to establish a retreat center for the Baptist community. Today, the property is home to the Tampa Bay Baptist Conference Center for local churches to use as a center of faith renewal, seminars, and youth activities.

Three

WEST TAMPA, YBOR CITY, AND EAST TAMPA

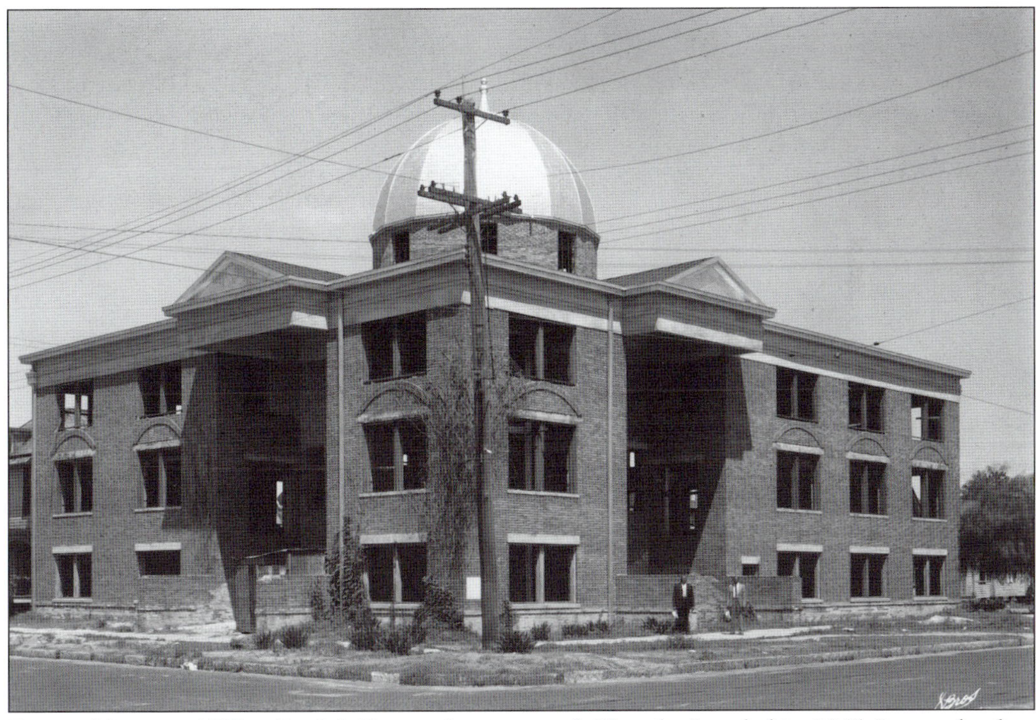

Pictured here in 1937 is Beulah Baptist Institutional Church, founded in 1865. It was the first Baptist church for African Americans in Tampa. When the Civil War ended, the faithful who attended services with their former owners were given financial aid by First Baptist Church of Tampa to build a separate church. The church pictured here was completed in 1937 at 604 Tyler Street and dedicated on October 10, 1938. (HCPLC.)

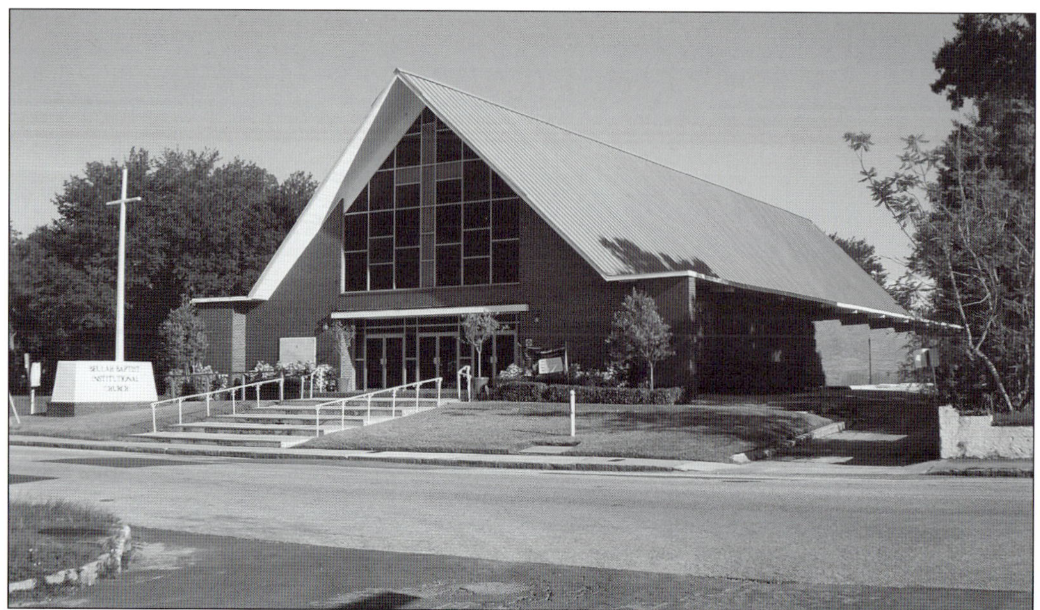

Pictured here is Beulah Baptist Institutional Church, one of the most historic congregations in Tampa. Founded in 1865, the first pastor was Rev. Elder Hadley. The first church was built on a parcel of land donated to the church at the corner of Harrison and Jefferson Streets. In 1881, the original church was moved to the corner of Tyler and Pierce Streets. In 1926, Rev. H.E. Jones became pastor. Among his accomplishments was the organization of the White Robe Choir, which later became the first African American church choir to broadcast live on a Tampa radio station. In 1931, Rev. W.M. Davis was assigned pastor and established a fund-raising campaign for the construction of a new sanctuary, which was completed in 1937. Pictured below is the choir in 1942.

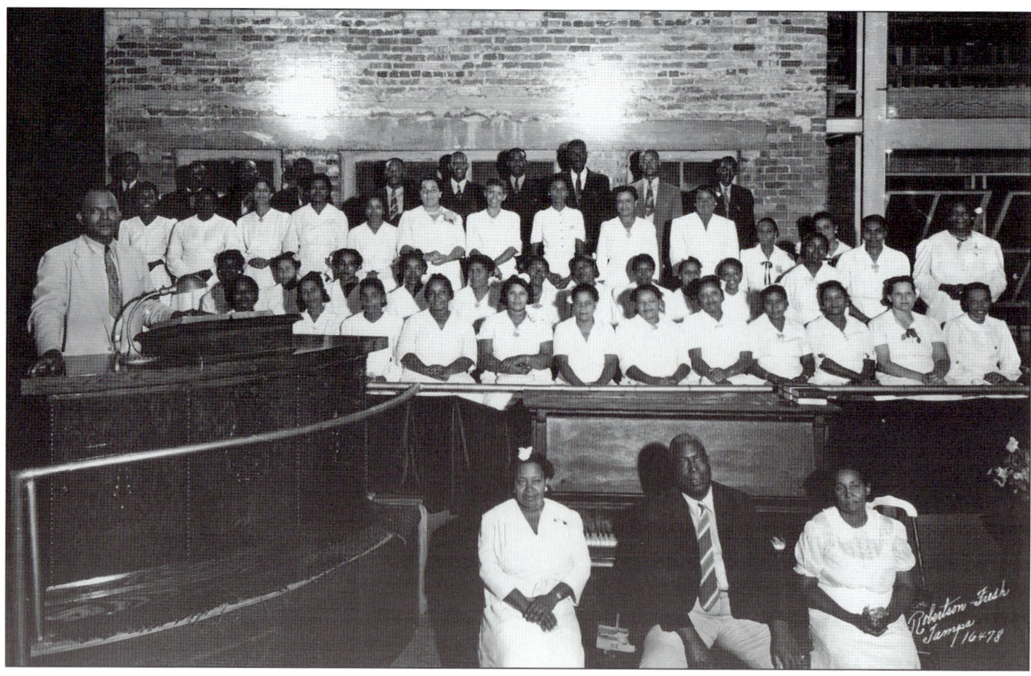

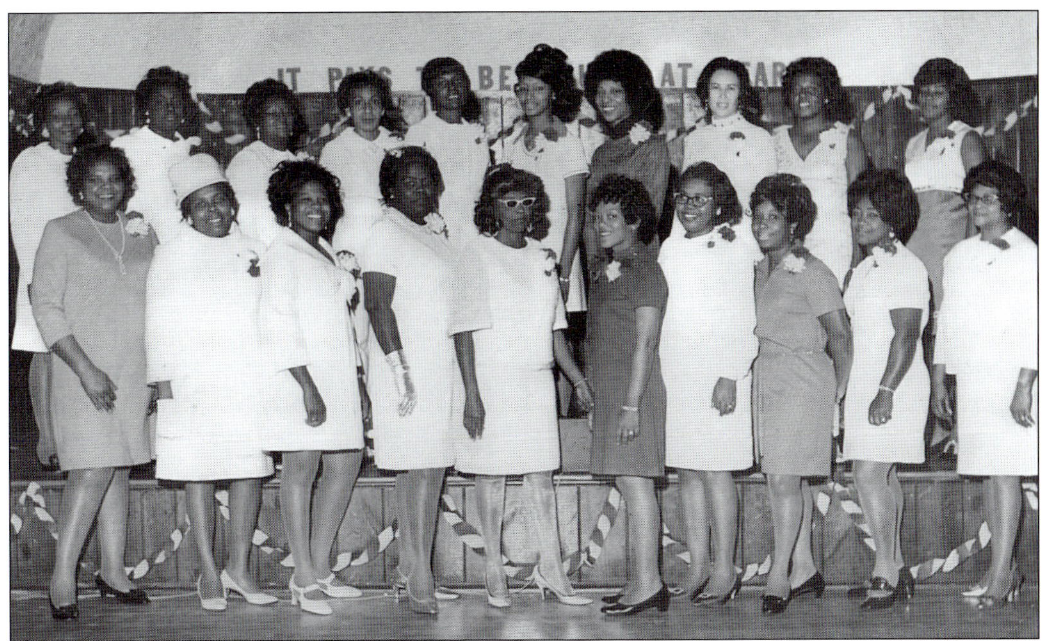

In 1956, Rev. A. Leon Lowry became the 13th pastor of the church. That same year, the congregation purchased property at 1006 Cypress Street with plans for a new church. In 1965, architectural plans were drafted and in 1966, the congregation launched a sale of bonds to finance construction of the new church. In 1968, ground-breaking ceremonies were held, and construction commenced. On Sunday, December 21, 1969, consecration services for the new church were held. In 1990, the church hosted the Florida General Baptist Convention and also constructed a new family services center that was named in honor of Rev. Dr. A. Leon Lowry. Pictured above in 1972 is the Beulah Baptist Sanctuary Ladies Society. Pictured below at the 150th anniversary celebration in 2015 is the Beulah Baptist Deaconess Ministry.

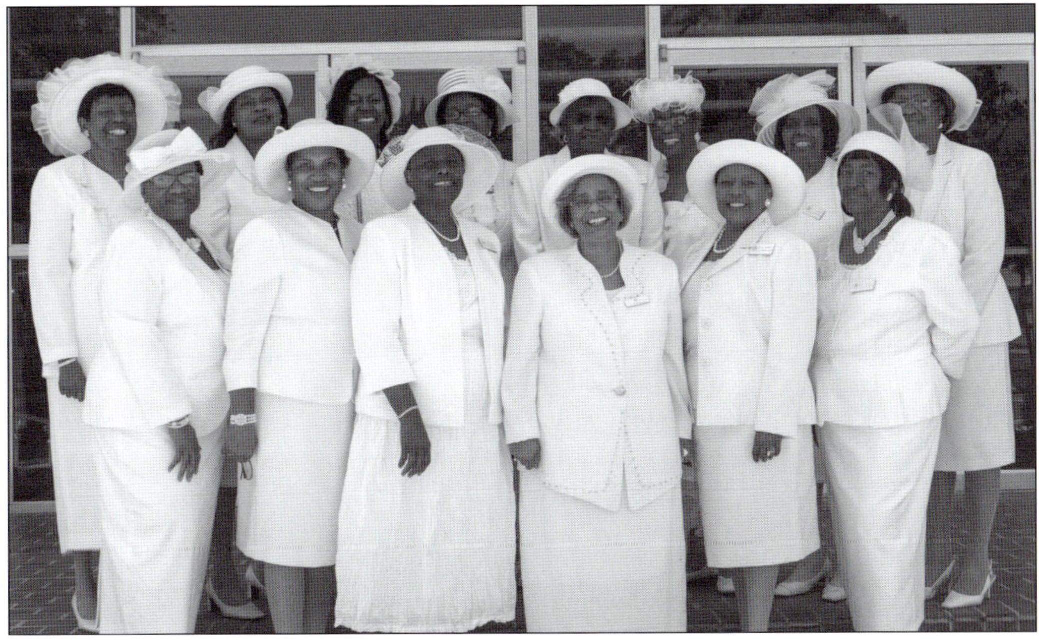

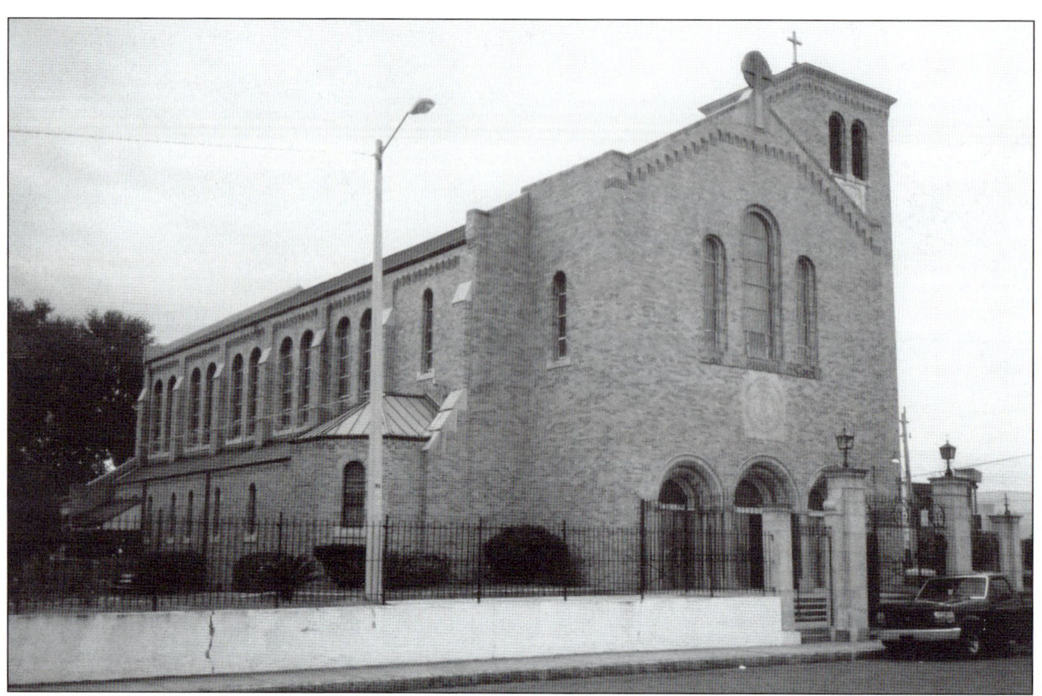

Our Lady of Perpetual Help Catholic Church is an Ybor City historic landmark at the corner of Palm Avenue and Seventeenth Street. This church has a rich history in ministering to the many diverse cultures represented in Ybor City and the surrounding community. The church property was purchased from Vicente Martinez-Ybor with a donation of $1,000 from Henry Flagler. The Jesuit Fathers then moved forward with plans to establish a Catholic church for Spanish-speaking immigrants. The original church, Our Lady of Mercy Catholic Church, was dedicated on April 19, 1891. The Jesuits guided the parish from its inception in 1891 until 1926, when Italian-speaking priests of the Salesian Order took over stewardship of the parish.

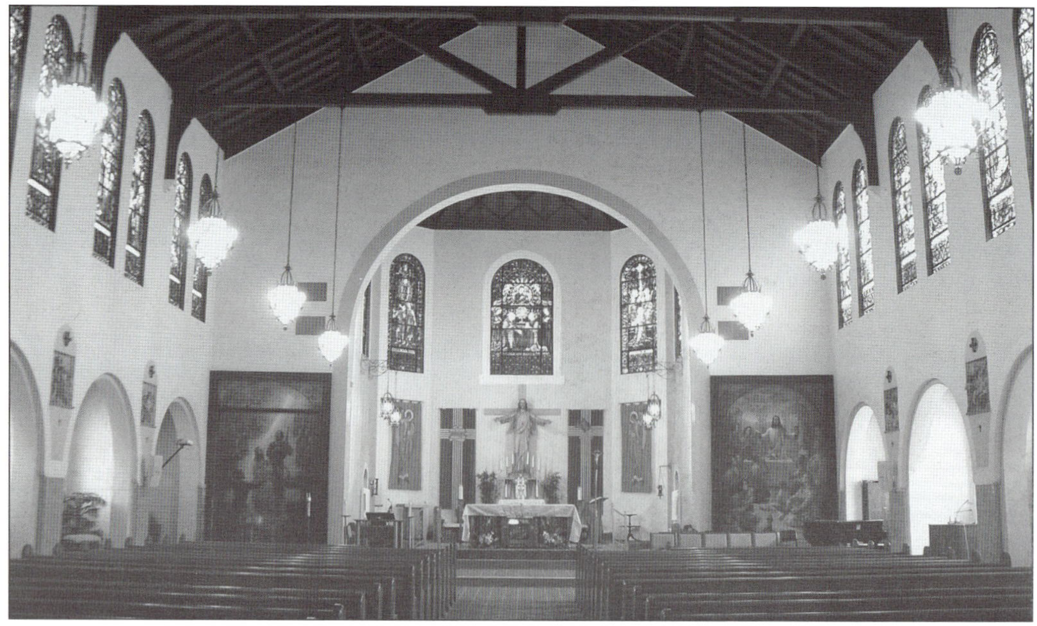

In 1934, the Redemptorist Fathers accepted care of the parish and moved forward with plans for a larger church. The new church was dedicated on July 15, 1937, as Our Lady of Perpetual Help Catholic Church in honor of the special devotion of the Redemptorists to Mary. The church features beautiful stained-glass windows built in Innsbruck, Austria, featuring the joyful, sorrowful, and glorious mysteries of the rosary, and scriptural scenes rendered in exquisite detail spanning the nave of the church. In 1986, the Marist Fathers accepted care of the church. Pictured here is the first communion service in 1947.

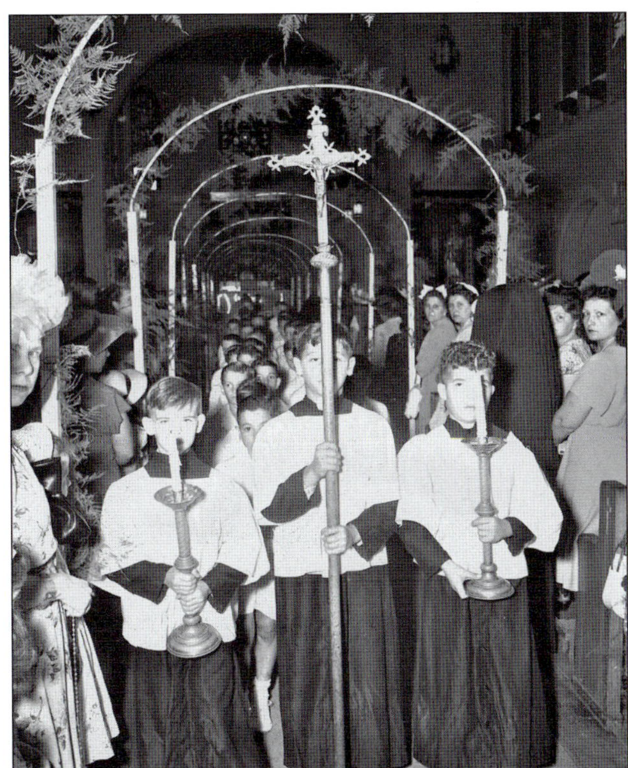

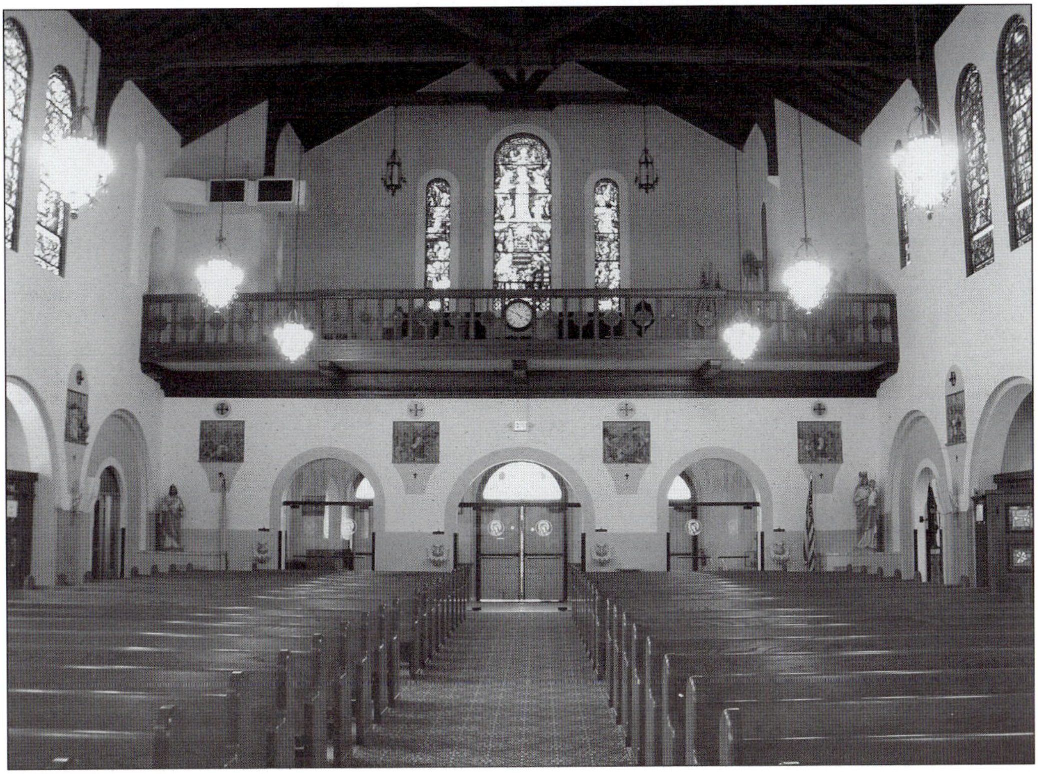

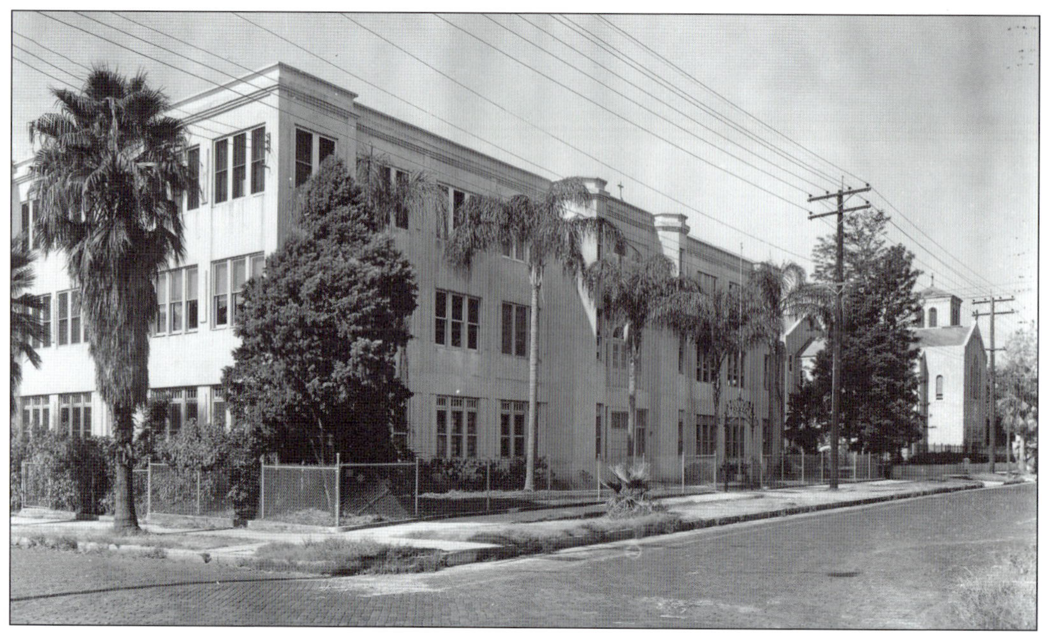

Shortly after the establishment of Our Lady of Mercy Catholic Church, the Sisters of St. Joseph established St. Joseph Academy at the church on September 23, 1891. Among the first students were the sons of Vicente and Mercedes Martinez-Ybor, Salvador and Ralph. The first school was a two-story frame building completed on October 1, 1892. The first convent was dedicated May 5, 1895. In 1921, Fr. William Tyrell constructed a larger three-story school building at a cost of $20,000, pictured above in 1947. In 1937, when the Redemptorist Fathers completed the new church, the school was renamed Our Lady of Perpetual Help (OLPH) Academy. Pictured below in 1917 is the school choir with Sr. M. Rosalie Andreu, Sisters of St. Joseph music teacher. (Both, SSJSA.)

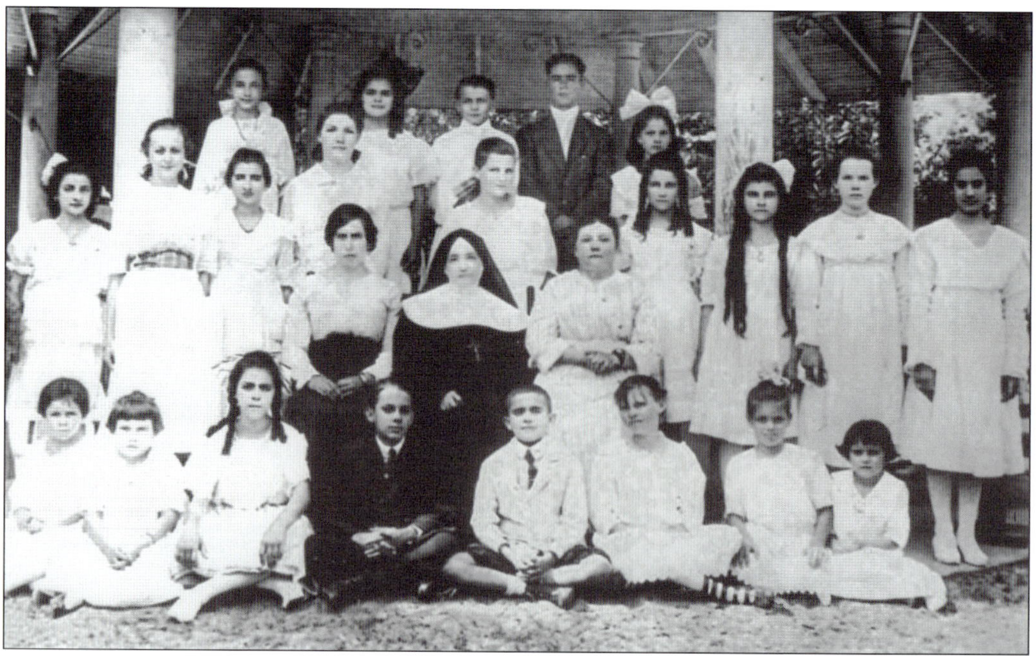

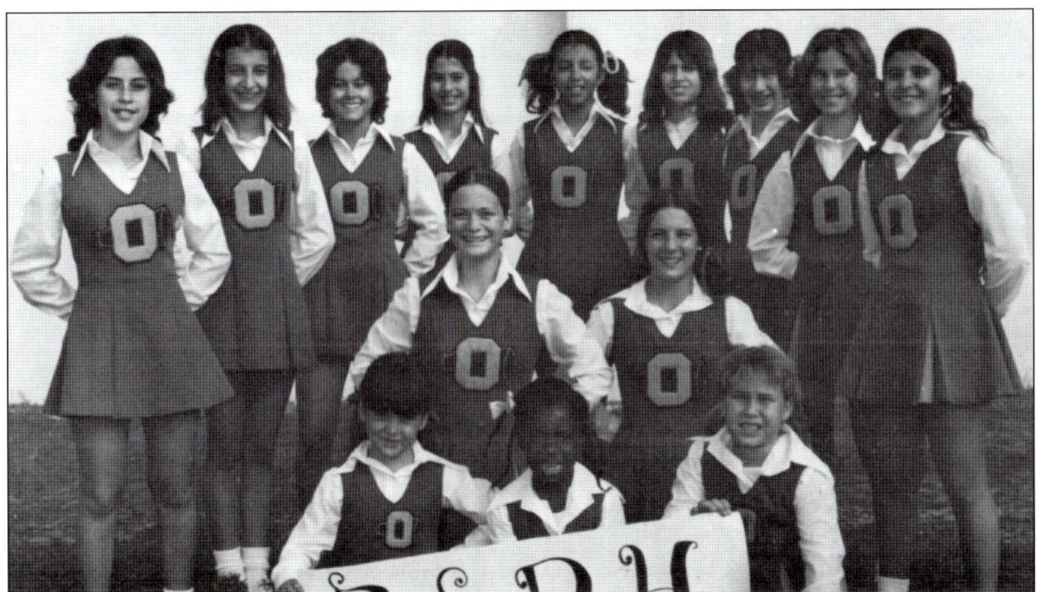

Pictured above in 1973 is the OLPH Academy cheerleading squad. For generations, the school children were often a reflection of the vibrant immigrant cultures the church and the academy served in Ybor City. OLPH Academy served the needs of this culturally diverse community, empowering the students to become responsible and productive citizens. Thousands of children walked through the school gates into the loving care of the dedicated sisters who selflessly devoted their lives to serve them. Pictured below in 1925 are the Sisters of St. Joseph who served at OLPH Academy from 1891 to 1944, when they transferred care of the school to the School Sisters of Notre Dame. The sisters continued their ministry until 1975, when the school closed due to a change in the demographics of the neighborhood. (Below, SSJSA.)

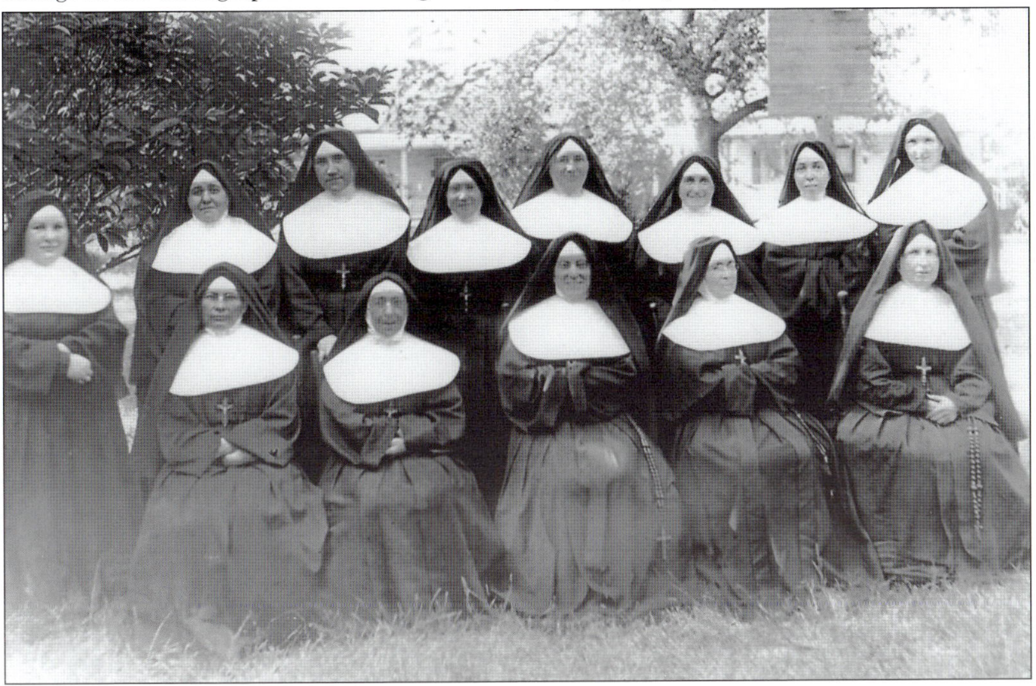

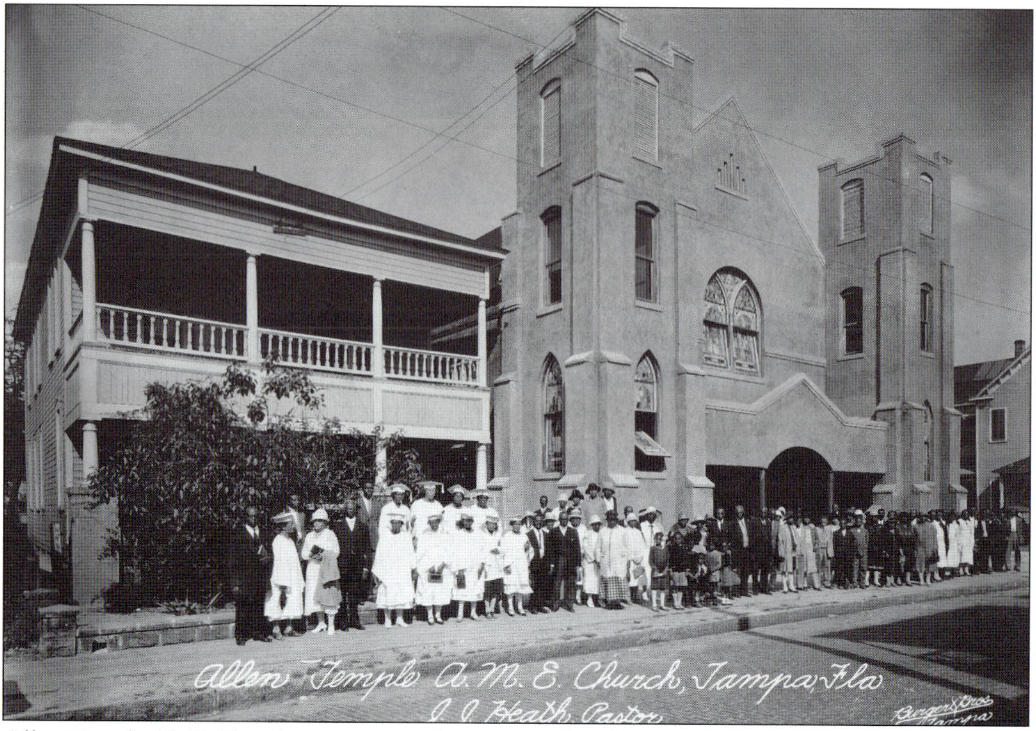

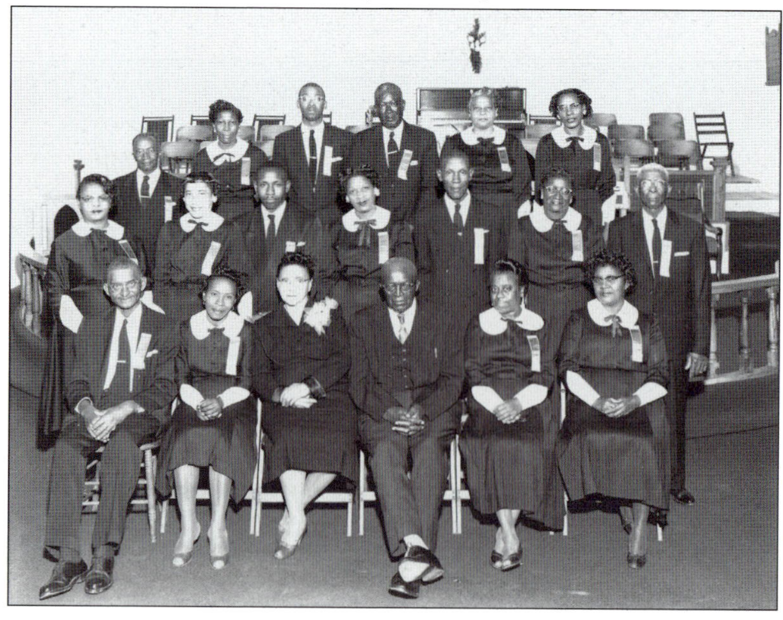

Allen Temple AME Church was organized in 1891 at the Ybor City home of Rev. Morris Allen, and held services there until construction of their first church at 1100 Seventh Avenue. The congregation then moved to property at Scott and Governor Streets in 1902. The first structure was a wood-framed building that was later remodeled into a larger brick church building under the pastorate of Rev. R.D. Lewis in 1908. The church community expanded the structure in 1924 and officially dedicated the church in 1928. Pictured above is the congregation in front of the church on November 8, 1926. Below is the Ushers Board inside the sanctuary of the original church in 1959.

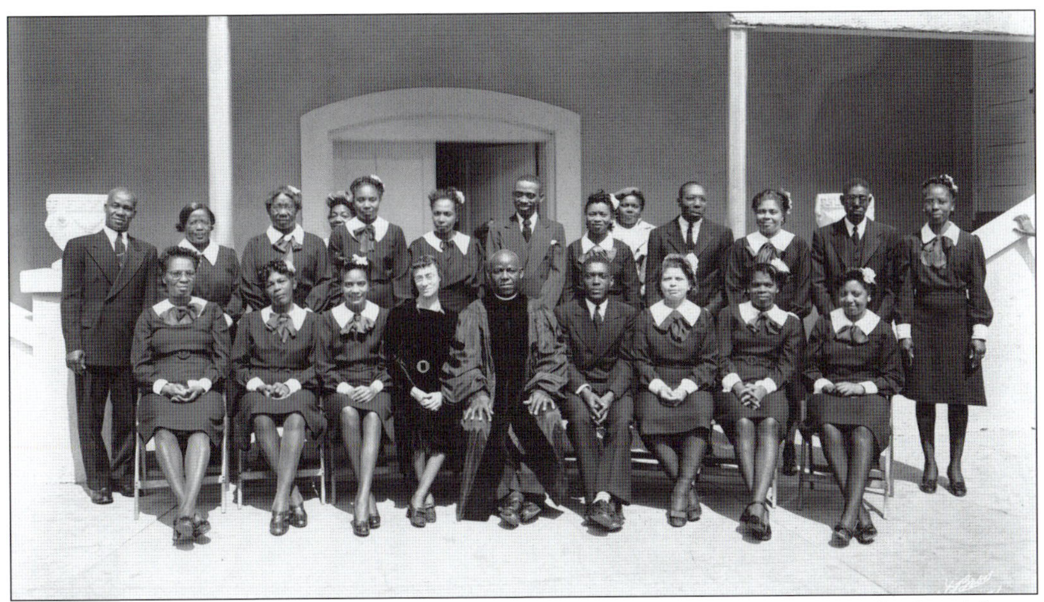

In 1972, the church hosted US presidential candidate Shirley Chisholm, who was the first African American woman elected to the US Congress. In 1977, Rev. John Wesley Burroughs became pastor and furthered efforts for the construction of a new church. In 1979, Rev. J.D. Stonom became pastor, and facilitated purchase of the property at 2101 Lowe Street for future expansion. In 1987, Rev. John F. Green led the effort to complete construction of the new church. This historical congregation has commissioned members that have served on the connectional, Episcopal, conference, and district levels of the AME Church. The above photograph of the Allen Temple AME Ushers Board was taken on March 11, 1942. Pictured below in 1945 is the Allen Temple AME Parsonage Aid Ministry Banquet. (Both, HCPLC.)

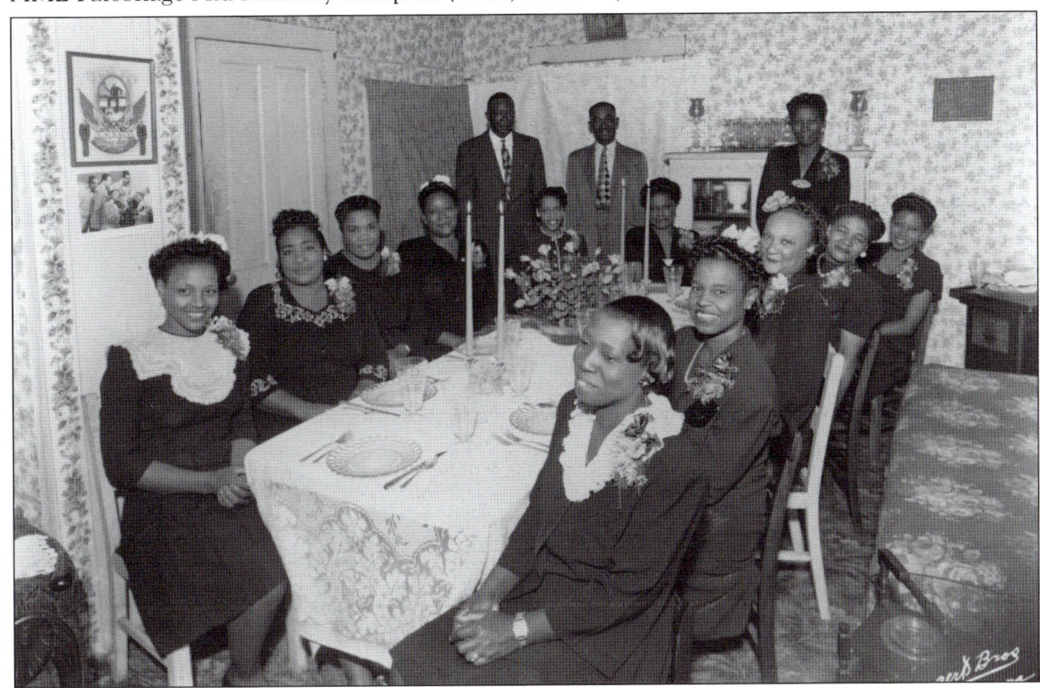

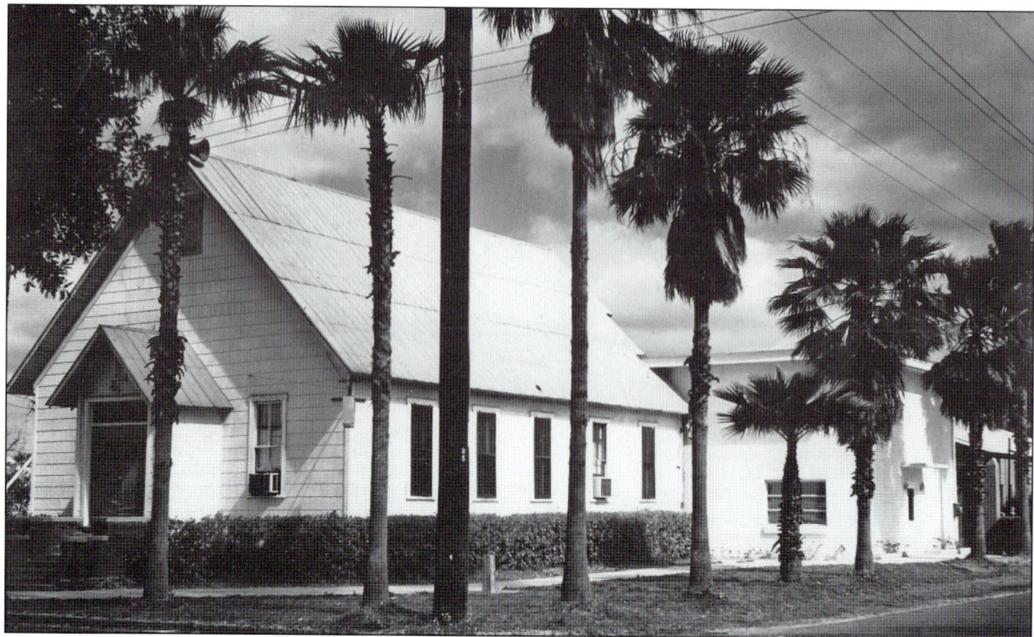

The history of Concord Baptist Church begins in 1909, when First Baptist Church established a mission that gathered in a tent on the corner of Twenty-Fourth Street and Corrine Avenue in Palmetto Beach. Messenger J.Q. Brantley took on the lead role in building the first church, a chapel constructed at a cost of $1,000, which Brantley donated. On March 9, 1909, the new church was constituted with 58 charter members. It was named Concord Baptist Church to honor the home church of the Brantley family in Mississippi. The first minister assigned was Rev. E.M.C. Dunklin. Pictured above is the original church building, which served the congregation from 1909 to 1964, when the new church was constructed. Pictured below in 1953 is the Sunday school graduating class.

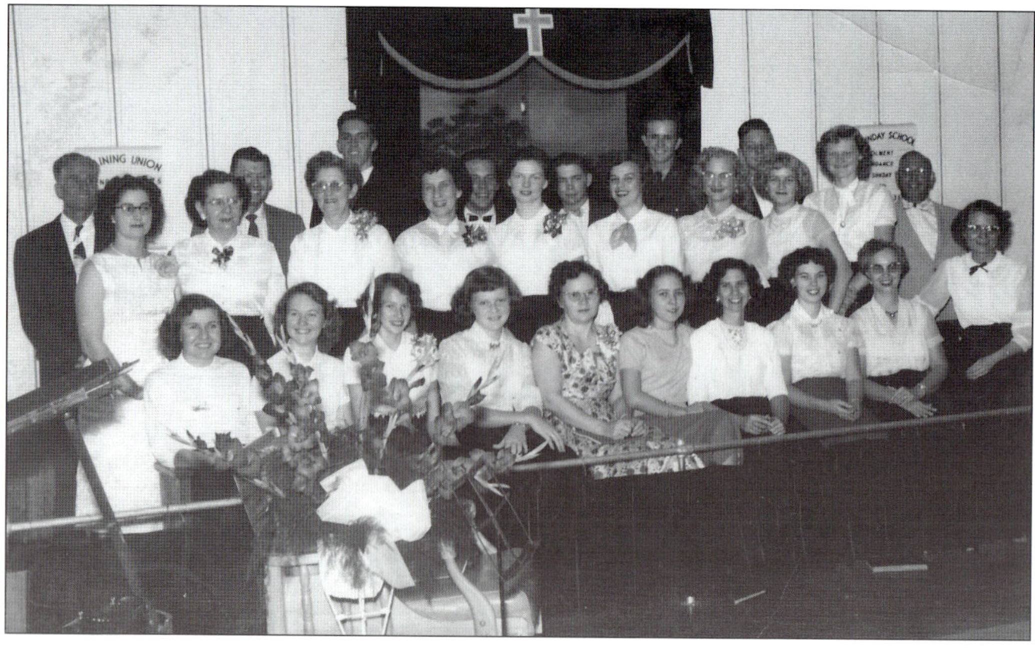

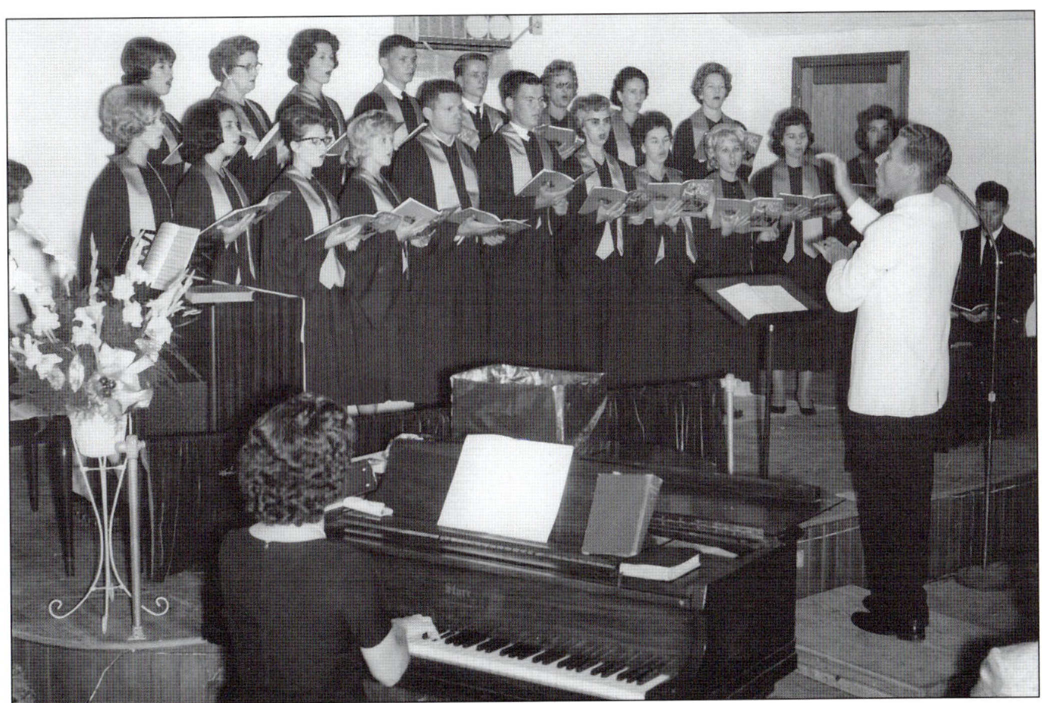

Concord Baptist Church is the oldest church in Palmetto Beach and has a long history of missionary service. In 1955, through the efforts of church members, a new church was built in the city of Matanzas, Cuba. Other supported ministries of the church have included the Youth for Christ Association of Hawaii and the International Board of Jewish Missions. In 1959, the congregation established a mission in Clair-Mel City, which became Community Baptist Church. The above photograph of the choir was taken in 1964 at the last service in the original church, shortly before it was demolished to begin construction of the new church. Pictured below is the congregation in their new sanctuary in 1986.

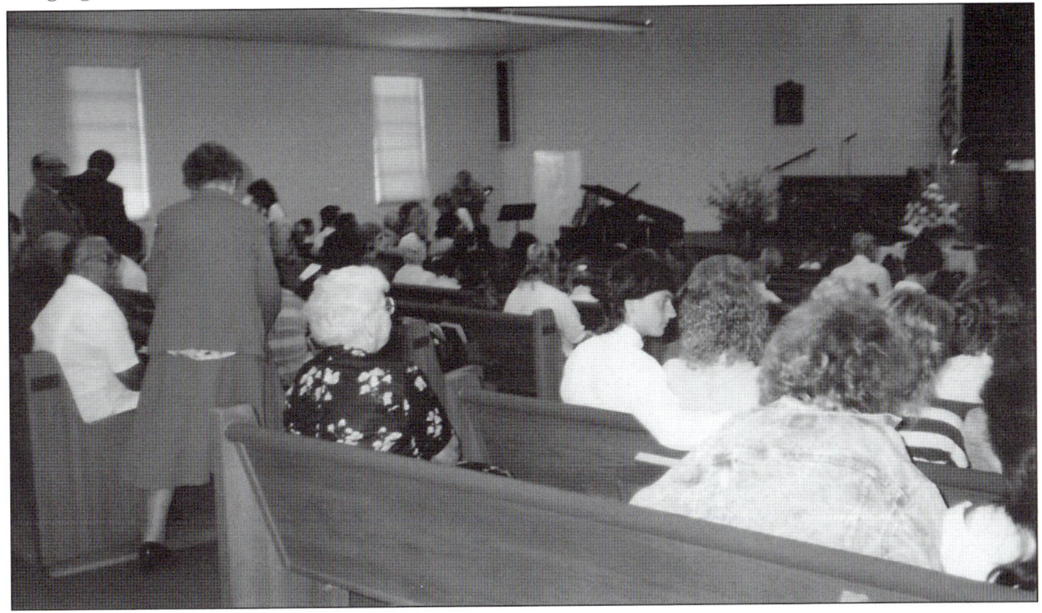

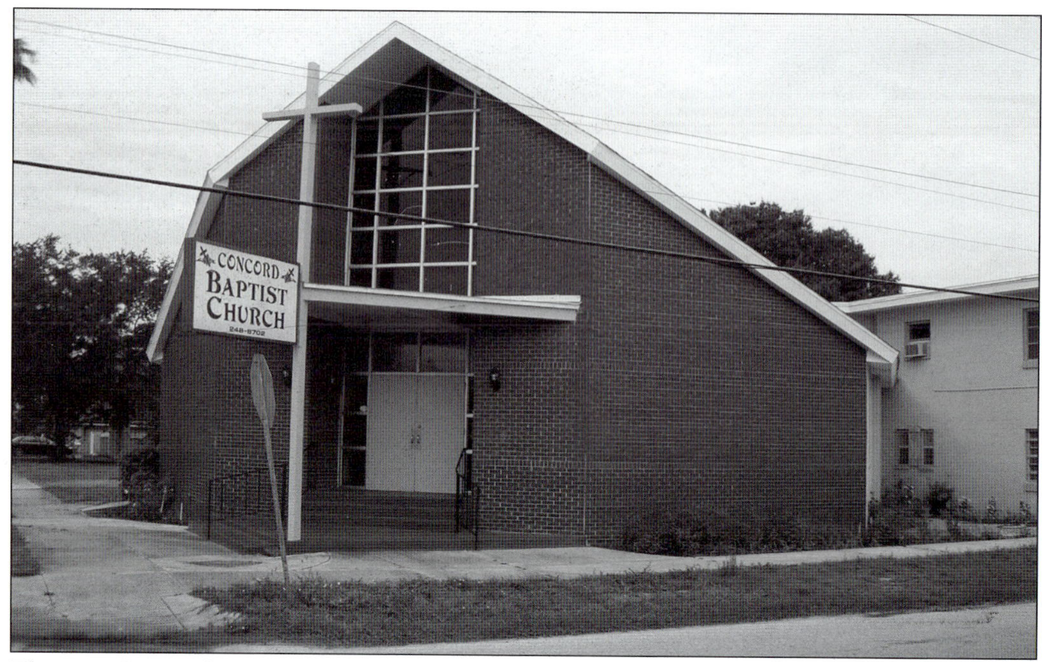

The new Concord Baptist Church was completed and dedicated in January 1965 at a cost of $35,000 and featured a 300-seat sanctuary and church offices. In 2016, Rev. Raul Fernandez celebrated his 30th anniversary as pastor, the longest tenure in the history of the church. Concord Baptist Church continues the legacy of those founding families who met in a simple tent on a street corner in 1909.

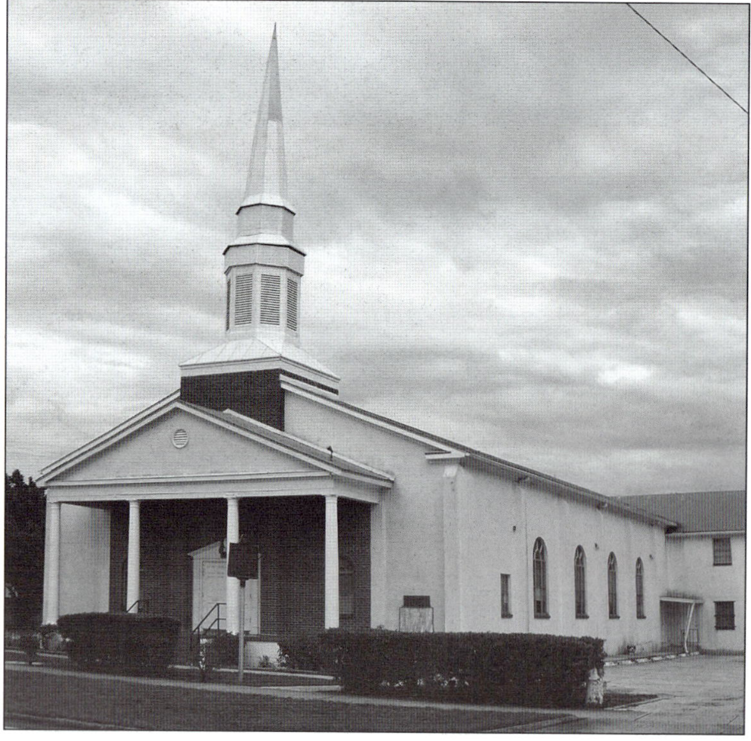

Greater New Salem Primitive Baptist Church was established in 1905 and later built a church at 914 Second Avenue. In 1966, the Urban Renewal project leveled the church and the community had to meet in a local hall. In 1969, the congregation dedicated their new church at 1605 Nebraska Avenue. In 2010, the city of Tampa designated the church a historic landmark to honor the legacy of the congregation.

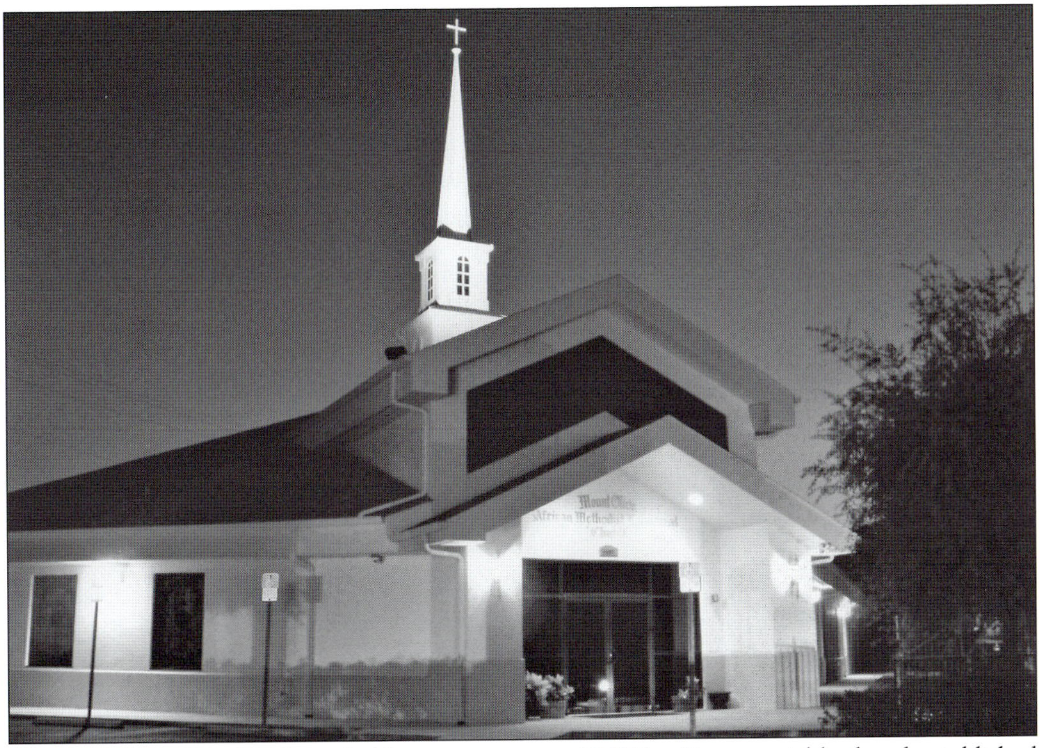

Mount Olive AME Church is a hidden treasure in an Old West Tampa neighborhood, established in 1908. In 1909, the first church was completed at LaSalle and Fremont Streets and Rev. A.M. Adair became first pastor. In 1939, the faithful constructed a larger church where they worshipped until the occasion of their centennial, dedicating their new church on June 22, 2008. The church continues to offer many programs of outreach to the community.

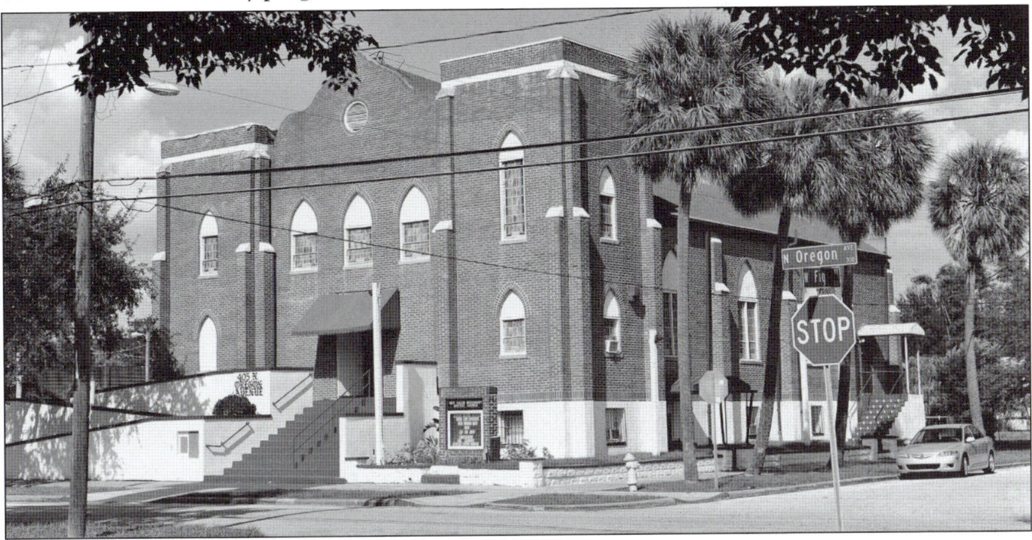

New Salem Missionary Baptist Church dates to 1904, when a dedicated group of faithful established a Sunday school. In 1906, Deacons J.C. Price and J.L. Stanley established the church at 400 North Oregon Avenue, with Rev. H. James as the first pastor. In 1950, the new church was dedicated and stood until 2015, when it was destroyed by a fire. The faithful then relocated to North Tampa.

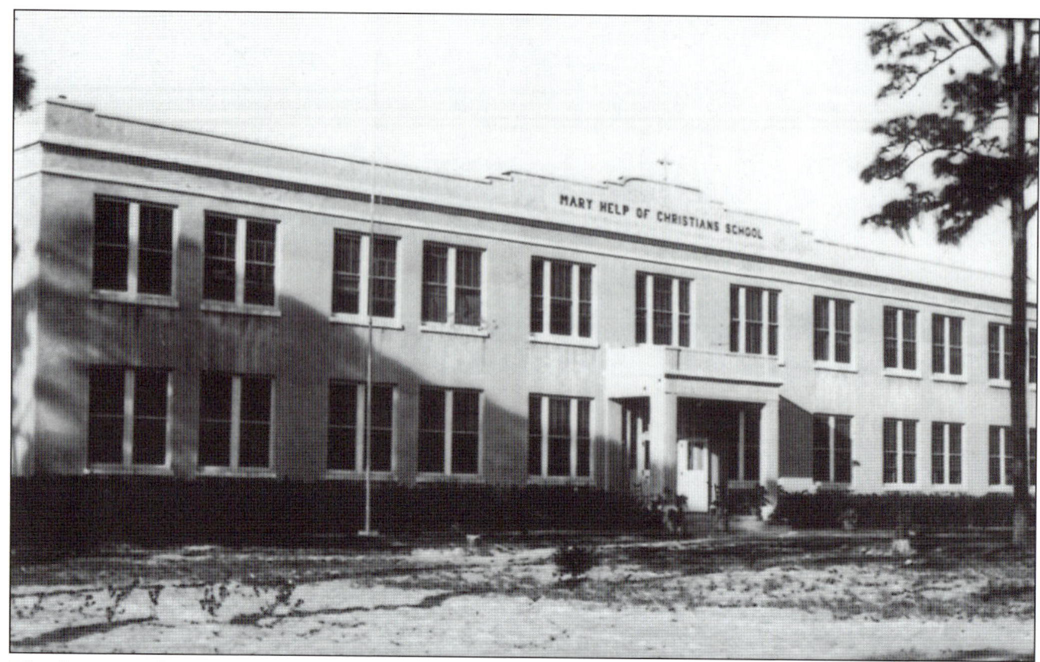

The history of Mary Help of Christians Catholic Church and School begins in 1926, when the Salesian Fathers arrived at Union Station in downtown Tampa. The call to Florida came from Alicia Gonzalez Neve, who donated the land to build a school for homeless boys. Neve was moved by the plight of the many homeless children in Tampa and recalled reading about the Salesians' work. In 1925, she offered to become a benefactor, with an appeal to establish an orphanage for boys in Tampa. Pictured above is the school in 1928 shortly after completion. The below photograph shows the students and staff of the school in 1950.

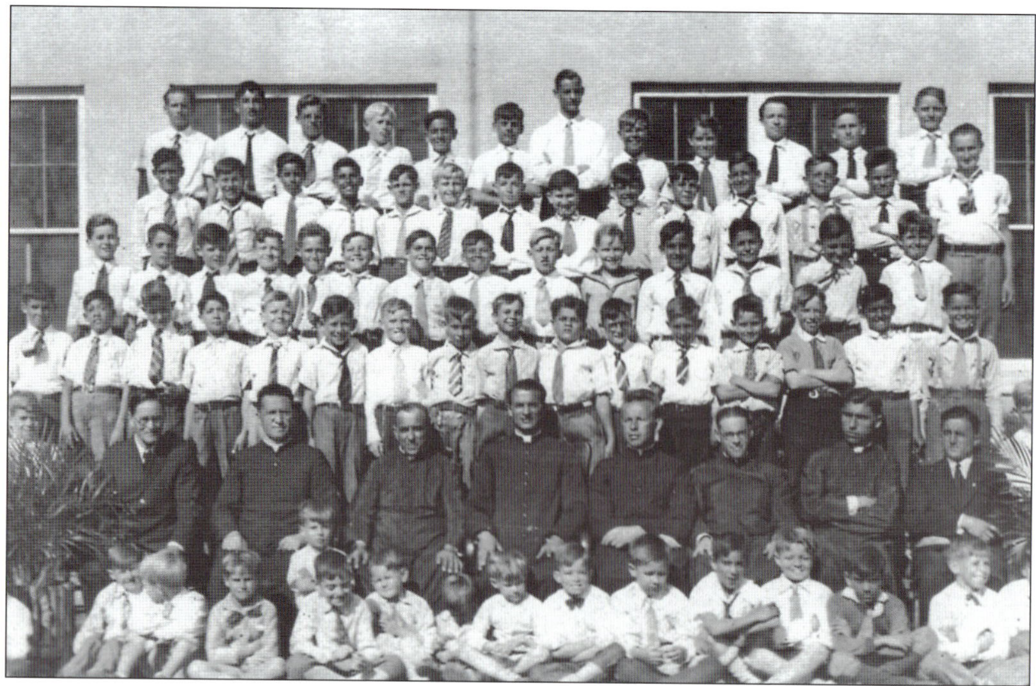

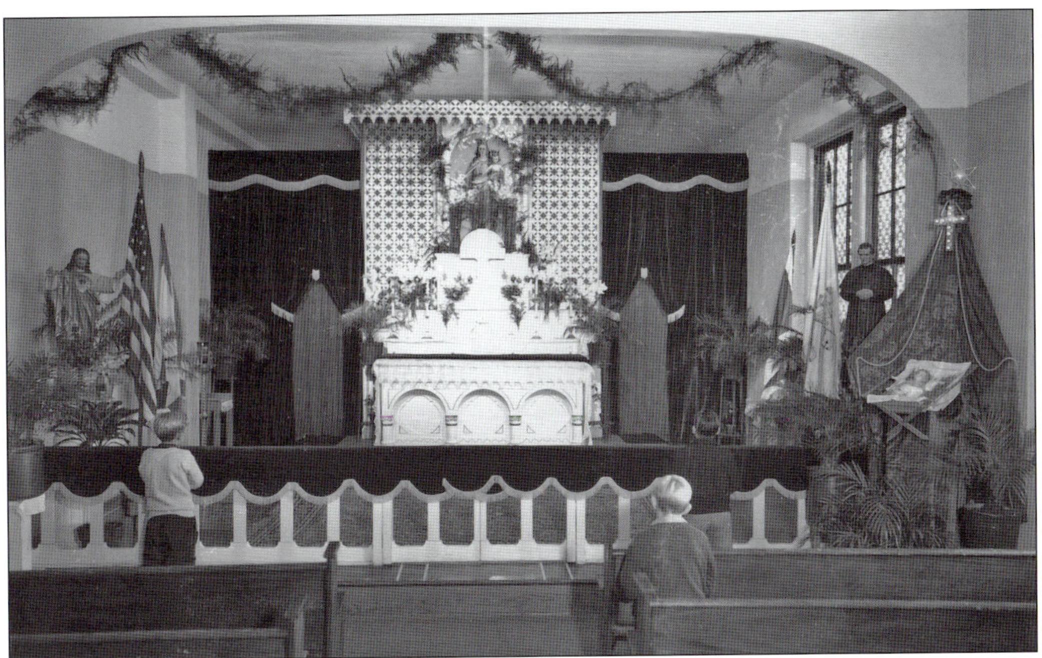

The Salesian Fathers and Sisters arrived with open arms to assist and nurture the Catholic community. After their arrival in 1926, work on the school began immediately on property bordering a picturesque lake in East Tampa donated by Alicia Gonzalez Neve, pictured below with students in 1943. The first building was a cottage constructed on the property and the first mass was celebrated there on November 13, 1926. The work of the Salesians was of great importance to the future development of the Catholic community in Tampa, requiring much courage and sacrifice. Mary Help of Christians Catholic School officially opened in September 1928. Pictured above in 1943 is the first chapel for the church and school.

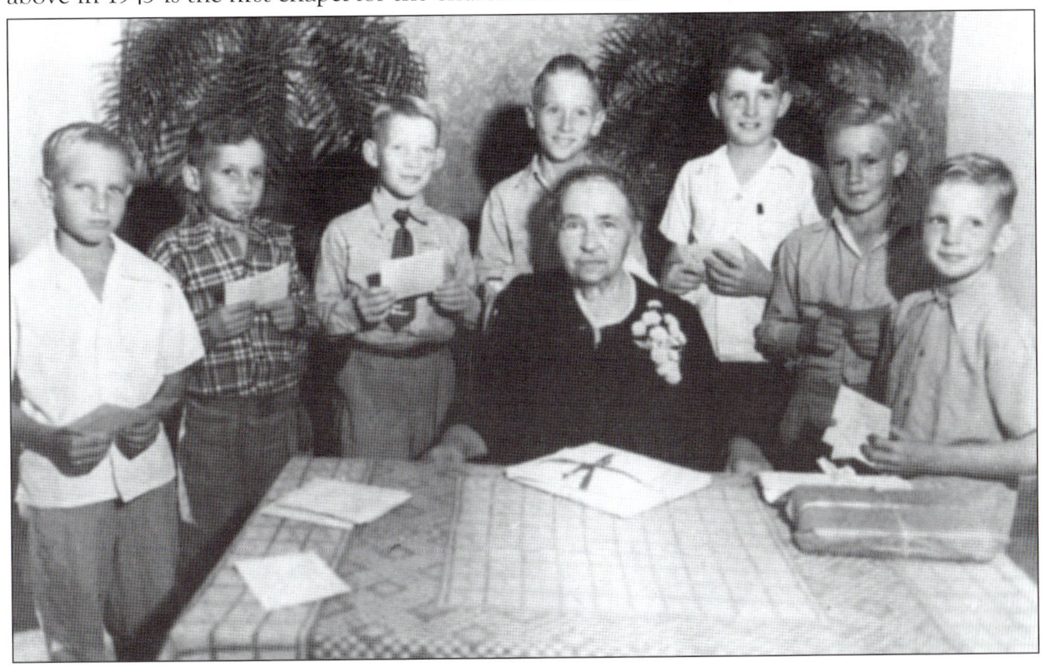

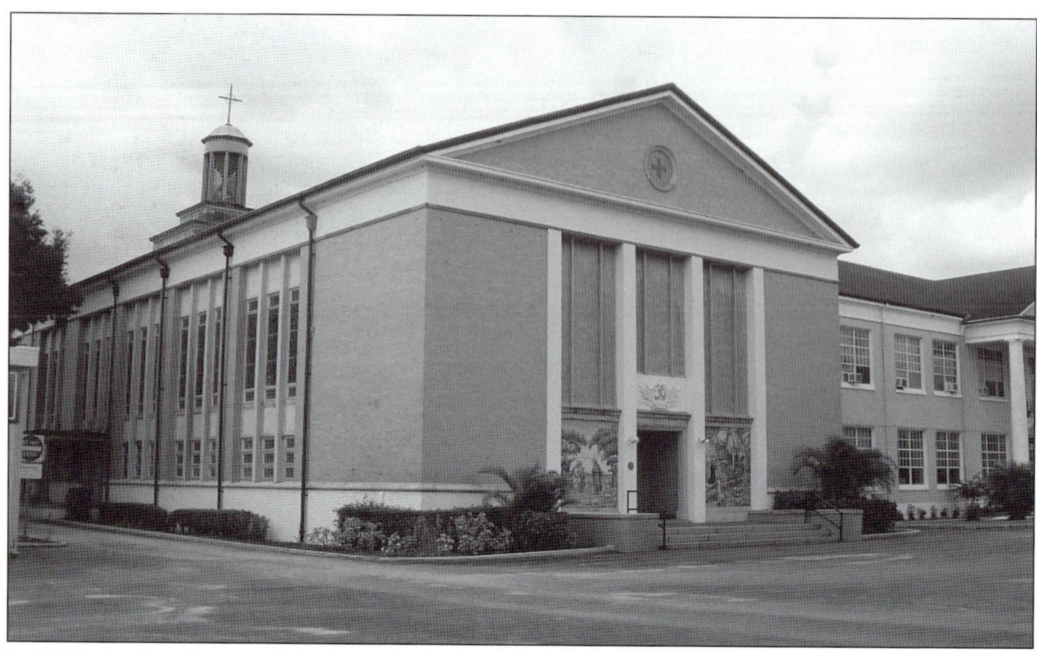

In 1928, the foundation of the Mary Help of Christians Catholic Church community began with the dedication of the school and orphanage for boys. The school offered a Catholic education and vocational training for trades such as carpentry and automotive repair. After worshipping in a small chapel for nearly 40 years, the community began making plans for a new church in 1961 under the guidance of director Fr. Alvin Manni. Ground-breaking ceremonies were held on October 23, 1963. On October 18, 1964, the cornerstone was laid, and on January 31, 1966, the Feast of St. John Bosco, the new church was dedicated by Archbishop Joseph Hurley. Pictured below is the dedication ceremony in 1966.

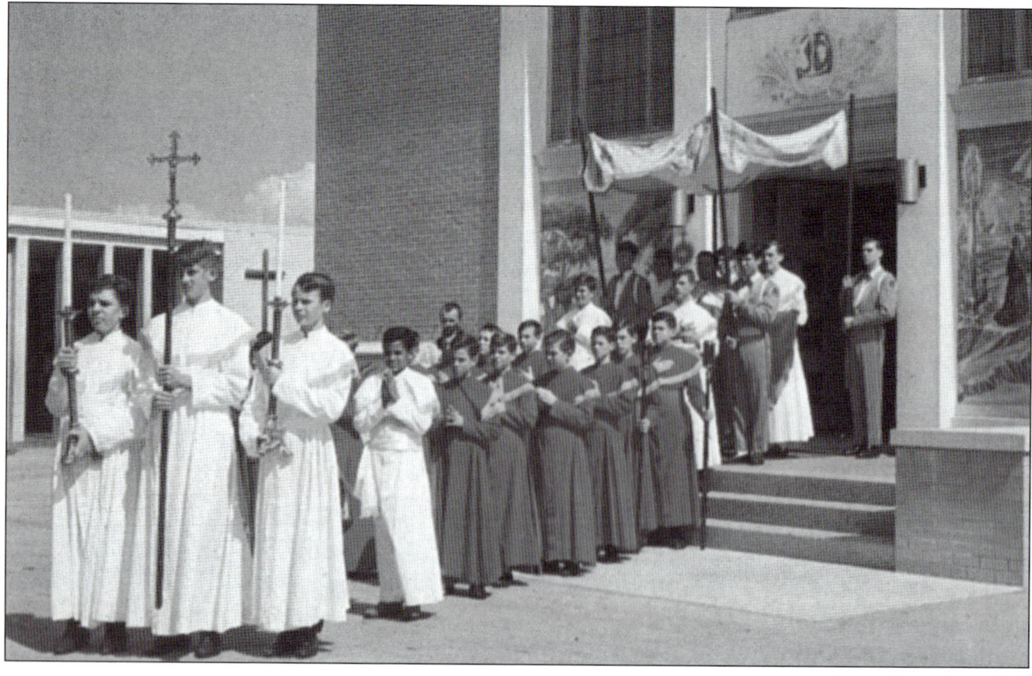

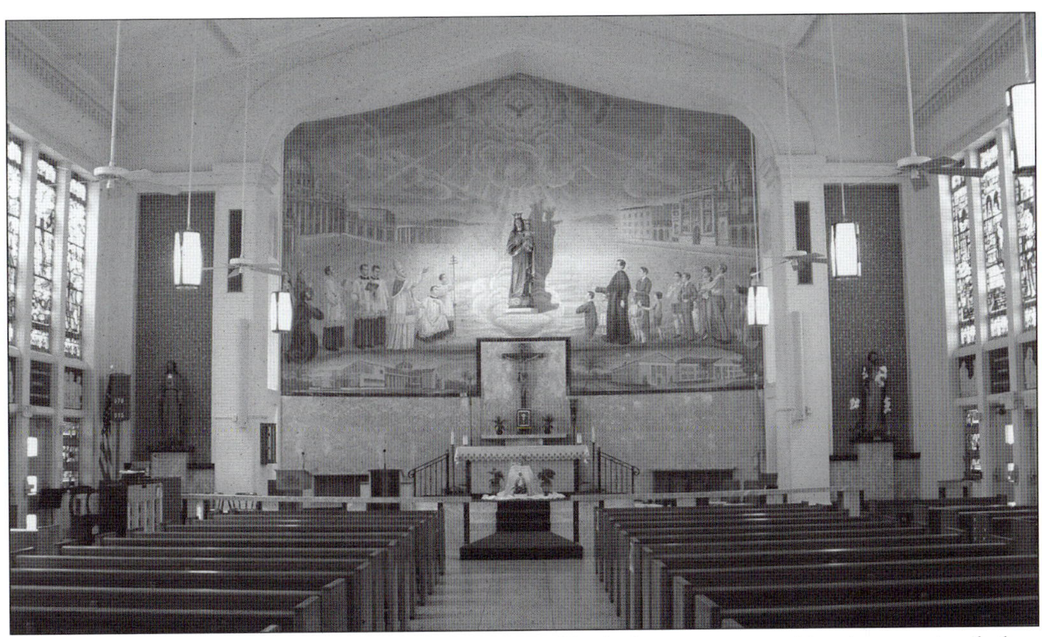

The church features Venetian glass mosaics created by Italian artists, and intricate stained-glass windows depicting the joyful mysteries on the east wall and the glorious mysteries on the west wall. The parish is also home to the Korean Catholic Mission. Another institution of the community is Cristo Rey High School, providing a college preparatory education along with the foundational skills offered through a unique internship program with local businesses. Mary Help of Christians Catholic Church is modeled after the Oratory of Valdocco in Turin, Italy, founded by St. John Bosco, founder of the Salesian order. The Salesian Fathers and Sisters spend their time with youth welcoming, evangelizing, and preparing them for life.

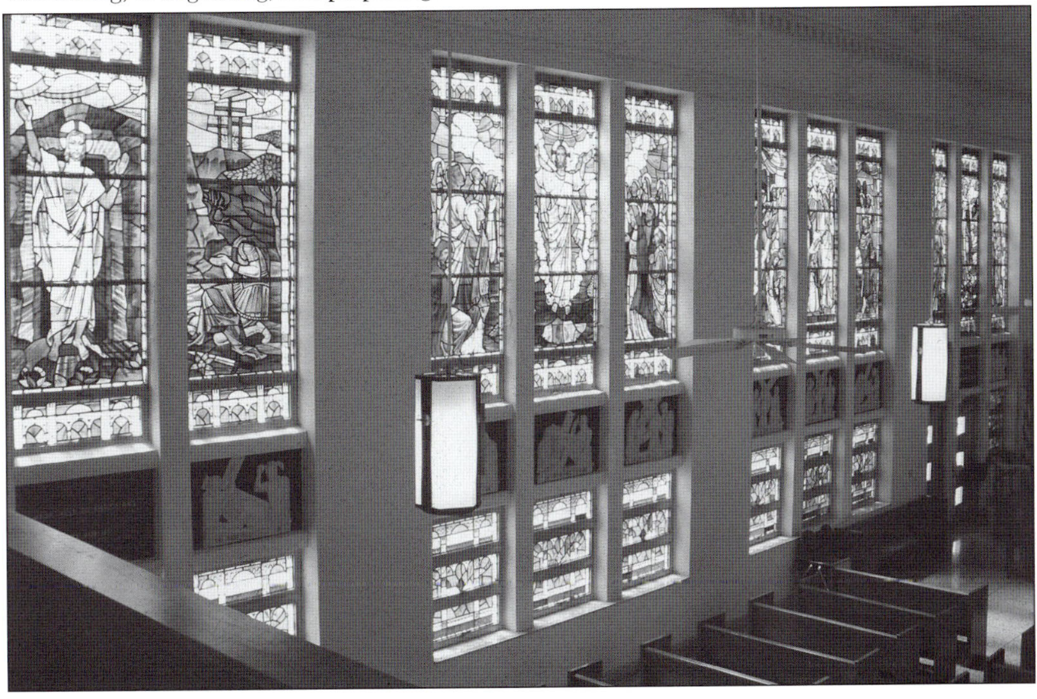

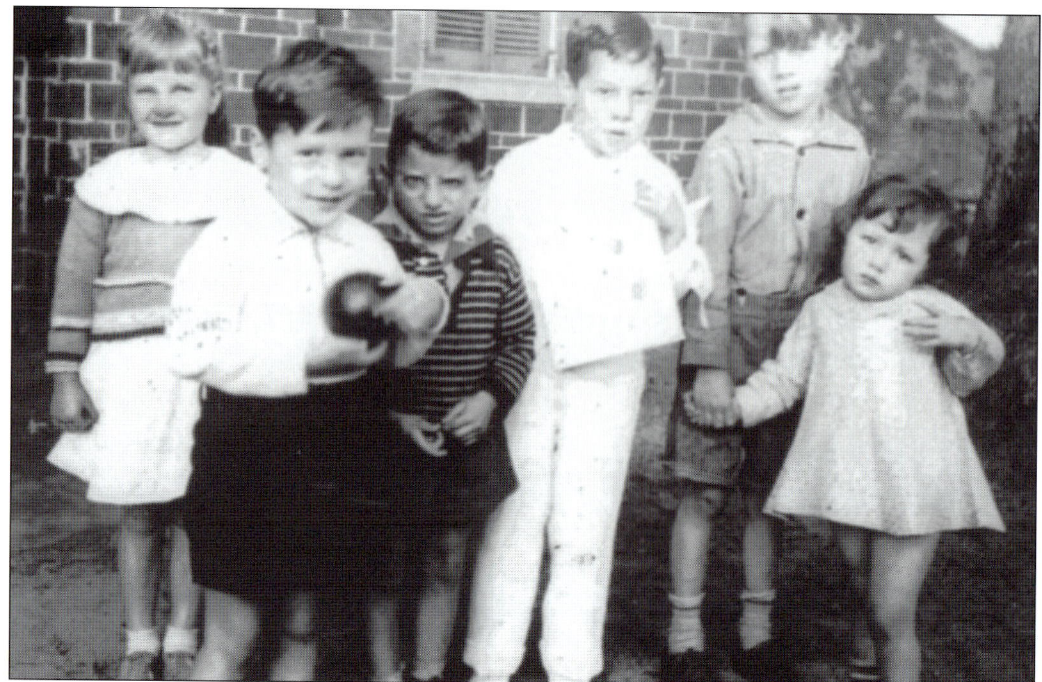

Since 1928, the Salesian Fathers and Sisters have served selflessly to care for the children at St. Joseph School and Villa Madonna School, pictured above in 1936. Salesian benefactor Alicia Gonzalez Neve donated her home on Columbus Drive, which was converted to Villa Madonna School. Pictured below in 1959 are the Salesian Sisters at Villa Madonna School and St. Joseph School. From left to right are (first row) Sr. Angelina, Sr. Vincent, Sr. Theresa, Sr. Rose Bucci, and Sr. Mary Palatini; (second row) Sr. Frances, Sr. Lena, Sr. Mary, Sr. Christina, Sr. Felicia, Sr. Louise, Sr. Letizia, Sr. Amparo, and Sr. Anna; (third row) Sr. Roberta, Sr. Ofelia, Sr. Mary Bertha, Sr. Rose Segarini, Sr. Bertha, Sr. Mary DiCamillo, and Sr. Theresa; (fourth row) Sr. Esther, Sr. Philomena, Sr. Maria, Sr. Marie, Sr. Cecilia, Sr. Rose Farina, and Sr. Inez.

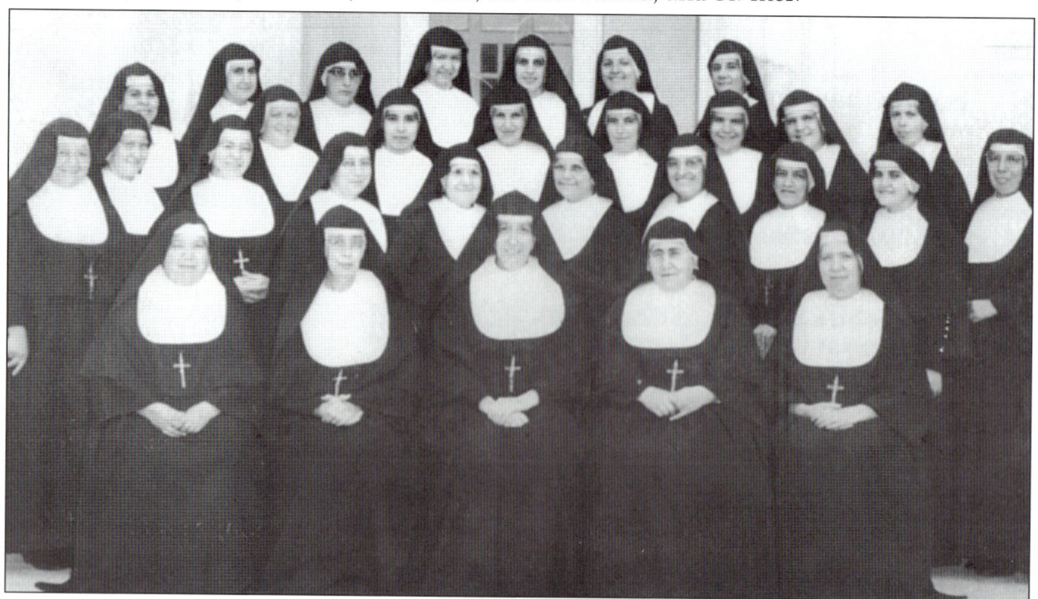

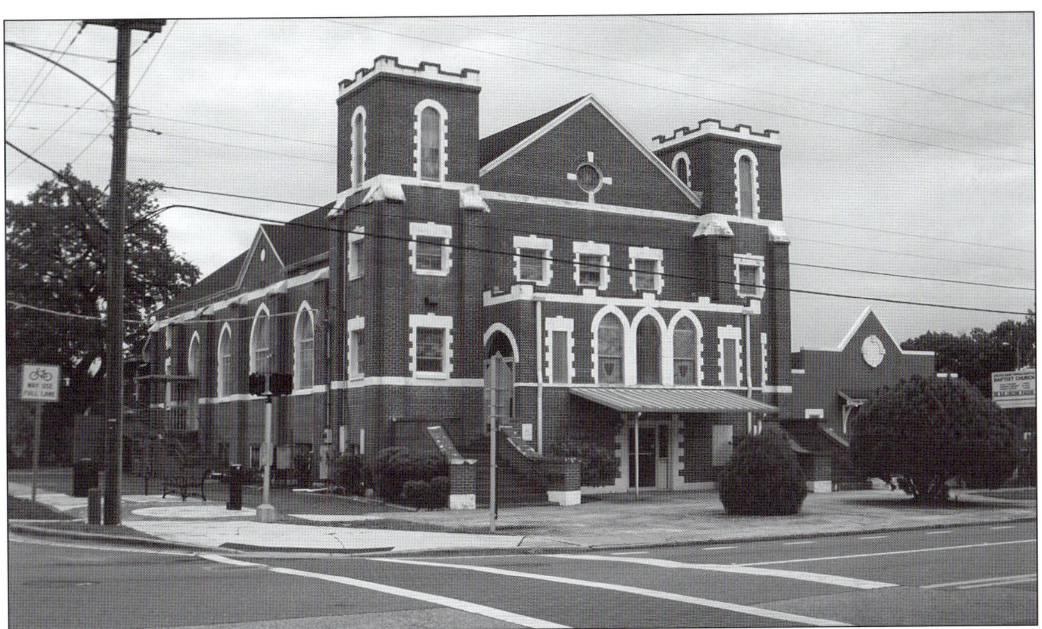

Pictured here is the historic Mount Moriah Primitive Baptist Church, established in 1886 by Rev. A. Wallace in a small chapel at the corner of Twiggs Street and Nebraska Avenue. In 1905, the church established a mission that became Greater New Salem Primitive Baptist Church. The congregation later moved to 1228 Nebraska Avenue and completed the dedication of their new church in 1948, which features four-story twin bell towers, stained-glass windows, and a gallery in the sanctuary. The chancel features an extraordinary hand-painted mural of the Last Supper. The congregation has lovingly maintained and preserved their historic church, which features the original vintage pews and organ.

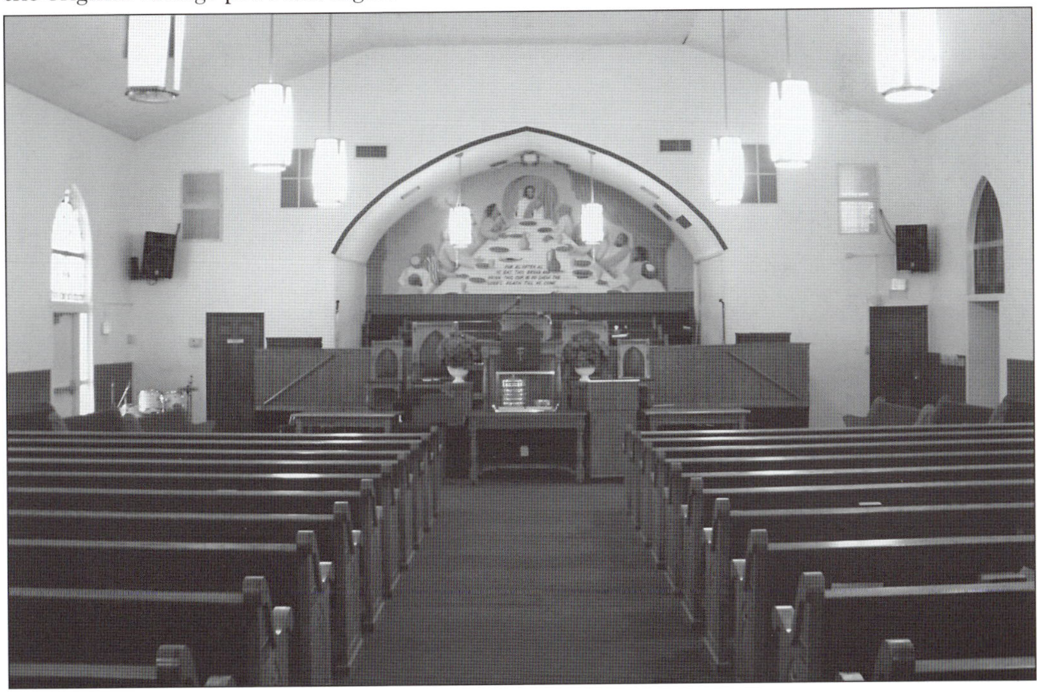

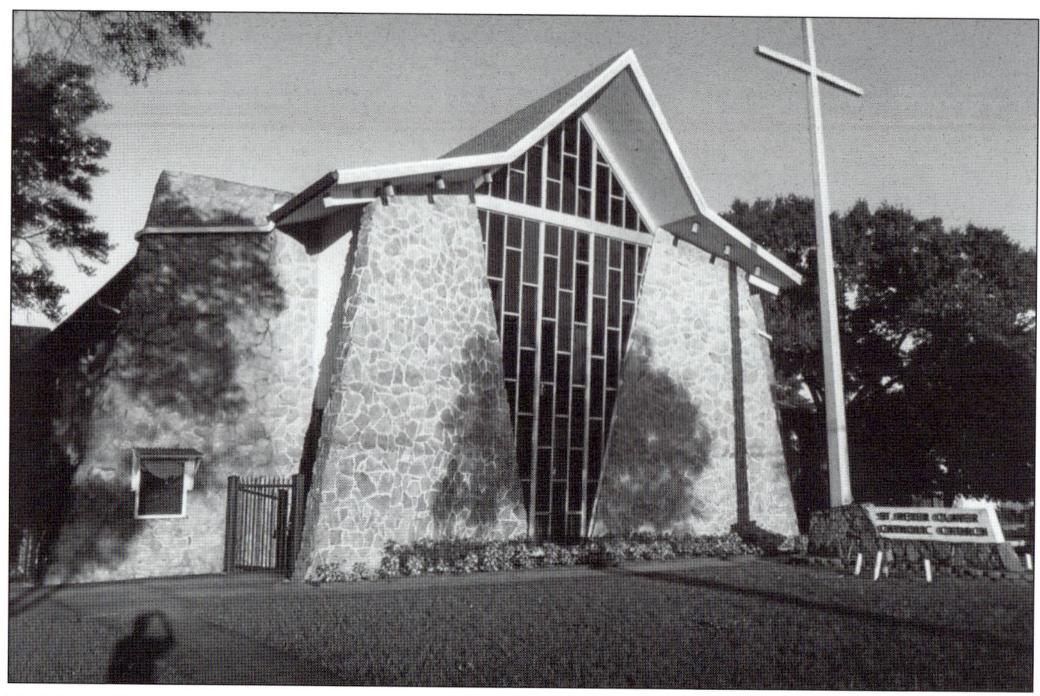

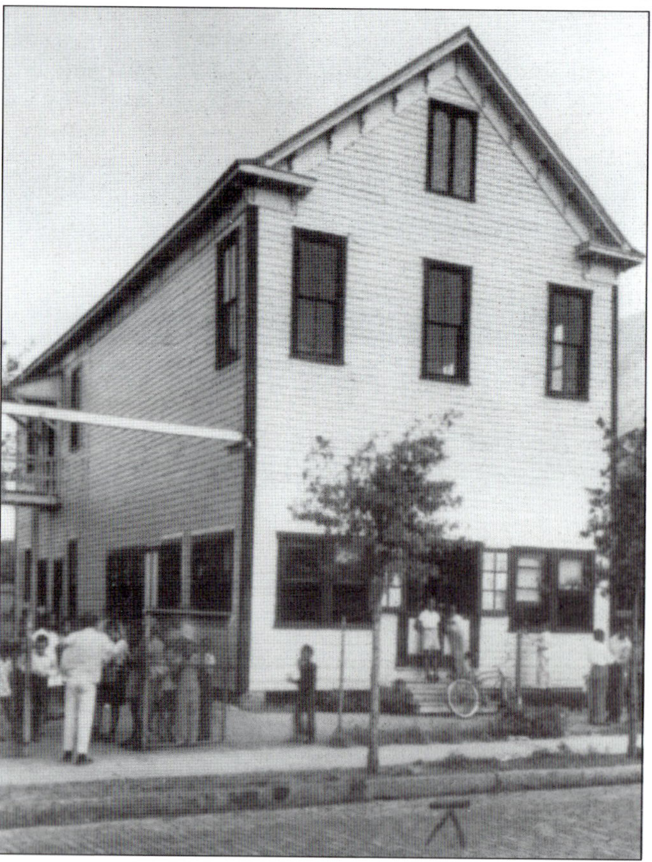

The history of St. Peter Claver Catholic Church and School begins in 1893 when the Jesuit Fathers purchased an old former Methodist church in downtown Tampa with plans to establish a Catholic school and mission church there. On February 2, 1894, the school officially opened under the care of two Sisters of the Holy Names. On the night of February 12, 1894, the school was burned down by arsonists who opposed the establishment of a school for the African American community. Plans were immediately made to rebuild the school. Fr. William Tyrell purchased property on the corner of Scott and Governor Streets, and the school was rebuilt and reopened on October 2, 1894. Pictured here in 1925 is the original school building. It is the oldest Catholic school in the state of Florida for the African American community.

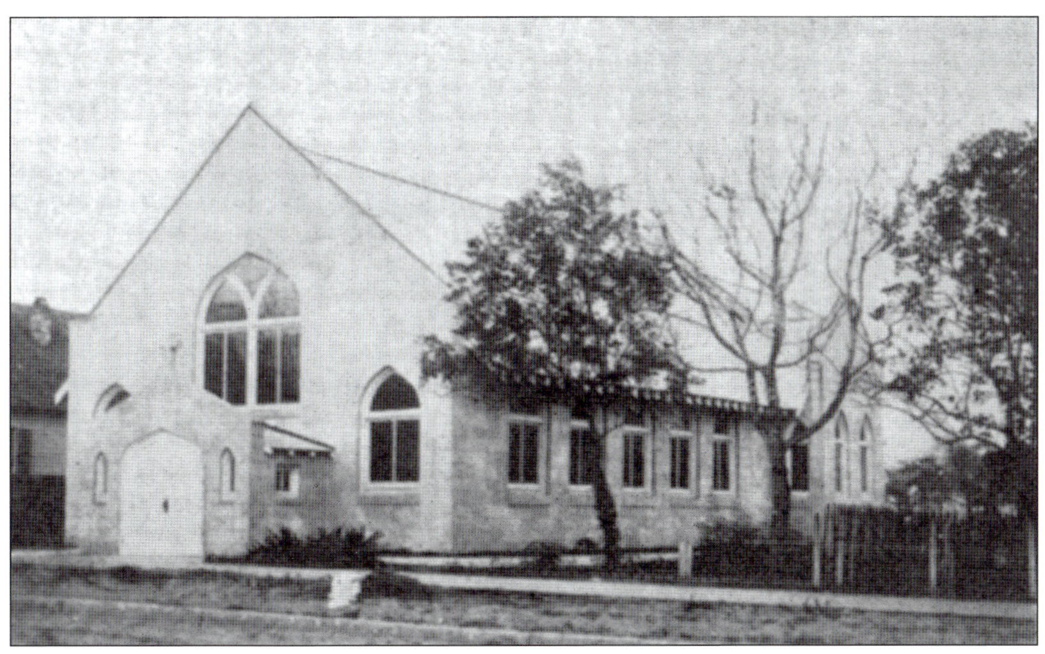

The first worship space for St. Peter Claver Catholic Church was the second-floor chapel of the school. The first church was built in 1915 with a gift from Mrs. L.D. Morreil, the sister of Mother Katharine Drexel, the founder of the Sisters of the Blessed Sacrament. The first mass was said on Christmas Day, December 25, 1915, by Fr. William J. Tyrell, the first assigned pastor. Pictured here is the original church and sanctuary in 1929. The statues of the Blessed Mother and Jesus were formerly used in the old St. Louis Church, which had been replaced by Sacred Heart Church and were given to St. Peter Claver Parish as a gift from Sacred Heart Parish in 1915.

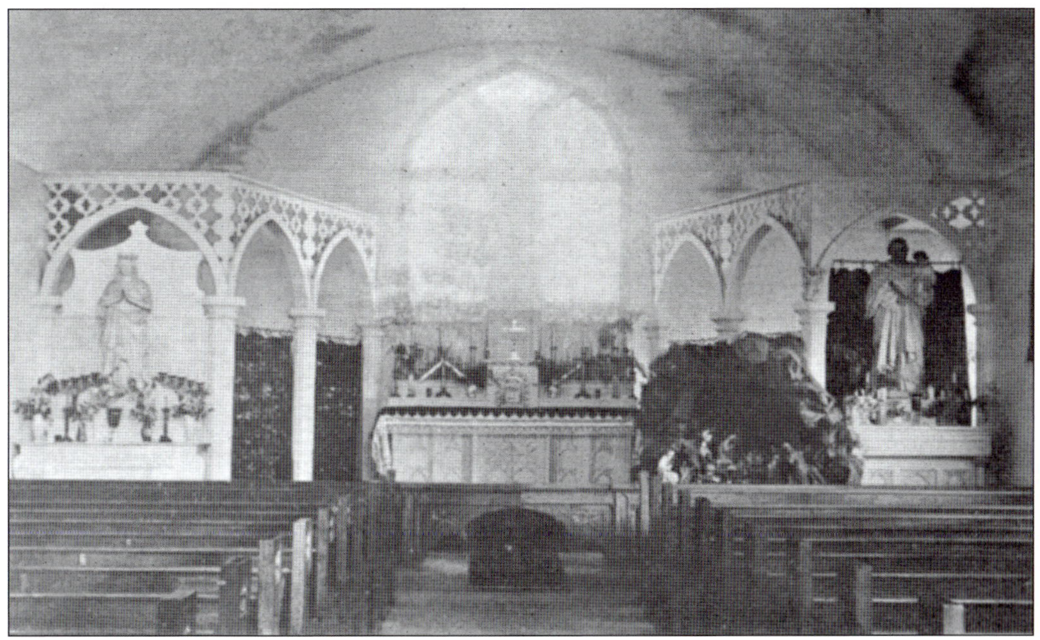

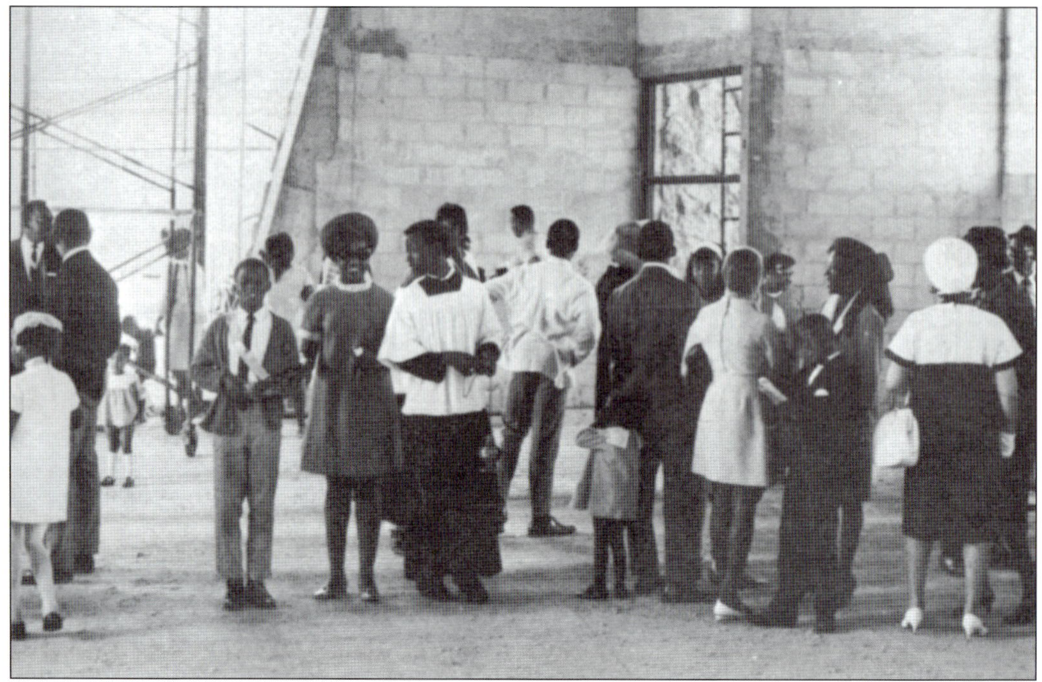

In 1968, the congregation secured property for a new church at 1203 Nebraska Avenue. The ground-breaking ceremony was held on September 15, 1968. Pictured above is the cornerstone dedication ceremony on February 2, 1969, with parishioners touring the construction site. The total cost was $138,900, and it was designed by architect Cesar Alfonso. Charles B. McLaughlin, bishop of the Diocese of St. Petersburg, dedicated the new church on June 8, 1969. Pictured below in 1986 is the congregation in the new church.

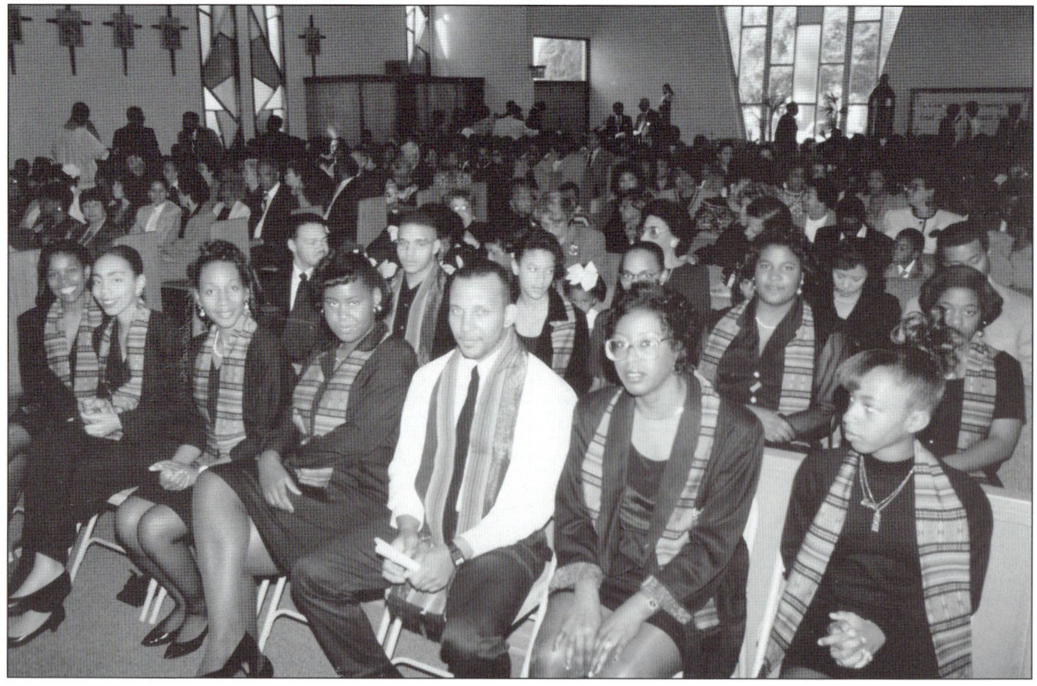

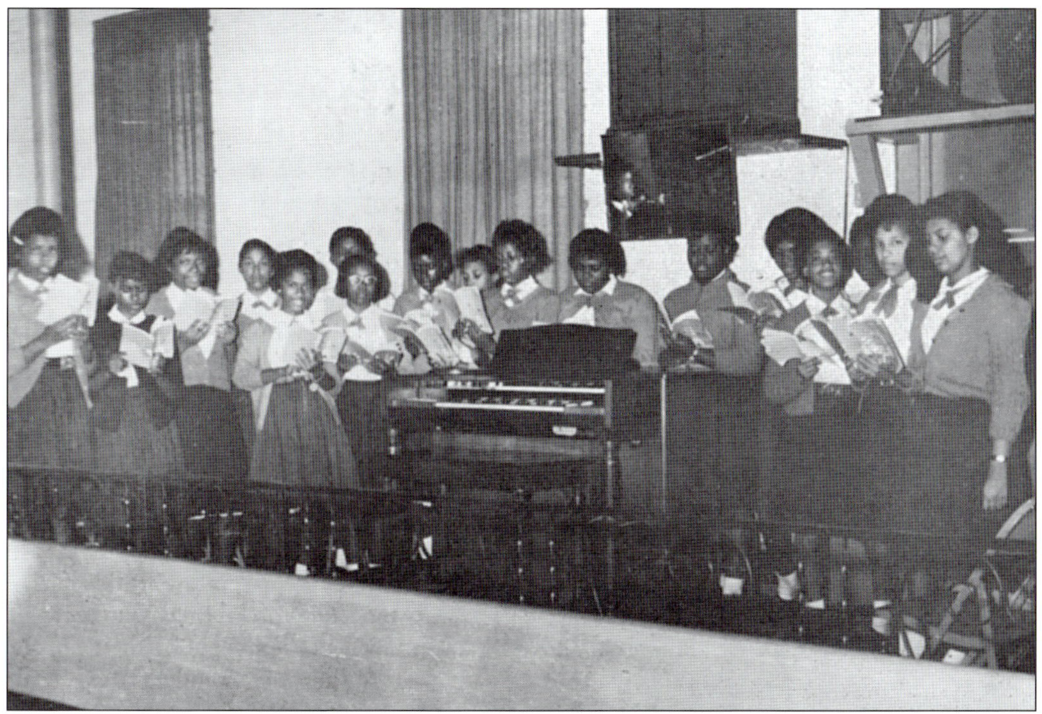

The parish of St. Peter Claver has been blessed since its establishment with many who have served the community with great dedication. Among those who have served are the Jesuit Fathers, the Josephite Fathers, Diocesan priests, Sisters of the Holy Names, School Sisters of Notre Dame, Sisters of St. Chretienne, and Sisters of St. Joseph of St. Augustine. Pictured above is the school choir in 1964. The St. Peter Claver Gospel Choir is seen below in 1996.

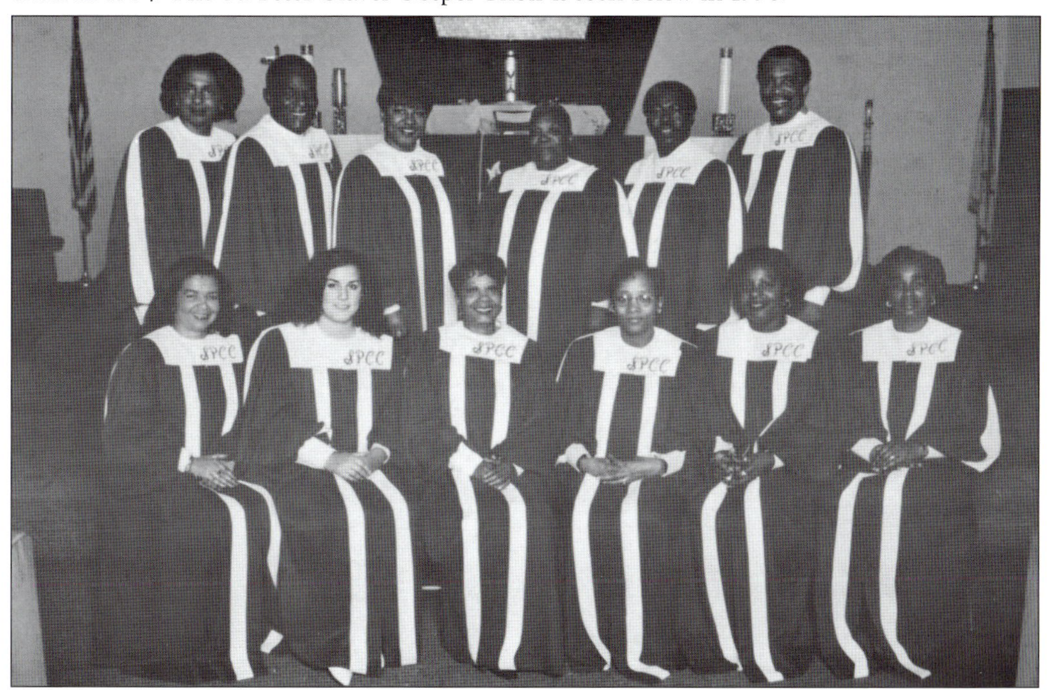

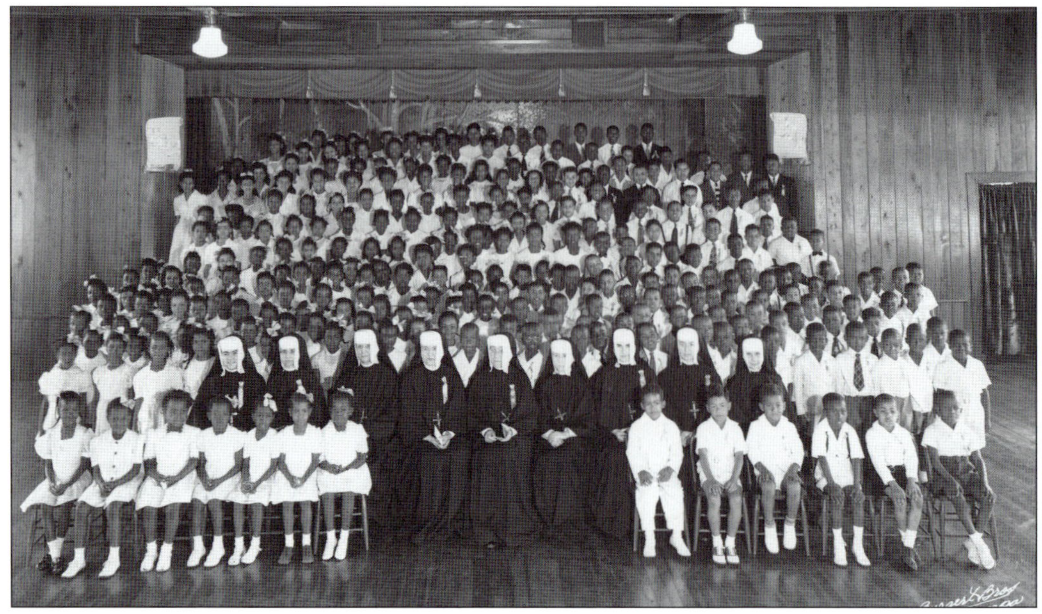

St. Peter Claver's new school was dedicated by Bishop Michael Curley in July 1929. In 1952, students from St. Benedict the Moor School were transferred to St. Peter Claver School after their school closed due to a fire. In 1953, Archbishop Joseph Hurley dedicated a new school annex. Pictured above in 1945 are the students with the Sisters of the Holy Names in the new school. The below photograph from May 1964 shows the first communion class with the Sisters of the Holy Names and Fr. Timothy Holland. The school continues the mission of those first two Sisters of the Holy Names, who gave selflessly for the needs of the community.

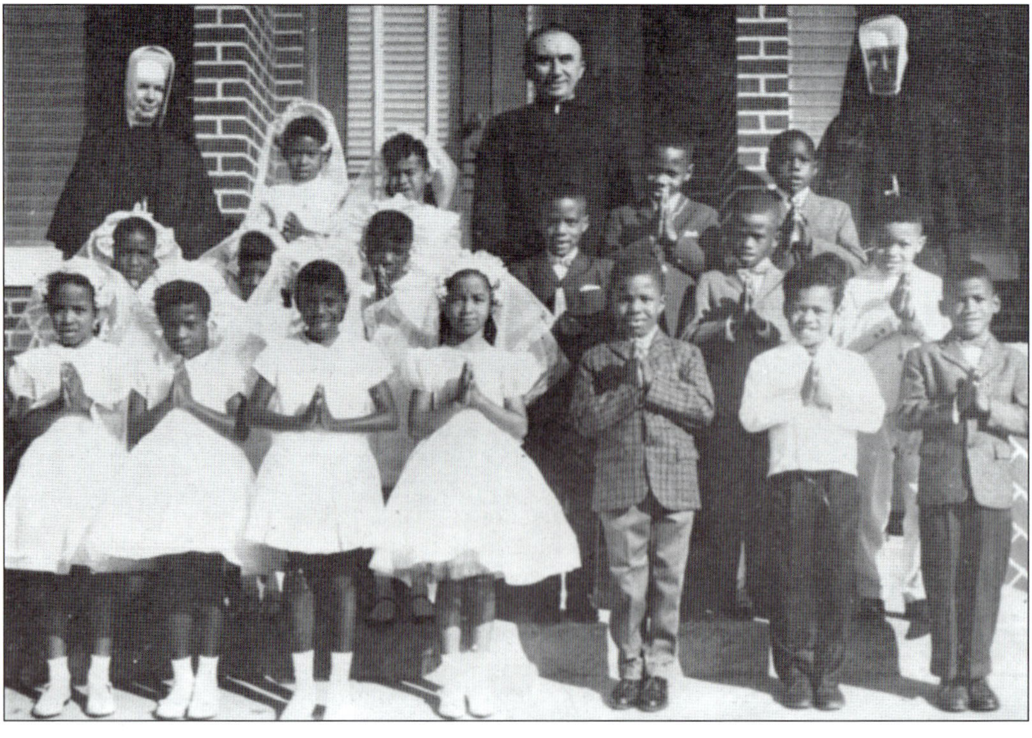

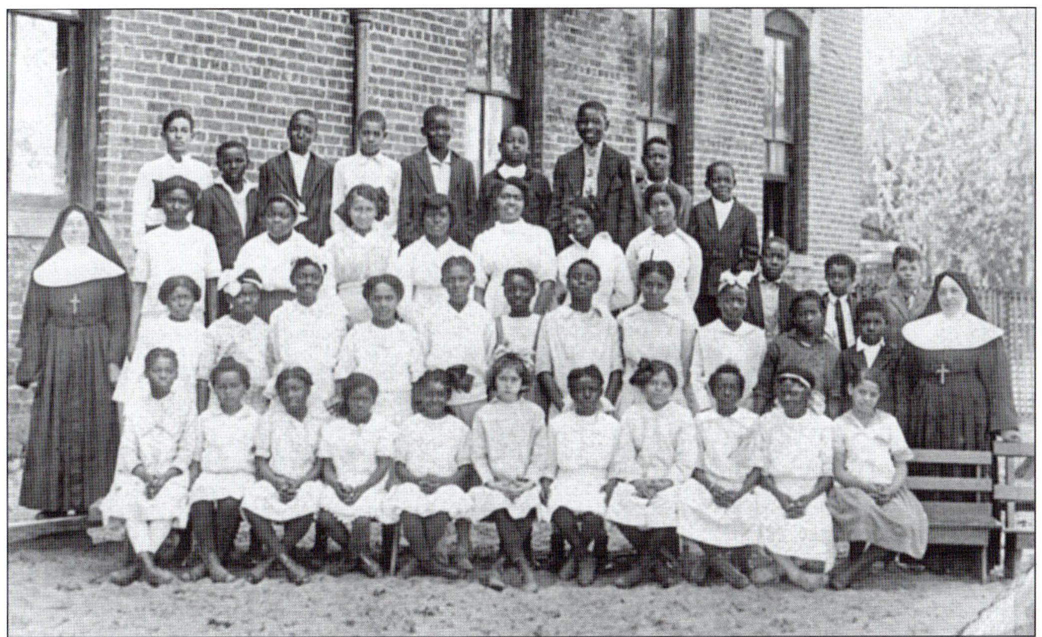

Pictured here in 1903 is St. Benedict the Moor Catholic School students and the Sisters of St. Joseph at 2600 North Twentieth Street. The students were children of families working in the cigar factories. In 1913, a law was passed by the Florida legislature to prohibit white persons from teaching African American students. In an act of defiance, the sisters refused to abide by this racist law and continued to teach the children. In April 1916, three nuns from the order were arrested, and the school had to temporarily close. One month later, a judge ruled the law did not apply to the sisters because they represented a private school. The school closed in 1952 when it was destroyed by an accidental fire. Pictured below are the sisters assigned to the school in 1935. (Both, SSJSA.)

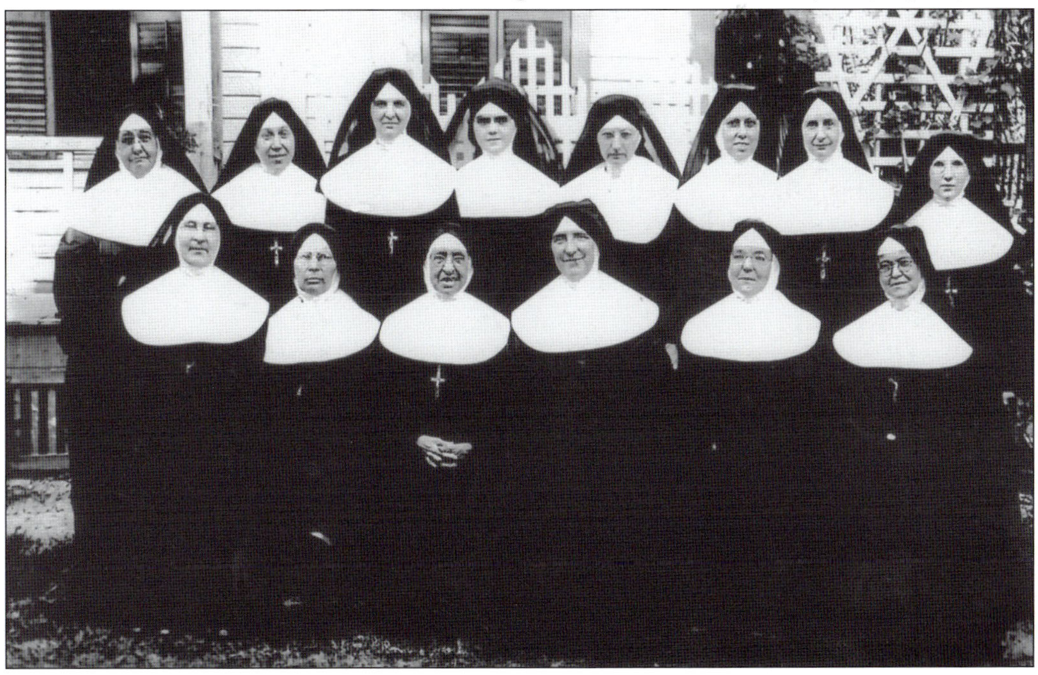

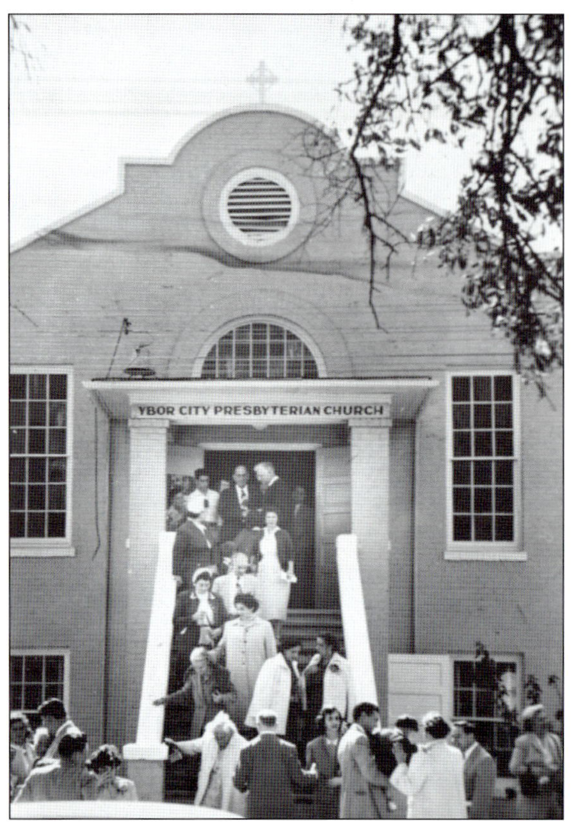

Pictured here in 1955 is Ybor City Presbyterian Church, which later became St. John Presbyterian Church. This church was founded in 1909 to serve the community of faithful in Ybor City at 953 Eleventh Avenue serving Cuban, Italian, and Spanish immigrants. From 1909 to 1935, five pastors led the church: Rev. P.H. Hensley, Rev. E.E. Someillan, Rev. Eladio Hernandez, Rev. H.Y. Beatty, and Rev. F. Boan. In 1935, Rev. and Mrs. Walter B. Passiglia arrived and began an evangelical visitation campaign to encourage new membership, which soon increased to more than 400. The congregation is pictured below in 1942.

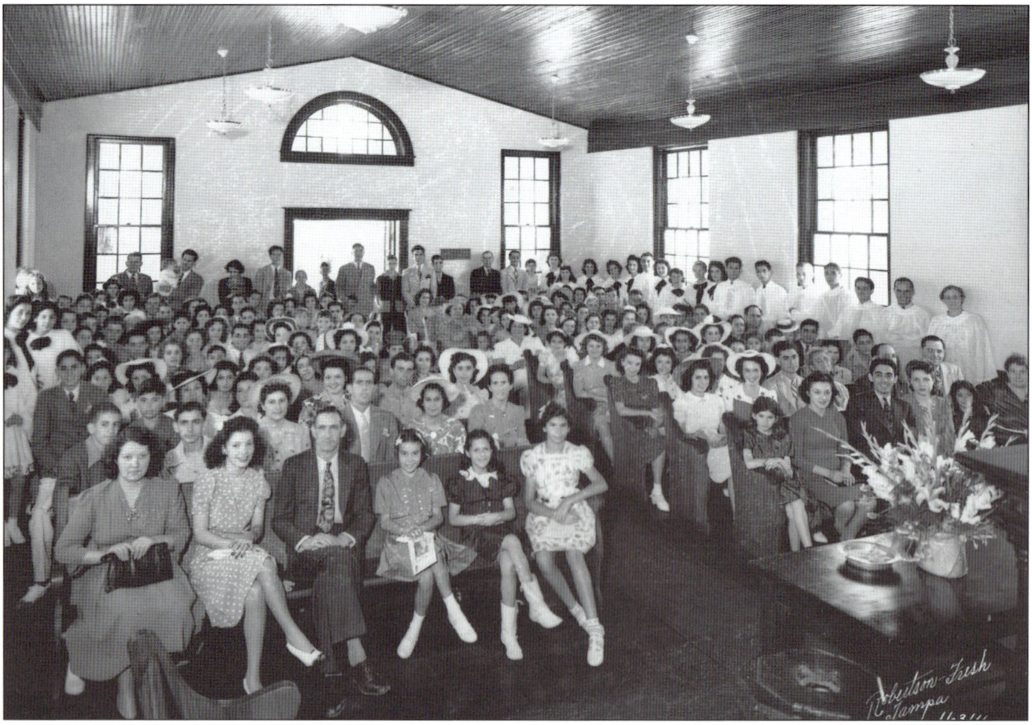

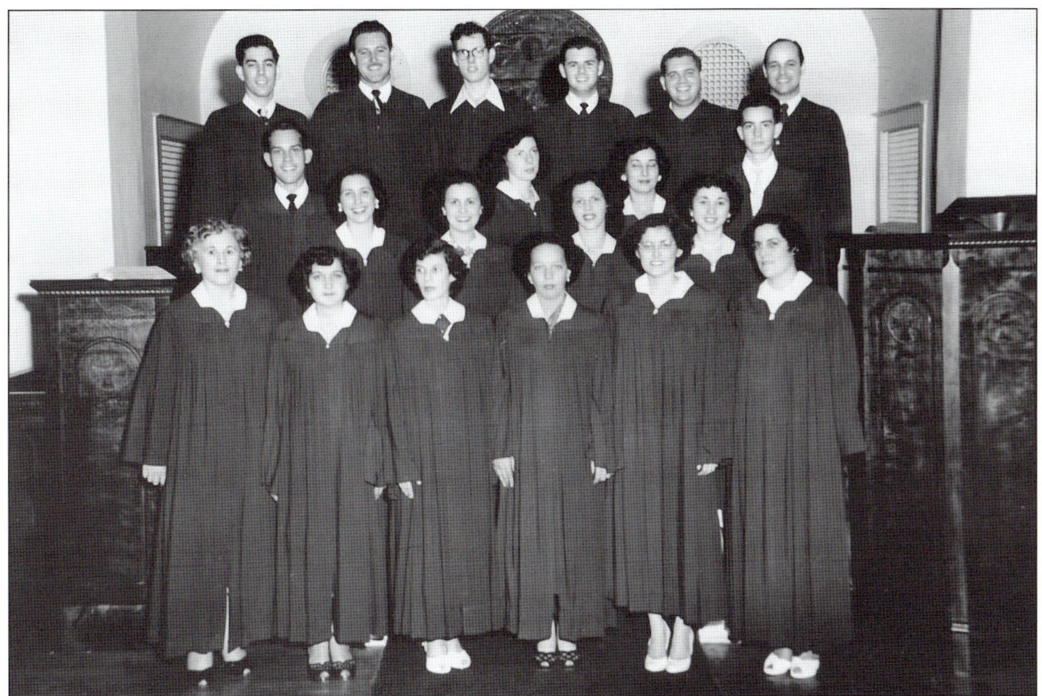

During the 1950s, the church continued to expand and made plans to build a larger church to accommodate the growth of the community. The pastor's wife served as choir director, developing what became a celebrated music ministry program, and five young members of the church were inspired to enter into full-time Christian ministry. Pictured above in 1956 is the church choir in the chancel of the Ybor City church. In the below scene captured outside the church in 1956, the church bus arrives with the congregation.

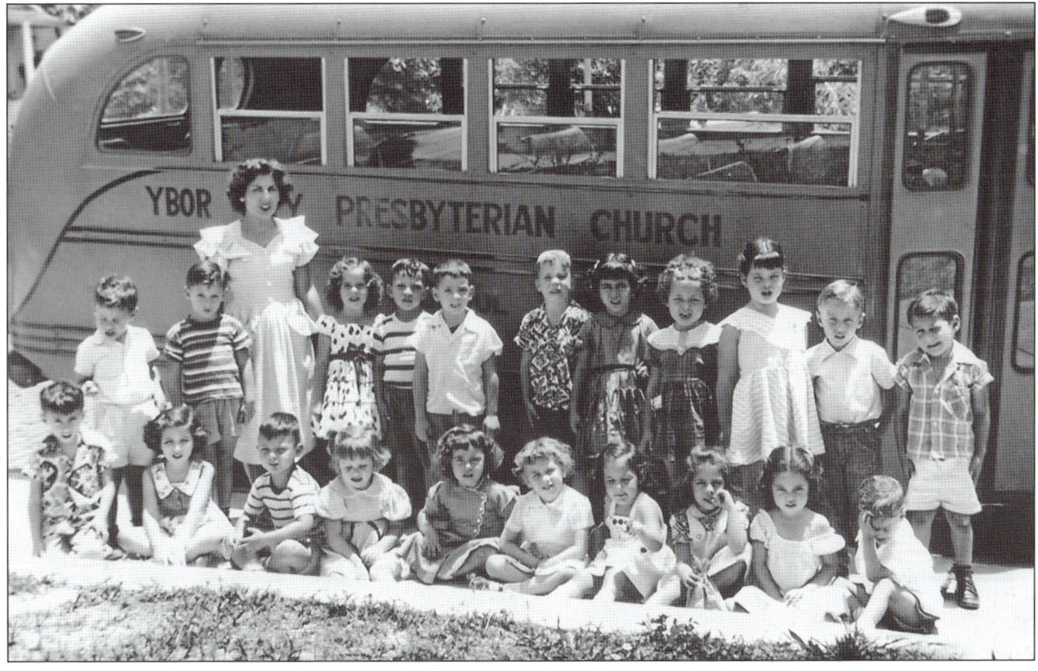

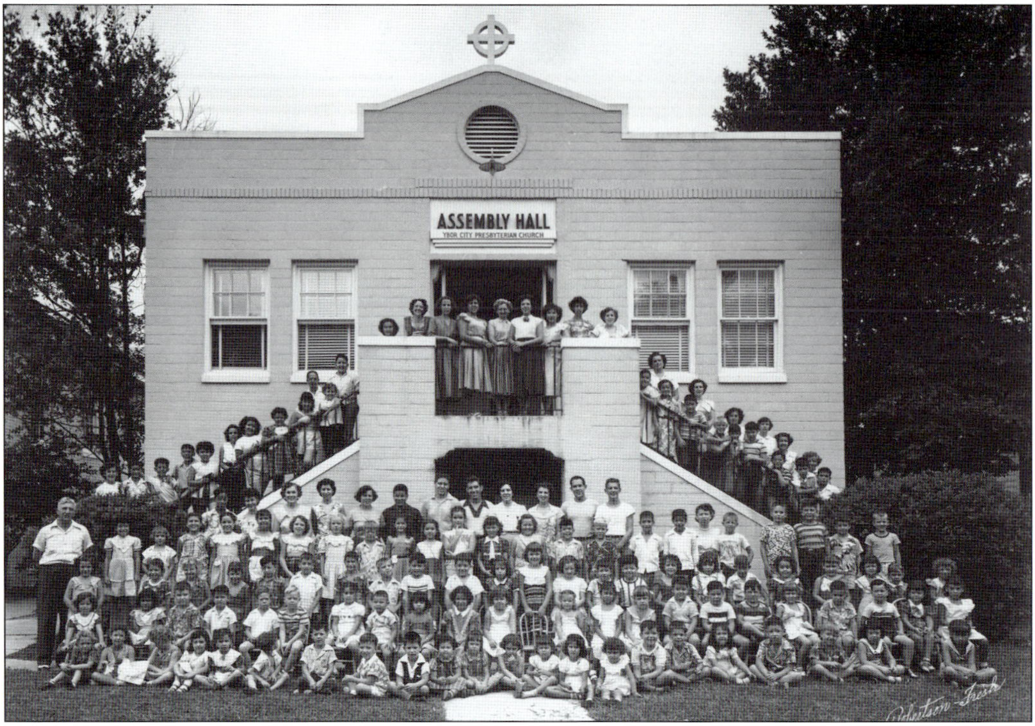

The history of St. John Presbyterian Church began in 1909 when the Ybor City Presbyterian Mission was established. After many years of service in the Ybor City community, in 1957, the congregation decided to relocate the church to a developing area of West Tampa, and a parcel of land was purchased at 4120 North MacDill Avenue. Ground-breaking ceremonies were held on January 13, 1957, pictured below with Mayor Nick Nuccio holding the shovel. Church services began on April 7, 1957, in the church parking lot and construction commenced. The photograph above shows the Sunday school class in 1950 at the Ybor City church site.

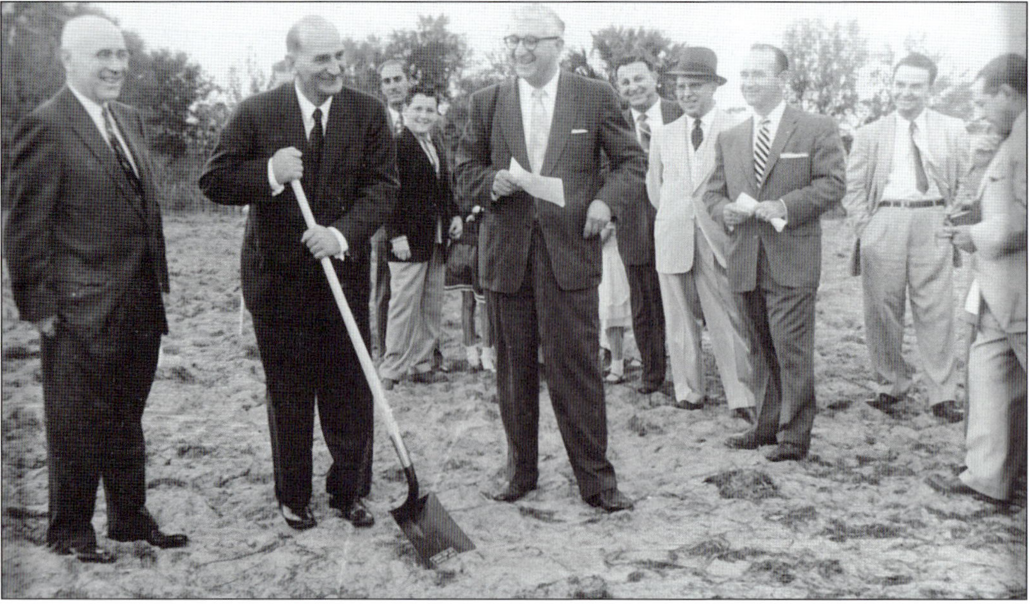

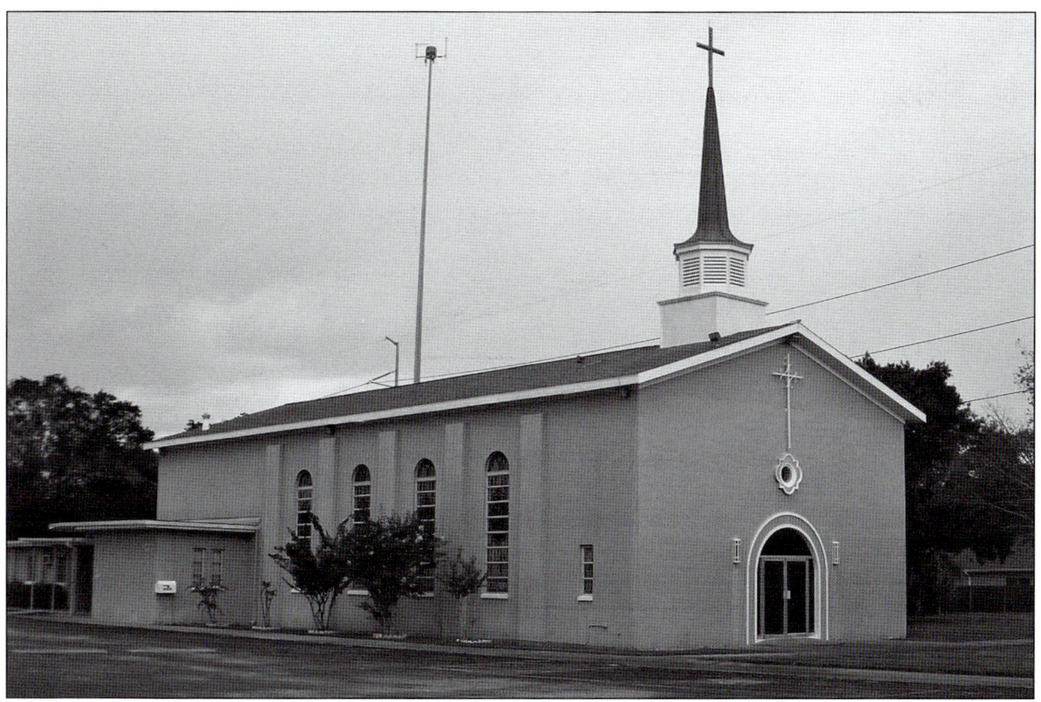

On July 21, 1957, the first service was held in the new church, pictured here shortly after completion. The facilities were dedicated on September 22, 1957, with an overflow crowd of faithful and many friends of the longtime parish joining in the celebration. Below, the sanctuary is decorated for Christmas in 1970. The church continues the good deeds of their founding faithful from Ybor City by offering many programs of outreach and assistance including the McClain Foundation Home, established in 1980, offering assistance to women with developmental disabilities.

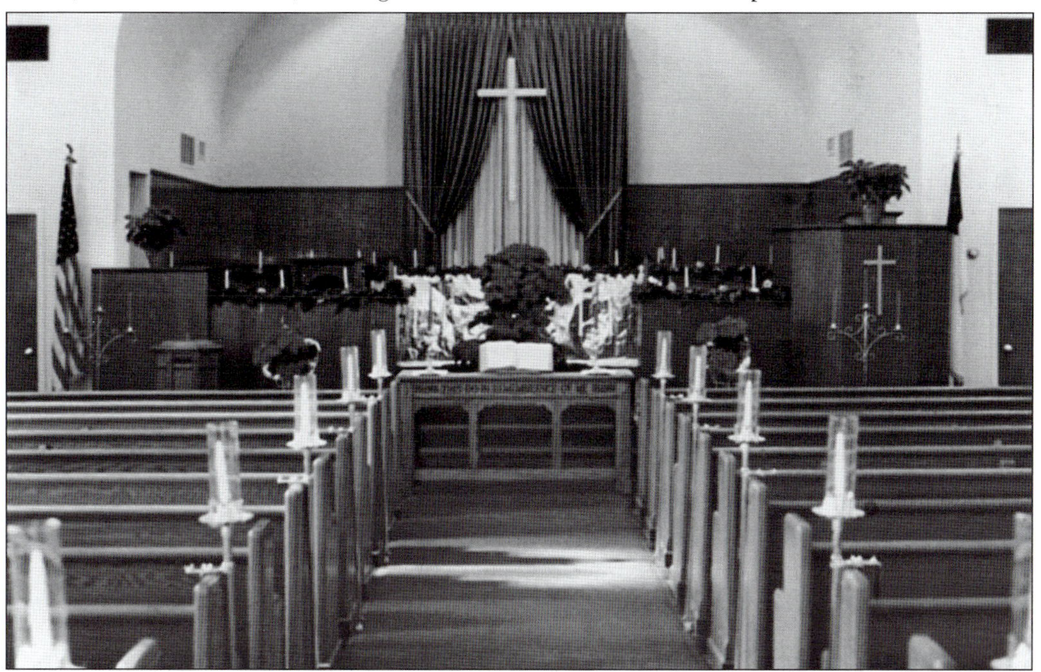

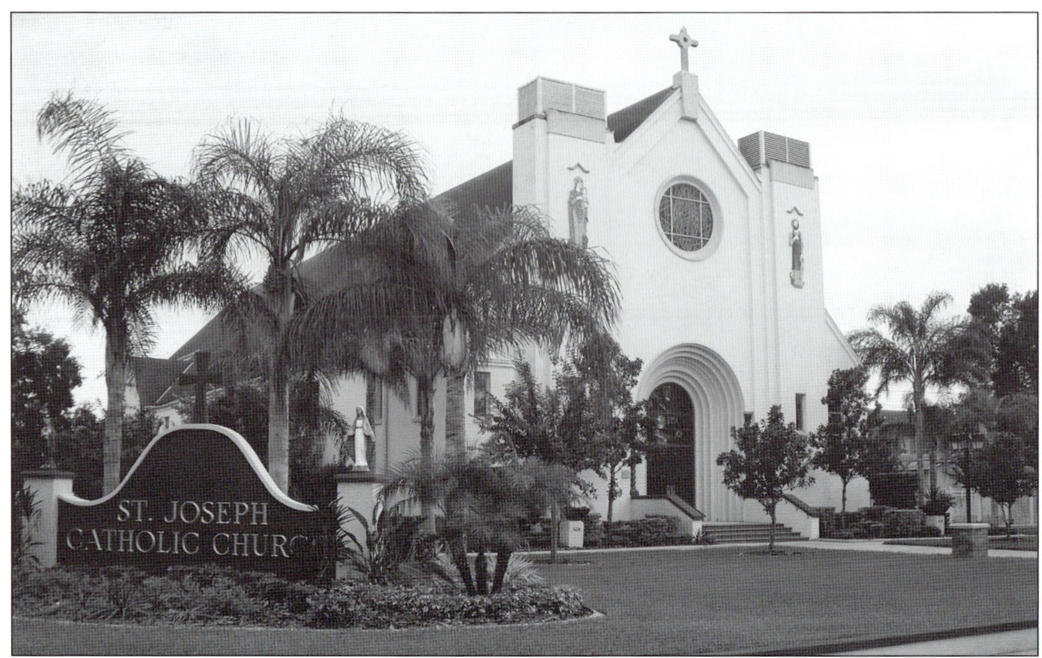

St. Joseph Catholic Church was established in 1896 through the efforts of the Sisters of the Holy Names and the Jesuit Fathers. In 1895, aware of the growing Catholic population in West Tampa, Bishop John Moore commissioned the Sisters of the Holy Names to establish a Catholic school in West Tampa. The first church building was at the corner of North Albany Avenue and Walnut Street, constructed at a cost of $15,000 and completed on May 3, 1903. The first pastor was Fr. Benjamin Roydhouse. Pictured below is the sanctuary and altar of the original church constructed in 1903; this photograph was taken from the choir loft in 1956 at the wedding of Delia Collera and John Cinchett.

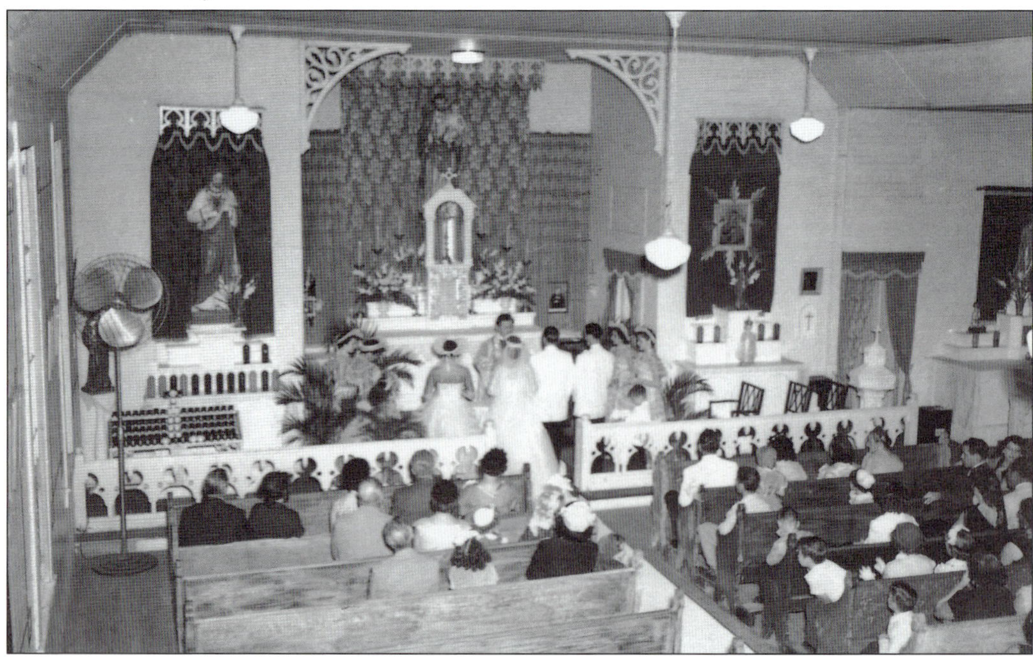

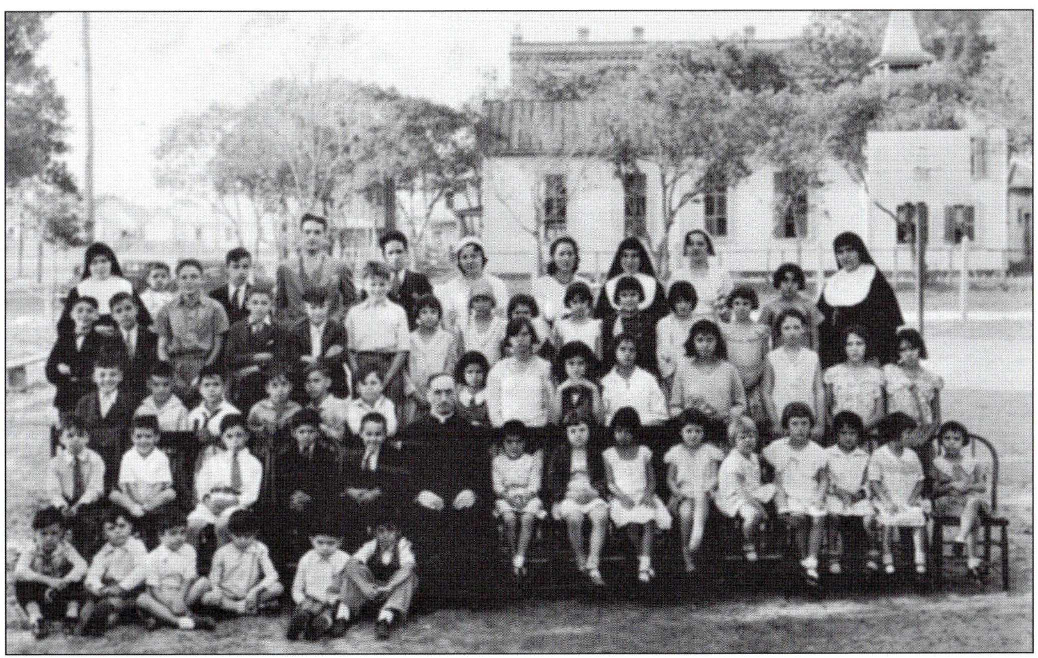

The school building was purchased on December 9, 1895, through the efforts of the Sisters of the Holy Names and opened on September 14, 1896. On November 29, 1896, Jesuit Father William Tyrrell arrived from St. Louis Church to assist with development of the church, and celebrated the first mass in the chapel. The Jesuit Fathers turned over care of the church to the Salesian Fathers in 1928, with Fr. Luis Conde as pastor. In 1930, through the efforts of Father Conde, the Salesian Sisters were commissioned to assume care of the school. Pictured above in 1931 are the school students and Salesian Sisters with Father Conde (first row, seated) next to the original church constructed in 1903. Below, a Salesian Sister conducts a sewing class in 1930.

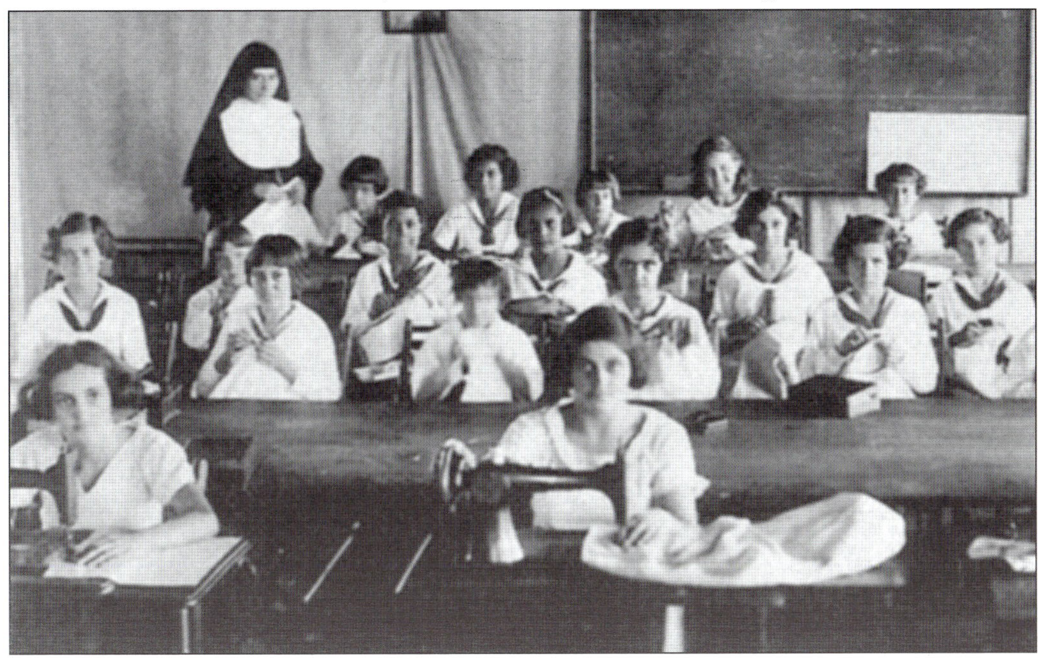

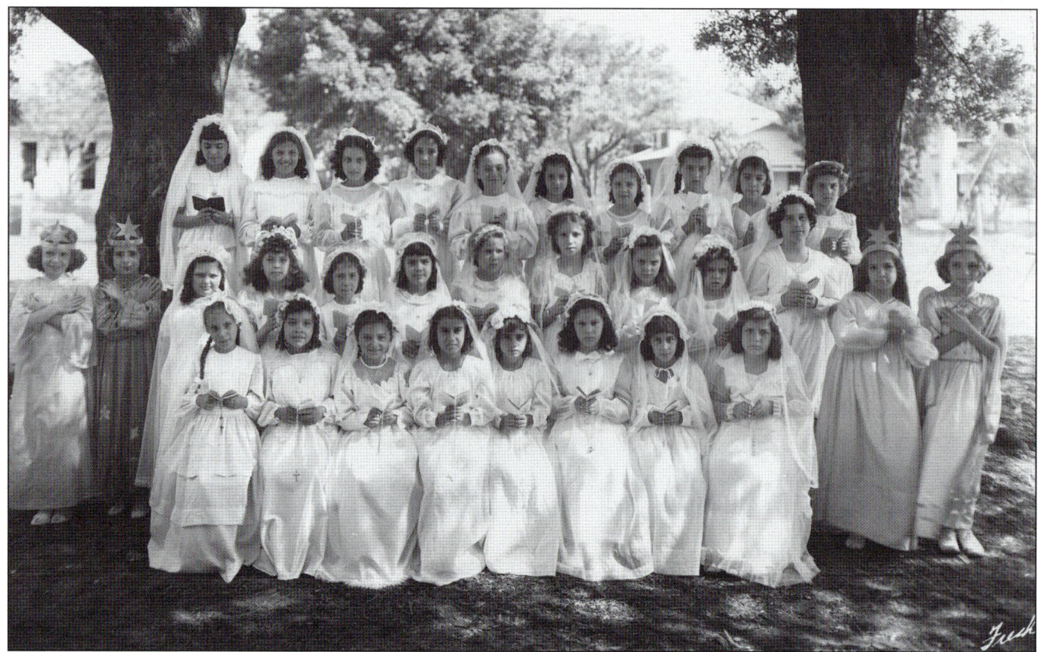

In 1934, the Redemptorist Fathers accepted care of the church and began making plans for construction of a new school and church on property they secured at Cherry Street and MacDill Avenue. In 1951, a new convent was dedicated, followed by the new school in 1955 and a school cafeteria in 1959. In 1961, a memorial program was established for fund-raising efforts, and in 1963, the contract for the new church was signed at a cost of $125,000. The ground-breaking ceremony was held on March 22, 1964. The first mass in the new church was celebrated on December 20, 1964. Pictured above is the first communion class in 1947. In the below image from 1953, the Ladies Altar Society and Salesian Sisters are pictured in the original church constructed in 1903.

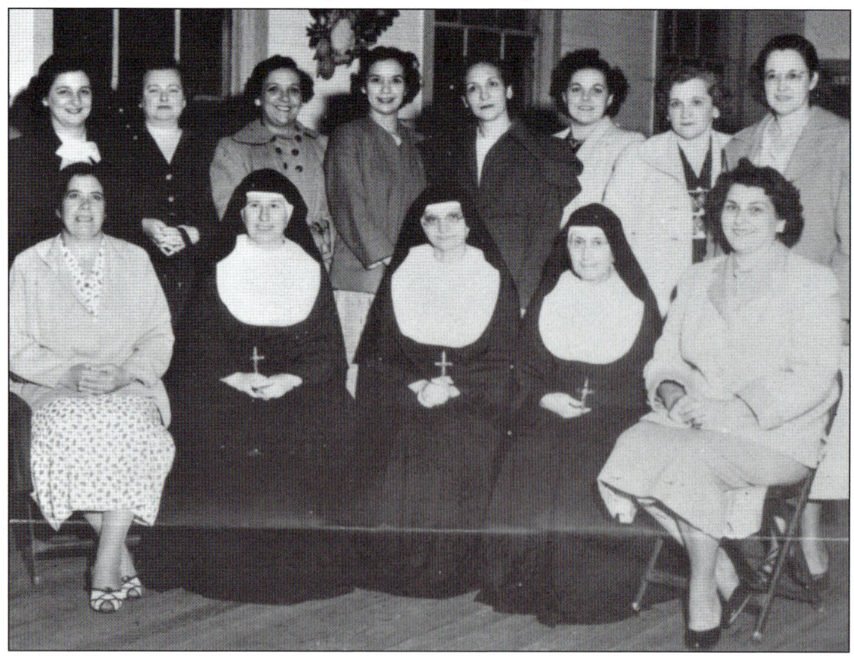

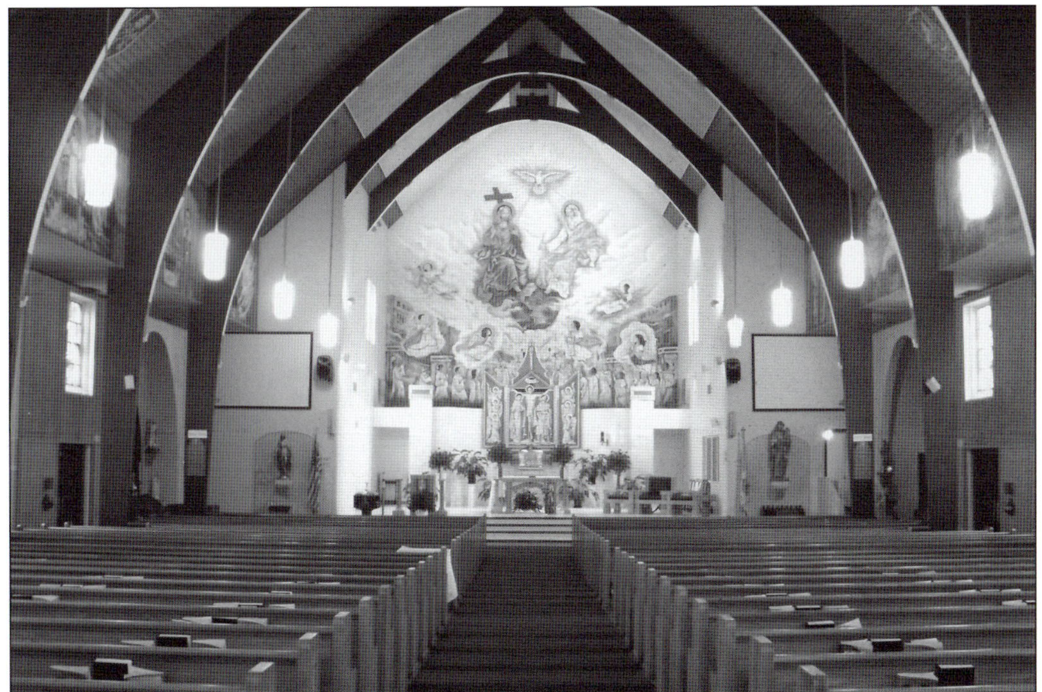

The new 800-seat church pictured here was dedicated on February 7, 1965. The tower facades feature mosaic tile reliefs of St. Mary and St. Joseph. Many articles from the original church were incorporated into the new church, including the St. Joseph statue and the steeple bell. In 1967, Fr. Tomas Gildea established a weekly mass for the Hispanic community. This was the first regularly scheduled Spanish-language mass offered at a church in the city of Tampa. In 1974, the church dedicated the Mother of God memorial pipe organ through the efforts of organist James Leone.

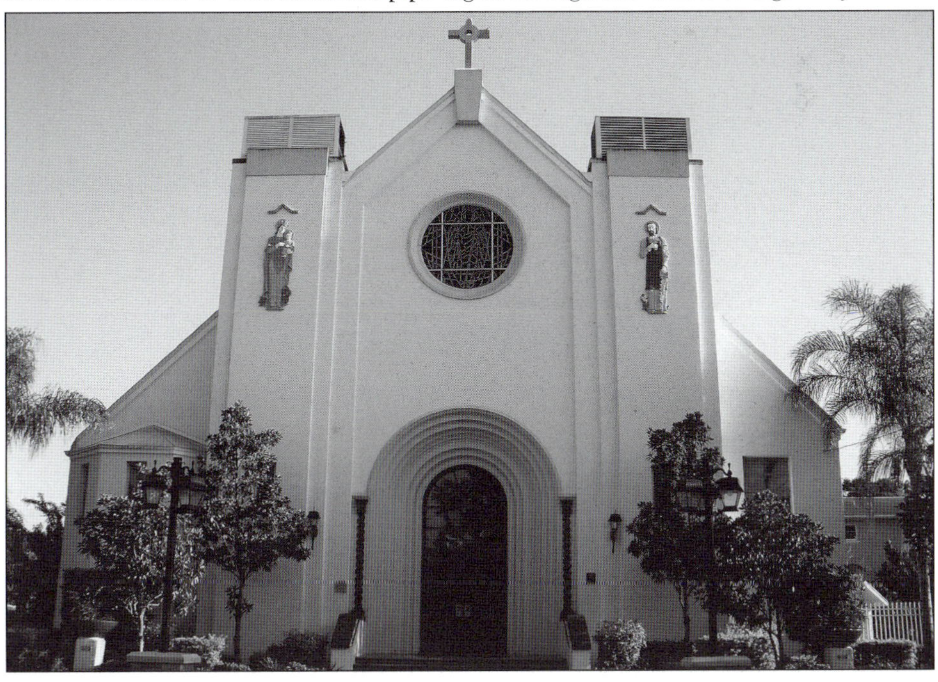

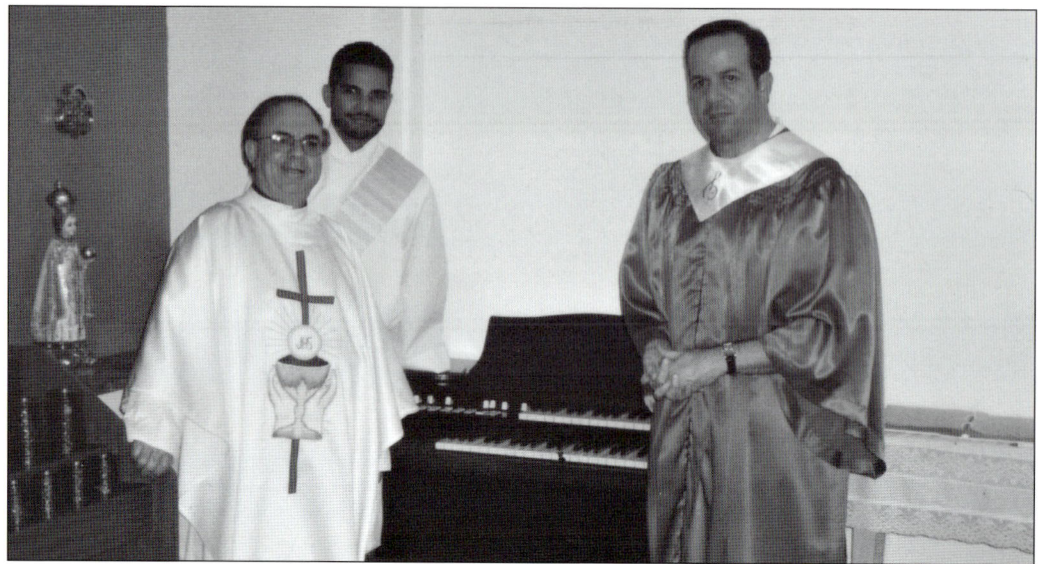

In May 2005, the original vintage organ from the old church was donated by former organist Jennie LoCicero. In 1974, the church installed a new organ, and this organ was given to LoCicero as a retirement gift from the parish. She wanted to return it back to its church home after more than 30 years. Pictured above at the rededication of the organ are, from left to right, Pastor Fr. Felix Sanchez, Fr. Carlos Rojas, and organist John Cinchett, who coordinated a fund-raising campaign for the restoration of the organ. Father Sanchez was pastor from 1999 to 2011, the longest tenure in the history of the church. Pictured below is the St. Joseph Spanish Choir at the centennial Christmas mass in 1995, with Pastor Fr. Karl Aschmann (first row, right).

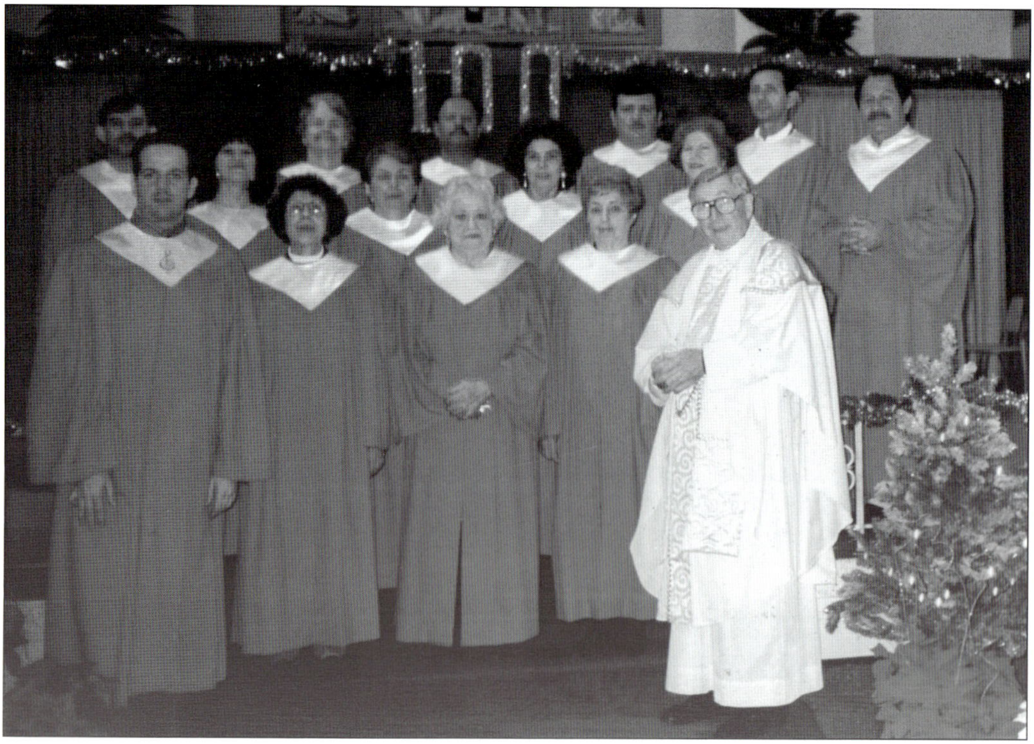

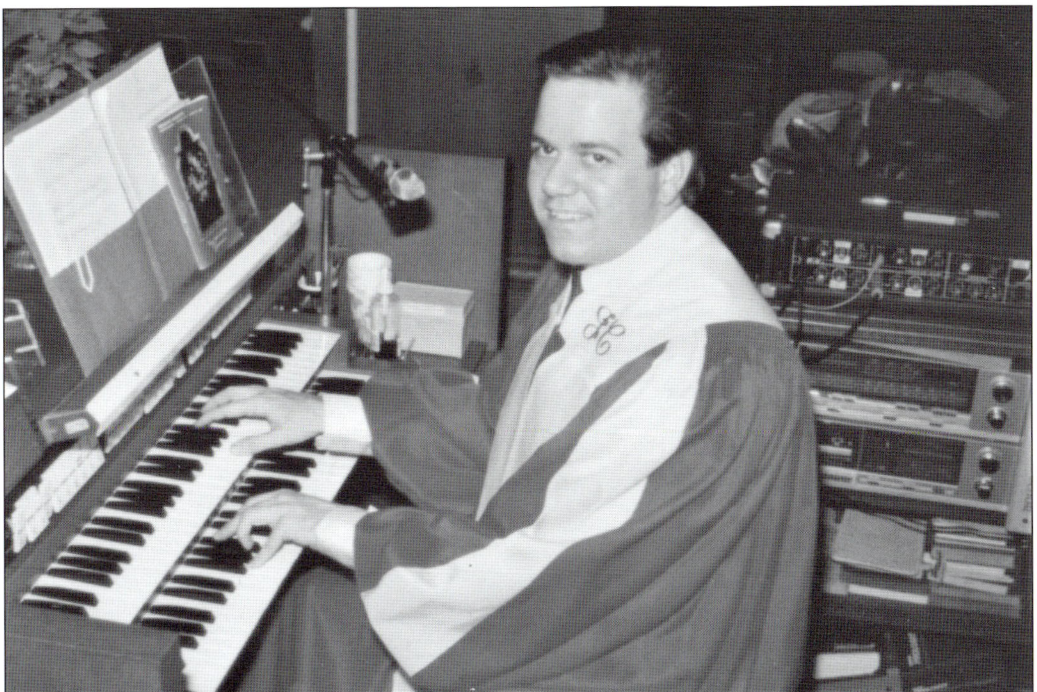

Pictured here on Christmas Eve, December 24, 1989, is organist John Cinchett at the organ of St. Joseph Catholic Church. On that day, the city of Tampa experienced a hard freeze and record-breaking cold temperatures. The city was forced to conduct rolling blackouts to maintain power. Many Tampa families found themselves looking for shelter in the homes of those not affected by the blackouts, which excluded city blocks with a fire station. On that same morning, the heating system in the church broke down. Once the congregation had gathered inside the frigid church for the Christmas Eve mass, Fr. Karl Aschmann announced that everyone gathered should sit closer together in the pews, to help keep everyone warm. Pictured below in 1993 is the Chancel Choir at the 90th anniversary mass of the church dedication.

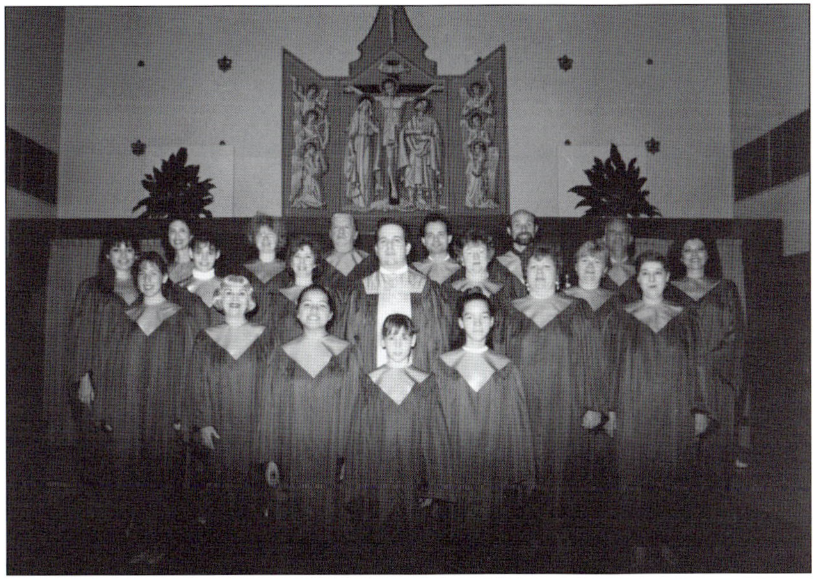

Discover Thousands of Local History Books Featuring Millions of Vintage Images

Arcadia Publishing, the leading local history publisher in the United States, is committed to making history accessible and meaningful through publishing books that celebrate and preserve the heritage of America's people and places.

Find more books like this at
www.arcadiapublishing.com

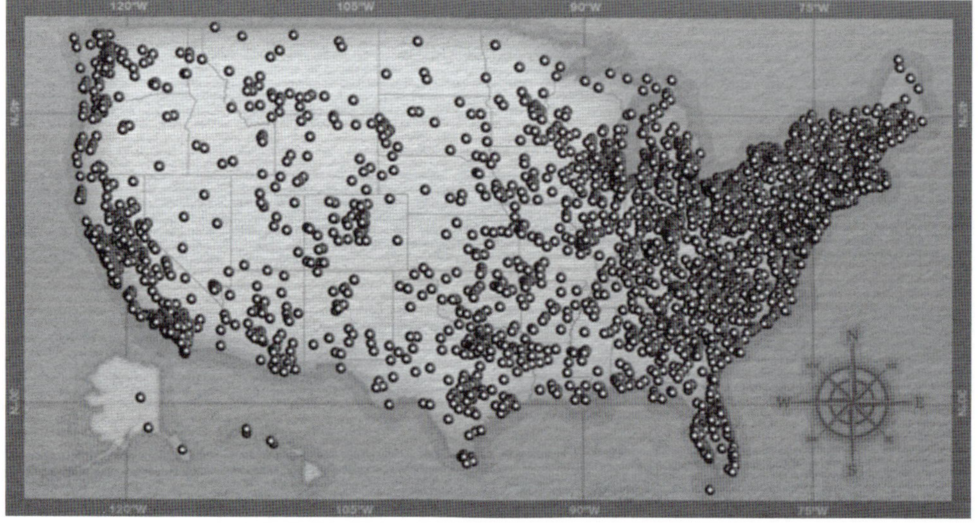

Search for your hometown history, your old stomping grounds, and even your favorite sports team.

Consistent with our mission to preserve history on a local level, this book was printed in South Carolina on American-made paper and manufactured entirely in the United States. Products carrying the accredited Forest Stewardship Council (FSC) label are printed on 100 percent FSC-certified paper.

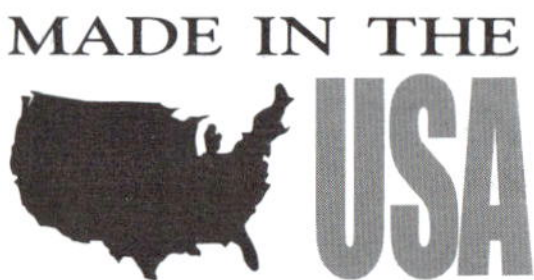